THE PARISH OF URR
CIVIL AND ECCLESIASTICAL

THE REV. DAVID FREW, B.D.
PHOTO. BY J. AND J. BROWN, CASTLE-DOUGLAS.

THE PARISH OF URR

CIVIL AND ECCLESIASTICAL

A HISTORY

BY

DAVID FREW, M.A., B.D.

WITH FORTY-SIX ILLUSTRATIONS

DALBEATTIE:
Published by Thomas Fraser
1909

Republished by

CASTLEPOINT PRESS
Barlay Cottage
Colvend
Dalbeattie
Kirkcudbrightshire
DG5 4QB
Tel: 055663 321

1993

ISBN 1 897604 01 7

Printed in Great Britain by Bell and Bain Ltd., Glasgow

CONTENTS

CIVIL HISTORY

	PAGE
Chapter I Introductory	1
Chapter II Name and Origin of the Parish	10
Chapter III From Robert Bruce to the Union of the Crowns	15
Chapter IV From the Union of the Crowns to the Union of the Parliaments, 1603-1707	22
Chapter V The Eighteenth Century	38
Chapter VI The Nineteenth Century: General and Agricultural Matters	60
Chapter VII The Villages	80
Chapter VIII Dalbeattie	109
Chapter IX Parish Boards and Associations	148
Chapter X The Antiquities of the Parish	171
Chapter XI Old Customs and Manners	187

VIII.

ECCLESIASTICAL HISTORY

Chapter XII
Before the Reformation - - - - - - 203

Chapter XIII
Ministers between the Reformation and the Revolution: 1560-1688 - - - - - - - 213

Chapter XIV
Rev. John Hepburn, M.A. 1688-1723 - - - - 226

Chapter XV
Ministers from 1723 to 1806 - - - - - 241

Chapter XVI
Rev. Alexander Murray, D.D. 1806-1813 - - 255

Chapter XVII
Ministers from 1813 to 1909 - - - - - - 265

Chapter XVIII
Ecclesiastical Matters Generally—Since the Reformation - - - - - - - - 275

Chapter XIX
Urr United Free Church - - - - - - 290

Chapter XX
The Churches of Dalbeattie - - - - - 296

APPENDICES AND INDEX

Appendix A: Names and Owners of Lands - - - **323**
Appendix B: Elders in the Churches - . - - **329**
Appendix C: Members of Public Boards - - - **332**
Appendix D: Commissioners and Town Councillors of Dalbeattie - - - - - **335**
Index - - - - - - - - - **337**

LIST OF ILLUSTRATIONS

1.	Portrait of the Author:	Front.	
2.	Dalbeattie:	To face page	2
3.	Mote of Urr—Plate 1:	,,	6
4.	Milton:	,,	26
5.	Portrait—George Maxwell of Munches: ...	,,	42
6.	,, Michael Herries of Spottes: ...	,,	46
7.	,, John Herries Maxwell of Munches:	,,	64
8.	,, Thomas Biggar of Chapelton: ...	,,	68
9.	,, James Biggar of Chapelton: ...	,,	70
10.	,, William Young-Herries of Spottes:	,,	76
11.	,, Alexander Young-Herries of Spottes:	,,	78
12.	Old Cottage by Spottes Burn:	,,	84
13.	Portrait—John Johnstone, Millbank: ...	,,	86
14.	,, William Harrison, Haugh-of-Urr:	,,	92
15.	Haugh-of-Urr:	,,	94
16.	Springholm:	,,	98
17.	Crocketford:	,,	106
18.	Dalbeattie Burgh Arms:	,,	108
19.	Portrait—Thomas Rawline of Little Firthhead:	,,	114
20.	,, David Paterson, Dalbeattie: ...	,,	116
21.	,, James McLaurin, Dalbeattie: ...	,,	118
22.	,, Homer Newall, } Dalbeattie: ...	,,	124
23.	,, Joseph Newall, }		
24.	,, Thomas Maxwell, Dalbeattie: ...	,,	130
25.	,, John Patterson Lewis, M.D., Dalbeattie.	,,	134
26.	,, Thomas McKnight, Surgeon ⎫		
27.	,, Thomas Helme, ⎬ Provosts of		
28.	,, Joseph Heughan, ⎬ Dalbeattie:	,,	140
29.	,, David McNish, ⎭		
30.	,, John Lowden, Haugh-of-Urr: } ...	,,	150
31.	,, William Allan, Hardgate: }		
32.	,, Wellwood Herries Maxwell of Munches:	,,	164
33.	Mote of Urr—Plate 2:	,,	172
34.	Milton Loch:	,,	182
35.	Spottes Hall:	,,	200
36.	Urr Church and Manse:	,,	212
37.	Auchenreoch Loch:	,,	234

38.	Portrait—The Rev. James Muirhead, D.D.:		,,	248
39.	,, The Rev. Alexander Murray, D.D.			
	(in the text):		,,	256
40.	,, The Rev. George M. Burnside: ...		,,	270
41.	,, The Rev. John Macrae Sandilands,			
	M.A.:		,,	272
42.	**Urr Parish Church**:		,,	276
43.	**Manse of Urr**:		,,	280
44.	Portrait—Robert Kerr, Redcastle:		,,	288
45.	Dalbeattie Loch:		,,	296
46.	Portrait—The Rev. David Kinnear, B.A.: ...		,,	308

PREFACE

BY way of excuse for the issue of this volume, the author may almost plead inability to help himself. The Parish of Urr presents so many features of interest, and contains so much matter of a historical and antiquarian kind, that some account of it seemed to be desirable; and circumstances combined with his official position and the suggestions of friends to impose upon him the duty of giving it. What was begun as a duty was continued as a pleasure, until the work grew to the proportions embodied in the following pages.

The general aim has been, not only to cover the whole course of the parish history, but to make a continuous narrative of it, and indicate the various points at which it came into touch with the wider movements of political and ecclesiastical life in the country. In carrying out this aim, the author has had the inhabitants of Urr in view, and people elsewhere connected with the parish; accordingly he has sought to weave into the story such details as may be of interest to any of them, and provide explanations of such historical and ecclesiastical allusions as some of them might find obscure. Matter of this sort, however, has been treated as briefly as possible, to avoid being tedious to the readers for whom it is superfluous.

The annals of the parish have, of course, been brought

down to the present day, and some notice has been taken of its existing condition; but, for obvious reasons, the references to living persons are sparing and brief, having only been introduced so far as necessary to render the story complete. Similarly, the illustrations have been drawn almost entirely from past figures in the life of the parish.

The substance of Chapters X and XI has already appeared in the form of articles in "The Glasgow Herald," and is here reproduced by the kind permission of the Editor. For useful information, both oral and written, the author has been indebted to too many people to be able to make individual acknowledgment, but he gladly avails himself of this opportunity of offering them all his warmest thanks. In particular, however, he must mention the kindness of Mr John F. Brown, Editor of "The Galloway Gazette," in lending his copy of the manuscript Account of the Parish in 1627; the great help received from Mr and Major Herries of Spottes, who have taken a lively interest in the History from its inception, and have furnished the author with much valuable material, in the form of books, documents, and family papers; and the valued assistance of Mr Thomas Fraser, Dalbeattie, whose well-known knowledge of Galloway matters and collection of Galloway literature have been freely put at the disposal of the author, and who is not only responsible for the form of the book, but has been of great service in its passage through the press.

In connection with the illustrations, the gratitude of the author is also due to many kind friends for the use of photographs, miniatures, and paintings. He desires particularly to thank Messrs J. and J. Brown, photographers, Castle-Douglas, for the views in the upper division of the parish specially taken for this work; also, Messrs Robert G. Mann of "The Dumfries and Galloway Courier and Herald" and Ivie A. Callan of "The Stewartry Observer," for the use of some interesting blocks in their possession.

CIVIL HISTORY

CHAPTER I

INTRODUCTORY

THE Parish of Urr is situated in the Eastern District of the Stewartry of Kirkcudbright. Longer and narrower than the neighbouring parishes, it almost intersects the county in a direct line from north to south. Its higher limit, among the Irongray hills, brings it within a few miles of Dumfriesshire: at its other extremity it touches the head of Rough Firth, an arm of the Solway. Its length is over fourteen miles: its breadth varies from one to six miles: its total area, accordingly, is about thirty-five square miles. On the east, it is bounded by the parishes of Lochrutton and Kirkgunzeon: on the south, by Colvend: on the west, by Buittle and Crossmichael: on the north-west and north, by Kirkpatrick-Durham and Kirkpatrick-Irongray. For a distance of ten miles upon its western side it is skirted by the river Urr, which takes its rise in a loch of the same name, far up among the hills that border the county, and, after a devious course of twenty-six miles through a lovely valley, empties its waters into the Solway at Rough Firth. A tributary stream from Kirkpatrick-Durham flows down through the picturesque glen of Spottes, and joins the Urr at a point below Spottes House, thereby obtaining the name of the Spottes Burn. The only other considerable water is the Culmain Burn, on the eastern side of the parish. Rising on the heights of Crochmore, it passes down through several farms, besides that from which it derives its name, and at length joins the Kirkgunzeon Lane, which in turn finds its way into the Urr at Dalbeattie. There is good fishing in all these streams, especially in the Urr, from which every season some large-sized salmon are taken. The hills of the parish, though numerous, are of no great consequence: none of them rising to a height of a thousand feet above sea level. The most conspicuous are the hills of Larg and Larglanglee: Auchengibbert and Bar hills: Crochmore: and Dalmun. The last-named is particularly striking, as it rises abruptly out of the deepest part of the valley of the Urr, that is to say, almost from sea level, and is faced across the water by a still higher hill, Barsoles, in Buittle Parish, with which it forms a natural gateway to the broader country that lies beyond. In the upper portion of the parish, there are two lochs or lakes of considerable size and attractiveness: Auchenreoch Loch, which is quite a mile in length, and about a quarter of a mile in breadth: and Milton Loch, which is somewhat larger, but nearly circular in shape. In general, these lochs are shallow round the verges, but soon dip down to a dangerous depth. There is some boating upon them in summer, with fishing for perch and pike; in winter they afford sport and recreation to the curlers of the neighbourhood. There are other smaller sheets of water at Spottes, Edingham, and Richorn.

As a rule the soil of the parish is fertile and kindly, especially in the lower lands which lie round the valley of the Urr. The portions not amenable to cultivation are a comparatively small proportion of the whole, probably not more than one-twelfth, and consist of the higher hills, some moss-lands, and the usual granite excrescences and whinstone scaurs characteristic of Galloway. Plantations are plentiful, and mostly comprise oak, ash, elm, and Scotch fir, all of which grow rapidly in the district. These not only provide cover for game and shelter for stock, but greatly enhance the appearance of the landscape. The prevailing rock formations are whinstone and granite; and iron ore is said to be plentiful, but the want of coal prevents it being exploited.

The greater part of the population is concentrated in the town of Dalbeattie, which occupies a fine situation in the lower end of the parish, about five miles from the mouth of the

DALBEATTIE.

PHOTO. BY A. BROWN AND CO., LANARK.

Urr. Being tidal up to the town, the river affords communication with the Solway by vessels of a small tonnage. In the upper or landward district, besides several large mansion-houses and many comfortable and commodious farm-buildings, there are five villages of varying size: Haugh-of-Urr, about four miles from Dalbeattie, with the parish church and manse standing above it: Hardgate, half a mile further on, containing the United Free church and manse: Springholm, three miles to the north, on the coach road to Dumfries: (part of) Crocketford, two miles beyond Springholm, on the same road: and Milton, about two miles east from Crocketford, on the old military road.

The early history of this tract of country belongs to the general history of ancient Galloway. That has been written by various competent authorities, and is so easily accessible that a brief summary of it, so far as it concerns the Urr district, may here suffice.

The earliest inhabitants of Galloway, of whom definite information has been obtained, belonged to the Gaelic branch of the Celtic race. If, as has been conjectured, there was a previous aboriginal population of small dark-haired people, it has entirely disappeared; no traces of it are to be found, either in the traditions or sepulchral remains of the province. Our knowledge even of the Celts is largely inferential and uncertain. They seem to have been a fair-complexioned people of large stature, who spoke a dialect of the Gaelic language common over Ireland and the rest of Scotland. In their time, as the numerous mosses and marl pits of Galloway testify, the face of the country was almost covered with forests, in which, besides the animals afterwards domesticated, there lived and roamed various wild species that are now extinct; among them the wild boar, the wolf, the bear, a large sort of deer, and the urus, an animal of the buffalo kind. Ignorant of agriculture, the Celtic denizens of the forests depended for subsistence upon the natural produce of the earth, and the fruits of the chase. The flesh of wild animals was their staple food, the skins of the same their only clothing; hence, it is presumed, they were given the name of Selgovae, by which they were known for a time, and which is supposed to be derived from the Gaelic word for hunters. In common with other early inhabitants of Scotland, they were also called Picts or painted people, from their custom of tatooing their bodies with colours and figures of beasts, probably to render themselves more formidable in battle. Their original dwellings were, in winter, the natural dens and caves of the earth; in summer, rude shelters in the woods, formed by driving stakes into the ground, and covering them over with the leafy branches of trees. Afterwards they improved upon these primitive habitations, and built themselves huts of wattled sticks and mud; then, in course of time, more solid houses of thick hewn beams, filled in with clay, and roofed over with straw, fern, or turf. This last style of building remained to comparatively modern times, only rough unhewn stones were used in the walls, instead of the old wooden beams. As a measure of safety, many of the ancient habitations were built within the margins of lakes, either upon a small island, if such presented itself conveniently, or upon piles driven into the shallow bottom. There is a rocky projection in Milton Loch, on and around which there seem to have been such lake dwellings. Many of the lochs of Galloway, and indeed of Scotland generally, have preserved remains of them, from the refuse of which much information has been derived regarding the food, utensils, and occupations of the Celts. It is not quite clear whether these lake-dwellings were the only habitations of the people for a time, or were used contemporaneously with houses upon land, though the latter seems the more probable opinion. Of land-dwellings numerous traces remain in the hill-forts, hut-circles, and burial cairns which abound in Galloway, but of which, of course, it is impossible accurately to determine the date. Sometimes a considerable population seems to have been gathered together into a settlement or town, probably to be near the residence of the prince or chief. If we may trust the geography of Claudius Ptolemaeus, a Roman surveyor of the second century, such a settlement existed in his time in the parish of Urr. In his map he places Caer-bantorigum, one of the four towns of the Selgovae, in the vicinity of the Mote of Urr, with which well-known earthwork some authorities accordingly identify it. Besides these substantial monuments, the Celts have left abundant traces of themselves in the place-names of the district, many of which are clearly derived from the old Gaelic tongue.

Isolated from the rest of Scotland by their geographical position, the old inhabitants of Galloway preserved their separate existence as a people, with chiefs and kings of their own, down to the twelfth century, when the province was formally annexed to the Scottish Crown. Their language even lingered on in the province so late as the sixteenth century, when it fell into desuetude through the influences of the Reformation, and the spread of the Lowland Scotch in the parish churches and schools. During the course of their career, however, they did not escape immigration and warlike invasion, any more than continual intestine feud, with the usual consequences of admixture of race, and modification of habits and life. The first outstanding event of their history was the appearance of the Roman legions in 79 A.D., during the second campaign of Agricola. For over three hundred years, these southern conquerors maintained a kind of intermittent sway in Britain; and, though there is scarcely any record of their operations in Galloway, their presence is widely attested by the Roman camps, weapons, and fragments of ware found in the province. It seems certain that they occupied the valley of the Urr, and used the site of the Mote, if not the Mote itself, as a place of encampment; indeed, they must have held it more or less continuously during the whole period of their stay in Britain, if it is really to be identified with the ancient Caer-bantorigum. At the beginning of last century, some remains of Roman outworks were said to have been seen in the neighbourhood of the Mote. Occasionally Roman relics have been unearthed in the parish, especially in the peat-mosses, when they were being dug up for fuel. A Roman javelin was discovered on the farm of Auchengibbert early last century, and presented by Mr Joseph Train of Castle-Douglas to Sir Walter Scott, who left it in his collection at Abbotsford. In May 1832, a beautiful specimen of the Roman tripod was turned up by the plough at Edingham. In 1834, two Roman tripods were unearthed in Richorn moss; and about the same time several brass spearheads, such as were used by the Roman legionaries, were discovered at Munches, within a few miles of the Mote of Urr. Roman coins are also said to have been found at different times in the neighbourhood. A more doubtful trace of the Roman occupation was discovered about thirty years ago on the farm of East Glenarm, by Mr John Reid, son of the tenant of the time. In ploughing the field on the left-hand side of the road leading to the farm-house, he came upon a square cavity, 4½ feet long, 2½ broad, and 1½ deep, hollowed out of a rocky knoll, and containing an earthenware jar with some markings upon it. The jar, which was about 7 or 8 inches in height, and had the appearance of a funeral urn, was handed over to Mr Thomas Duncan, of Ottley, the proprietor of the farm, and the cavity carefully covered up again, without, however, any expert opinion having been obtained regarding the matter.

For several centuries after the departure of the Romans in 407 A.D., there is scarcely any light to be had upon the progress of events in Galloway. During that period the inhabitants were probably engaged, for the most part, in resisting the incursion of enemies from various quarters. In the seventh century the province is supposed to have been invaded and subdued, after a great battle, by the men of Ulster; but this supposition rests upon a wrong identification of the site

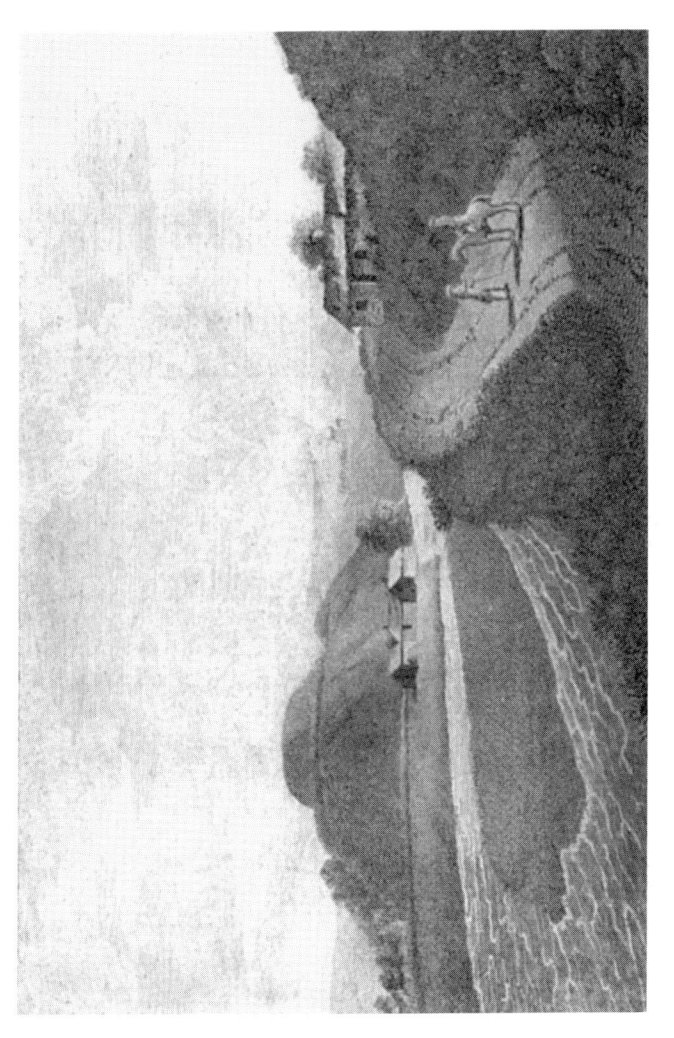

MOTE OF URR.—Plate 1.

FROM ENGRAVING IN GROSE'S "ANTIQUITIES," 1797.

of the battle, which is in Antrim, not in the south of Scotland. There would doubtless be considerable intercourse and intermarriage between the Picts of Galloway and those of the neighbouring Irish coast; but no good reason exists for believing that at this time they came under their dominion. On the other hand, it is clear that they did at this time come under foreign sway—that of the Northumbrian Angles of Bernicia. The kings of Bernicia had allied themselves with the Galloway Picts in the fierce disputes and complicated hostilities of the time, and in consequence acquired a suzerainty over them. For nearly two hundred years they maintained their position as overlords in the province, though they allowed the actual government to remain in the hands of the native chiefs and princes. To this arrangement the modern name of Galloway is probably due; at any rate, it was at this period it came into use, as a term of distinction for the part of the country ruled by the Anglians. The inhabitants were called by other Gaels Gallgaidhel or Gallwyddel, stranger Gaels; whence the transition was easy to the name by which Wigtownshire and the Stewartry of Kirkcudbright are now known.

The Anglian dominion came to an end about the beginning of the ninth century. Thereafter the Norsemen made their appearance in Galloway, and established settlements along the Solway coast. For the next three hundred years the history of the province is bound up with the presence of these daring sea-warriors, who found its shores a convenient basis for their operations against Cumbria, the Isle of Man, and Ireland. At first the inhabitants seem to have had an amicable understanding with the invaders, and to have permitted them more or less willingly to settle in their midst, if they did not actually make common cause with them, and join them in their piratical expeditions. Some authorities find in this fact, and not in their subjection to the Anglians, the cause of the name Galwegians being applied to them; but if, as has been asserted, they were already so denominated, their relations with the Norsemen must have intensified their alienation from the general Gaelic brotherhood, and confirmed the name upon them. Henceforth they were stranger Gaels indeed, in taking part with the common enemy; and that enemy subsequently repaid them for their defection by usurping dominion over them. After a period of more or less complete independence, the Norsemen asserted their supremacy, and held the province in subjection till Malcolm Canmore ascended the Scottish throne. By that time their power was broken, and they were forced to retire northward. Galloway passed accordingly into the possession of the Scottish king. In 1107 it was granted as an earldom to his youngest son David, on whose succession to the crown in 1124 it was formally incorporated into the Scottish kingdom. Attempts were afterwards made by a succession of the lords of Galloway, Fergus, Uchtred and Gilbert, Roland, and Alan to get rid of their Scottish allegiance, but without success. Towards the close of the thirteenth century, when the Scottish crown was in dispute, the lordship was divided between four descendants or relations by marriage of the ruling family, among them John Baliol and Alexander Comyn. Under their leadership the men of Galloway found themselves in opposition to Robert Bruce in his struggle for the Scottish kingship. Warlike operations were undertaken by Bruce against the province, and in 1308 it was finally subdued by his brother Edward. In 1369 the eastern part of it was conferred upon Archibald Douglas the Grim, who built Thrieve Castle, the ruins of which still exist, on an island in the river Dee. The excesses and pretensions of his descendants ultimately brought about their downfall, and in 1455 the lordship of Galloway was transferred to the Scottish crown.

The chequered history of those early years had a lasting effect upon the development of the province. The successive dominations to which the inhabitants were subjected had each its share in determining their ways of thought and life, if not also their physical characteristics. In old customs and superstitions hardly yet extinct, and perhaps in the physical features of the people, no less than in their place-names, it is still possible to trace such old-world influences as those of the Anglian and Scandinavian occupations. The turmoils and contentions, too, of which it was the scene, had a great effect in retarding the general progress of the province, especially in agriculture, for which it was well adapted. A turbulent disposition was begotten in the inhabitants, which rendered them averse to pastoral pursuits, and inappreciative of the benefits of law and order.

CHAPTER II

NAME AND ORIGIN OF THE PARISH

THE name of the parish, though practically remaining uniform in sound, has varied considerably in spelling at different periods. The oldest form of the word is Vr; but Ure, Hurr, Urre, Whur, and Wur are also found. Until the beginning of last century it was, and had been for a long time, written Orr; an orthography which is still reflected in the pronunciation of the natives. It is now, however, definitely fixed as Urr.

The original application of the name would be to the river which continues to bear it. This may be inferred from the generally accepted derivation of the word, which associates it with water. In most primitive languages, the word for water is more or less akin to Urr; in that of the Basques of France and Spain—a race supposed to be older than the Celts, and one of the separate folk-stems of Europe—it is exactly the same. In the Gaelic language, Ur has the kindred significance of the brink, border, or edge of the water, and so is found in various parts of Britain under the modified forms of Orr, Ure, and Ore, as the name of lakes and rivers. The sound expressed by it recalls the rippling or murmuring of water, and suggests a root of onomatopoetic origin; that is, a phonetic imitation of the object it was designed to represent. We may believe, therefore, that Urr perpetuates the name given to the river, in early times, by the Celts who lived upon its banks.

Another explanation of the name derives it from the Latin urus or the Norse ur, the words in those languages for the wild ox or boar, and supposes it to have been first given to the country lying round the river, from the fact that it abounded in herds of that animal. This derivation is hardly so probable as that already given.

A third alternative has been suggested by popular humour, and may commend itself to the modern Anglo-Israelite. According to it, the name of the parish is derived from the region of ancient Chaldaea to which the patriarch Abraham belonged, and argues a connection between the original Celtic inhabitants and the ten lost Hebrew tribes. So far, it is hardly necessary to say, the evidence of such association is not convincing.

The earliest notices of Urr occur in charters of Holm Cultran, an abbey in Cumberland, of which Kirkgunzeon was a pendicle, and to which belonged considerable allocations of land in Galloway. These charters were granted by the Kirkconnel family of the time, and date from the period before the Scottish wars of independence. To one of them the name of Hugo of Hurr is appended as a witness; and to another that of his son Thomas. This person appears again, in 1296, as a subscriber to the Ragman Roll—the collection of instruments under which many of the nobility and gentry of Scotland promised allegiance to Edward I. of England, during his military progress through their country. In this document his name appears as Hughe de Urre del Counte de Dumfres; but the apparent discrepancies are of no great consequence, as Dumfres is understood to be the Stewartry, and the altered spelling of the proper name is the result of the usual inexactitude of those days. These notices imply that a tract of country in the vicinity of the Urr had already been defined and erected into a barony, and as such was in the possession of Hugo; who, according to old Scots law, would not only exercise manorial and hereditary rights over the land, but civil and criminal jurisdiction over the inhabitants. There is nothing to show how long the barony of Urr was in existence before his time; but the probability is that it was of previous creation, and that it took its name from the Mote of Urr being the seat of baronial government. From several subsequent notices we learn that it passed out of the possession of Hugo and his family. On 8th September, 1296, it was given by Edward I. of England, with various other lands, to Henry de Percy, whom he had appointed Keeper of Galloway, with its Castles of Botel, Wygton, and Crugeltoun. On the overthrow of the English power, and the accession of Robert Bruce to the Scottish throne, the lands of Percy were forfeited; and in 1308, one half of the barony of Urr was conferred by the king upon Thomas Randolph, who received at the same time many grants of land in other parts of Scotland, as well as the titles of Earl of Moray, Lord of Man, and Lord of Annandale. To whom the other half was given by Bruce does not appear; but later in the century it was conveyed, under charter of his son David II., to a person named Andro Buthergask. It is again mentioned in a charter of 8th May, 1566, under which the half of Urr is granted to John, second son of Robert fourth Lord Maxwell, who married Agnes, eldest daughter and co-heiress of William fourth Lord Herries.

The ancient barony of Urr probably determined the bounds of the parish, when it came to be formed, some time in the twelfth, or early part of the thirteenth century. To that period of religious revival in Scotland, under the influence of Margaret, wife of Malcolm Canmore, and her son David I., is ascribed the general division of the country into bishoprics and parishes. The latter, as a rule, were associated with the existing baronies, and made conterminous with them: the parish of Urr would be delimited accordingly, on the lines already fixed by the barony. The subsequent partition of the barony in the time of Bruce may be related in some way to the appearance of two parish churches in Urr simultaneously, which will be noticed later.

The condition of things in Galloway, and consequently in Urr, about the time of its erection into a parish, shows some improvement upon the rudeness of existence in former days.

The religious revival instituted by Queen Margaret, and other influences at work in the province since its incorporation into the Scottish kingdom, had not been without a salutary effect upon the social life of the people. The land was still, to a great extent, covered with wood and swamp; but agriculture had risen to the level of a recognised industry, and was as far advanced in its methods as it was for three or four centuries afterwards. Besides black oats, rye, and long-bearded barley, such quantities of wheat were grown, that Edward I. was able to draw upon them for the support of his army during his campaign in Galloway. The rise of monastic institutions in the province, and the distribution of parish clergy among the people, helped to spread the knowledge of agriculture, as well as other refining influences. Of course the cultivation of the soil still proceeded upon somewhat elementary lines. The possibility of reclaiming wet lands by drainage, and enriching poor ones with fertilising substances, was not yet understood, hence tillage was confined to the higher-lying regions, even practised upon the summits of considerable hills; and, when the portion of land utilised became worn-out and unfruitful, it was left to recover itself by the healing virtue of time. This explains the traces of past cultivation still visible on heights where no modern agriculturist would dream of attempting to grow a crop. The plough was of primitive structure, and was drawn by quite a herd of oxen, ten being no infrequent number. Where it could not be worked, or failed to take effect, the spade was brought into requisition. The harrows were simply bunches of whins or thorns tied to the tails of the oxen. When the grain had been gathered and dried, it was ground in a small stone handmill called a quern. This usually consisted of two round flat stones, the upper one having a narrow hole or funnel driven through its centre, and the lower one a wooden or metal pin inserted in it, on which the other revolved, and crushed the grain. Some of these stones have been found in and around the parish of Urr, after having been used for other purposes, and are now carefully preserved. Much of the grain was not put through the quern, but made into malt, and brewed into ale. The mountains, forests, and uncultivated parts generally were no longer given over to wild animals, but stocked with black cattle, sheep, goats, and swine; which, in the absence of fences, had to be assiduously herded off the cultivated lands. The clothing of the natives was still largely composed of animal skins; though wool had begun to be used, and, either in its natural state or spun into yarn, was woven into a coarse kind of cloth, which was utilised for raiment. Flax was grown in very few places, and linen consequently almost unknown. Shoes were hardly ever worn by the lower classes, though pieces of hide were sometimes tied upon the feet to cover and protect them. As usual in an undeveloped stage of society, the drudgery, and indeed most of the work, was left to the women, the time of the men being divided between idling and fighting.

The houses of the poorer inhabitants remained very much as they had been for centuries: small huts of wooden beams and branches, plastered over with clay or mud, and roofed with heather, sod, or turf, which the cattle shared with the owner and his family. Large castles, however, after the Norman style, with thick stone walls and numerous apartments, moats and draw-bridges and other fortifications, began to be built by the nobles; and it was at this period the abbeys and monasteries arose, and grew into the splendid proportions which may still be traced and admired in such magnificent ruins as those of New Abbey and Dundrennan.

CHAPTER III

From Robert Bruce to the Union of the Crowns

HAVING achieved the independence of Scotland and established a settled government, King Robert caused many wise and beneficent enactments to be passed, in the benefits of which Galloway duly shared, as by his time it had been admitted to a full participation in the general life and law of the country. The advantages of his statutes, however, were largely lost or discount d in the period that followed his death in 1329, through the renewal of civil strife, and conflict with the southern kingdom. The frequent calls of their superiors, to support them in their mutual contentions, or follow them to battle against the English, either as invaders or invaded, demoralised the inhabitants of the province, and unfitted them for peaceful employments. This state of affairs continued for nearly three centuries, and involved a succession of hardships, which must have been felt in Urr, no less than in the other parishes of the Stewartry.

It was particularly marked during the lordship of the Douglases. Throughout the century of their supremacy in Galloway, war and tumult were the order of the day. With the large forces at their command, these powerful nobles not only harassed and oppressed their own dominions, but menaced the authority of the Scottish kings, invaded England, and even took a hand occasionally in the wars of France. Among the Galwegians who followed their banners at home and abroad there would usually be men from the parish of Urr. Thrieve Castle, the headquarters of the Douglases, was not far distant: the stronghold of Buittle was still nearer, on the very confines of the parish: and, as existing indications continue to show, the road from the south passed over the Urr Water at this old castle of the Baliols, and thence onwards through the valley of the Urr to Dumfries and Edinburgh. In common with the rest of Galloway, Urr owed fealty to the Douglas family, and would require, as occasion called, to furnish its due proportion of fighting men. In addition to this duty, the parishioners would also be subjected to an annual tribute or exaction. The old Gaelic chiefs had been accustomed to demand and receive presents from their clans, called calpes or caupes, which usually consisted of a horse, a cow, or other article of value. The Douglases were careful to perpetuate this custom, and required every parish in the Stewartry to deliver annually at the Castle of Thrieve what was called the Lardner Mart Cow, that is to say, a cow in good condition to be killed and salted at Martinmas, for provision during the winter. This exaction was continued by the successors of the Douglases till after the Jacobite Rebellion of 1715, when it lapsed through the forfeiture of William, Earl of Nithsdale, the last possessor of the fortress and rights of Thrieve. Under these circumstances, it is evident that the inhabitants of Urr must have felt the full pressure of the Douglas domination, both in its civil oppressions and in its military demands. It was hardly to be expected that any records should remain of the part taken by them in the feuds and raids of their warlike masters; but there is scarcely room for doubt that they suffered and bled for them on many a well-tried field, and that their quiet valley frequently witnessed the passage of their armed adherents, if it was not sometimes the scene of their sanguinary encounters.

The downfall of the Douglases brought a measure of peace to the Galwegians, but did not exempt them from further experiences of the horrors of war. Under their new masters, they were still liable to military service; and, on each occasion of the renewal of warlike operations in the nation, had to follow them to the field. So far as the parishioners of Urr are concerned, there are sufficient historical notices to show that they bore their share in the great conflicts of the time. At the Battle of Flodden in 1513, one of the gentlemen of Galloway who fell with the Scottish king was Robert, second son of Alexander Gordon, who at that time was in possession of the lands of Auchenreoch. It is true that the Gordons did not reside in the parish; their family residence seems to have been at Clonyard in Kirkmaiden, and Robert is described as of Barharrow in Borgue; but, according to custom, they would draw upon all their retainers in going to war. The inference is, therefore, that men from Auchenreoch, and probably from other parts of the parish, were engaged in that disastrous battle. At Pinkiecleuch, in 1547, John Gordon of Blaiket was among the slain; and one of the prisoners taken by the English, either then or shortly afterwards, was Paul Redik of Dalbeattie, who seems to have been able to bring a considerable force into the field. In the list of the Talbot Papers, he is put down as "the Laird of Dabatie, of 20 marks land: his pledge his brother, with Sir John Tempest, for 41 men." In the Battle of Langside, in 1568, men from Urr were probably engaged upon the side of the unfortunate Queen Mary; for Lord Herries, one of her chief supporters, and the companion of her flight, held land at the time in and around the parish. The supposition is corroborated by the fact that, during the ensuing summer, the Regent Murray, in his progress through Galloway with a strong force to receive the submission of the queen's party, met and pardoned several gentlemen at "a strong house on the Water of Urr," which is generally supposed to have been Nether Place. It may also be noticed that Queen Mary, in the course of her historic flight, must have passed through the parish of Urr, as she proceeded from Corra in Kirkgunzeon to Dundrennan, to take boat for England, and cast herself upon the tender mercies of Elizabeth.

This last disturbance of the peace of Scotland was intimately associated with the Reformation of religion, which had taken place in 1560. However beneficial in its ultimate effects, as a great social upheaval it was naturally accompanied in its beginnings with strife and commotion. Old customs and manners were unsettled, old authorities discredited, and disputes generated over the property as well as the doctrines of the Church. The new faith early found lodgment in Galloway: indeed, it is supposed that, originated and fostered by the teaching of Wycliffe, dissatisfaction with the old religion, and desire for reformation, had long been simmering in the province. In 1562, and again in 1565, John Knox was directed by the General Assembly to visit the churches in the south of Scotland, and arrange their affairs in accordance with the Reformed discipline and doctrine. On one or other of these occasions, he may have found his way to Urr; at any rate, the Reformed faith was speedily accepted in the parish, and a reader was appointed to the church shortly after Knox's visits. Here as elsewhere, the immediate result of the change of religion would be the introduction of a new element of disturbance into the life of the people.

These wars and commotions, as may readily be imagined, entailed much misery and privation upon the inhabitants of Galloway, and effectually precluded the possibility of progress. Agriculture was necessarily neglected, and not only deteriorated in its methods, but even became more circumscribed in the extent of its operations. In their modes of living, and the habitations they occupied, the people were in no better condition than before the wars of independence; nor until the influence of the Reformation began to be felt, was there any improvement in their general character and intelligence. Under the Roman Catholic system, education was practically confined to the ranks of the clergy; who, in later years at least, were ignorant and corrupt. Religion lost its power of elevating the lives of the people, and restraining their vices and passions. Old superstitions, of heathen character and origin, though now associated with Christian festivals and saints, revived and flourished. Holy wells were visited with offerings for safety and health: witches were consulted, and their charms and specifics employed, for the cure of bodily and mental ailments; amulets were worn, and perforated stones hung up in houses and stables, to ward off danger and disease. Immorality abounded, and theft and murder were not uncommon. Several instances of crime are recorded, with which Urr and its inhabitants were more or less connected. In 1542, William Sinclair of Auchenfranco was murdered at Nether Place, the residence of Andrew Herries, brother of Lord Herries. The crime was charged upon John McNaught of Kilquhanity, who had to find security to underlie the law at the next Justice Court at Kirkcudbright. The tradition of this murder long lingered in the vicinity, and the field in which it took place went by the name of Sinclair's yard. In 1570, John McKinstray, John Smith senior, and John Smith younger, all from Grange, were associated with John Broune from Mollance and William Kurour from Blakerne, in a trial for battery and assault upon Catherine McKie, spouse to Robert Livingstone of Little Airds. They had gone to the lands of Bordland, near the Water of Dee, with lances, staffs, and swords, and attempted to carry off the hay; and, being opposed, had made a savage attack upon Mrs Livingstone. "For the quhilk," it is satisfactory to learn, "they were fynit, with the thesaurer." These incidents shed light upon the state of things at the close of the period under review; though in both instances, it is to be observed, the offenders were brought to justice. It is one of the few redeeming features of the time, that the law, though still tardy and uncertain, was administered with greater strictness and impartiality than it had been in former days.

The worst evils that afflicted Galloway, and were doubtless shared by the parishioners of Urr, in the old feudal times before the Reformation, were probably the famines and plagues that usually followed in the wake of the wars. Many instances are recorded in which they played sad havoc among the people. In the time of Robert Bruce, a grievous famine took place, in consequence of the long-continued war and suspension of ordinary employments. In the reign of David II., both famine and plague visited the country on two separate occasions. The visitation of 1349 was the worst that had so far been experienced; but that of 1360 even exceeded it in violence and disastrousness. The latter was a general devastation, in which it was estimated that nearly one-third of the total population of Scotland perished. In 1439, again, whole multitudes died of want and of the "pestilence without mercy;" and a similar result followed the exceptional turbulence that preceded the downfall of the Douglases, about the middle of the fifteenth century.

One result to be expected from all these troubles was a frequent change in the proprietorship of the lands. In many cases, especially in the earlier years of the period, the transference was effected simply by superior might, and of course no attempt was made to record it. In other cases, however, lands were acquired by purchase or marriage, or by deed of gift of the owner, either to his own relations or retainers, or to the Church; and many notices of these transactions have been preserved in old charters. Apart from the dispositions of the Barony, which have been already mentioned, the earliest historical notices of the transference of lands in Urr are mostly in connection with gifts to the Church. If the lands of Auchenreoch, as there is reason to believe, are to be identified with those of Auchencork, mentioned in the old charters of Holm Cultran Abbey, they were bestowed upon the monks of that religious establishment, by the old Lords of Galloway, in the thirteenth century. About 1260, in the reign of Alexander III., the lands of Blaiket, with the chapel of St. Bridget, were granted to the Abbey of Holyrood, by Eustace Baliol. In the grants of the church of St. Constantine of Urr, and of the chapel of Edingham, to Holyrood Abbey, it is not clear whether lands were included. In the case of Edingham, this is hardly likely, as a grant by King David II. to Dougall McDougall is recorded, of lands in the vicinity of Dumfries, and called Evinghame, which is supposed to be simply a variation of the name. According to an old tradition, which will be found under the account of the Mote of Urr, the lands of Mote were bestowed by King Robert Bruce in 1306 upon a family called Sprott or Sprotte. It is unnecessary to give the old charters in detail, or at any stage of our history to enter into particulars of the various proprietors of the different lands in the parish; for that has been carefully and laboriously done by P. H. McKerlie, in his *Lands and their Owners in Galloway*. In Appendix A, however, a list of the successive proprietors of the various properties is given, according to McKerlie, for the benefit of those who have not access to his volumes.

CHAPTER IV

From the Union of the Crowns
to
The Union of the Parliaments. 1603-1707

MORE than a century had still to elapse before any substantial improvement took place in the condition of Galloway. The Reformation, it is true, had awakened the dormant intellectual capacities of the people, and opened a new realm of moral and religious interests to them; it had raised their ideals of life, and set spiritual forces in motion, which were bound in the end to tell upon their material comfort and prosperity; but time was needed for the manifestation of its real character and bearings, and various disturbing experiences interposed to postpone the ripening and reaping of its fruits. By 1603, when James VI. departed for the south to assume the sovereignty of the United Kingdom, the beneficial effects of the Reformation were beginning to make themselves felt in the province. The manners and morals of the people had improved in response to the higher demands of the new faith; their minds had been roused to the understanding and appreciation of its purer teaching; and a feeling of reverence and responsibility had been diffused among them by the earnest preaching and catechetical and other labours of the Protestant ministry. In the succeeding century, however, a series of ecclesiastical and political disputes emerged; which, while they stimulated the religious zeal of the people, and quickened their love of freedom, entailed such distractions and calamities upon the province as completely arrested its social and material development.

Early in the century, a crime was committed in the immediate neighbourhood of Urr, which reveals the persistence of a passionate and lawless disposition among men of the better class, that ill accords with the principles of the Reformation Church. The name of a parishioner, David Maxwell of Newark, was associated with it; but, to all appearances, in an entirely innocent way. Between him and John McNaught of Kilquhanity, a meeting had been arranged for the 29th April 1612, at the Three Thorns of Carlingwark, which stood on the verge of the loch of that name, a little beyond the present town of Castle - Douglas, and the last of which disappeared about forty years ago. McNaught arrived first at the trysting-spot; and, while waiting Newark's coming, all unsuspicious of harm, was set upon by two men, who had conceived a deadly animosity against him, Thomas Maxwell of Arenyning, and John Maxwell his nephew, the brother and son of Alexander Maxwell of Logan. Dragging him from his horse, they carried him into the house of John Hutton, messenger, which was near at hand; and, while the older man held him pinioned by the arms, the younger one despatched him with two thrusts of his whinger or sword. Thomas Maxwell was brought to trial for the slaughter; but, for no apparent reason, except that he did not himself deliver the death wounds, was acquitted. Among the witnesses who appeared in his behalf was Sir Robert Maxwell of Spottes, a leading representative of the Maxwell family, which seems to have been numerous in the district at the time. It adds to the horror of this cold-blooded murder that McNaught left a widow and three children. The former, Margaret Gordon, was a sister of Lord Kenmure; and one of the children, Marion McNaught, became the wife of William Fullerton, Provost of Kirkcudbright, and was not only renowned in her day for her piety, but is still remembered as the friend and correspondent of Samuel Rutherford of Anworth.

Fifteen years after this event, an interesting light is thrown upon the state of things in the parish, by an old manuscript preserved in the General Register House in Edinburgh. It is a kind of early Statistical Account drawn up by Mr Alexander Robertson, minister of Urr at the time, and is subscribed by him at the Kirk of Urr on the 6th day of May 1627, before Robert Herries, elder, and George Reddik, notary. There is no hint in the document itself as to the occasion of its writing, which must have been some public demand, such as that made by the Lords of the Commission of 1617, appointed to revise and allocate the stipends, or the later one of the Stewartry War Committee, to which reference will shortly be made. Besides some ecclesiastical information, which will be noticed in its proper place, Mr Robertson records some general facts regarding the parish, and gives a list of the separate farms or "rooms," as he calls them, with the rent and stipend payable by each, either in meal, corn, or money. No estimate of the population is given; but from the number of communicants mentioned (600) we may infer that it was about fourteen or fifteen hundred. The fact that there was no school in the parish is suggestive of the state of education at the time, though it does not prove that absolutely no attention was paid to it, as there might be an occasional class, either in a private house or in the parish church. That some demand for education existed may be inferred from the further remark of Mr Robertson, that there was great need of a school, and that sufficient church funds were still available for its equipment and upkeep. Another felt want was a parish hospital, by which may have been meant a house of refuge for the very poor, the aged, and the infirm, of whom there would probably be a considerable number. The farms or "rooms" are located by Mr Robertson according to their distances from the parish church, and bear names differing in little but the spelling from their modern representatives. Curiously enough, the number of them, thirty-seven, corresponds exactly with the present number of properties in the parish, though that of separate holdings or tenancies has largely increased. The rents yielded by the individual farms, and the estimated annual produce or " stock," as Mr Robertson calls it, afford an indication of the extent and nature of the tillage. Reidcastell pays a rent of eight hundred merks, which in sterling money would be about forty-five pounds; the Mot and Merkland of Ur pays forty merks, or about two pounds sterling; the annual yield, in the one case, is estimated at twelve score bolls of corn, and, in the other, at twelve bolls; the rest of the " rooms," in rent and " stock," range between these two. The stipend allocated to the different properties bears a much greater proportion to the rent than it does at the present day, approaching in most cases to an actual teind or tenth, and in some cases to the higher proportion shortly afterwards fixed by Charles I. Rent and stipend were mostly paid in " stock," though occasionally, as in the case of Reidcastell, money had been substituted. Corn seems to have been the only crop; and the smallness of its yield, according to Mr Robertson's figures, suggests that it was only grown upon limited patches, and by the rudest processes. The cultivation of the ground had evidently deteriorated from the olden days, when wheat, as well as oats, was produced in considerable quantities. In this respect Urr would be like the rest of Galloway; which, as we learn from other sources, was chiefly pastoral at this time, and depended more upon its small native breed of white-faced sheep than upon its grain harvests. The mutton and wool of these sheep were of the finest quality, and are highly praised by Lithgow the traveller, who visited the district in 1628. Most of the wool was sent to Dumfries for manufacture, but some of it was made up locally into stuffs for raiment and household use. The pasturage, of course, was still unfenced; and a considerable proportion of the population found employment in herding the cattle and sheep. Travelling pedlars, periodical fairs, and weekly markets in the burghs, afforded opportunities of disposing of produce, and receiving other articles in exchange. Little money being in circulation in the province, barter was the ordinary method upon which business was done.

Such was the state of affairs when rumours of war again began to reach the parish. Even in the reign of James VI., which terminated in 1625, the Episcopal leanings and measures of the king had aroused suspicion and resentment in Scotland; but under his son and successor Charles I., these feelings, which had so far smouldered, burst into open flame. The immediate occasion of the outbreak was the order of the Court in July 1637, that the English Service-Book—a book of prayers and lessons, prepared by Archbishop Laud and other English prelates—should be used henceforth in all the Scottish churches. Within a year of the issuing of this order, most of the nobility, gentry, ministers, and burgesses of Scotland had banded themselves together in a compact for armed resistance, by subscription to a document called "The Solemn League and Covenant," which was thereafter to play a momentous part in the history of the country. The subscribers to this document became known as the Covenanters; and the name continued to be applied to those who adhered to its principles, long years afterwards, even when the danger it was designed to obviate had passed away. Remonstrances and petitions having failed to effect an alteration in the mind and policy of Charles, preparations were made for a resort to arms; and a War Committee was appointed for the Stewartry, to superintend the gathering in of its resources. Each parish had to guarantee a levy of fighting men, and every inhabitant of means was compelled to contribute to the purchase of horses and accoutrements. In the account of the transactions of the War Committee, as given in their minutes, published in 1855 by Nicholson of Kirkcudbright, Milton of Urr comes into prominence, as one of their meeting-places, and the ordinary rendezvous for the forces they collected in the district. At this time, it was a Burgh of Barony, with a market cross for

MILTON.

PHOTO. BY J. AND J. BROWN, CASTLE-DOUGLAS.

the weekly interchange of merchandise, and not only the sole village of the parish, but the most important and populous village in the eastern portion of the Stewartry. Four times during 1640, namely on 18th July, 25th August, 17th and 22nd October, the War Committee held its meetings at Milton; and twice, namely on 16th July and a day not specified in October, Milton was the scene of an assemblage of armed men, both foot and horse. Its situation had been found convenient in earlier days as a gathering-place for the forces of the Stewartry, and many a time bands of fighting Galwegians had been collected on its common, to begin their march against the southern enemy; so that this quiet village, now dwindled down to a few cottages, must have witnessed many a warlike scene, and teemed with life and excitement, even before the stirring times of the War Committee.

In the Minute Book of the Committee, there are other references to Urr and its inhabitants, which go to show that the parish, as a whole, stood by the Presbyterian cause, and loyally responded to the demands made upon it. On 24th July 1640, the ten parishes in the Presbytery of Dumfries, situated in Galloway, "under the water of Urr," of which Urr was one, were required to nominate the minister and two of their most considerable men, to give in certified valuations at the next Committee meeting, and learn the impost to be put upon them, both for horse and foot. On 16th September, the Committee received warrant from the Estates in Edinburgh to collect and intromit with the "haile tenth and twentieth penny" of the same ten parishes, as well as the rents and goods of all papists, anti-covenanters, and recusants within their bounds, and apply the same for the support of the South Regiment. The latter part of this commission authorises a certain amount of persecution, and would help to teach the anti-covenanters the use of that weapon, which they wielded with such disastrous effect in succeeding years. On 1st September, Grisell Gordon, relict of Mr Alexander Robertson, minister of Urr, was ordained to produce her six silver spoons, and two other pieces of silver bought by the parish for the use of the kirk. The need as well as the enthusiasm must have been great, when such articles, especially Communion Plate, had to be melted down to supply the wants of the army. On 2nd September, Andrew Chalmers of Waterside delivered up six silver spoons, which weighed nine ounces and a half; and on the same day, the Laird of Dalbeattie, the John Redik of the time, was ordained to bring money next Committee day for the baggage horse of the parish of Urr. That the strictest measures were taken to prevent people escaping from their obligations may be inferred from the Act of 4th November, ordaining the Captains of the parishes to send their constables, with two sufficient witnesses, to "rype" through their districts for suspected goods, and the fact that on other occasions loiterers and runaways were severely dealt with. Though John Redik of Dalbeattie declared upon 17th December that, to the best of his knowledge, there were no "cold or un-covenanters" in his district, some of the parishioners, it must be confessed, had been somewhat loath to take their share of the common burden. On 1st September, John Hamilton of Auchenreoch was cited for concealing his money to the prejudice of the public interest; and, pretending that he had lent it to George Rome of Irongray, before he knew that it would be wanted, was ordered to produce the writ between him and Rome at the next meeting of Committee. On 6th October, Thomas Thomson in Richerne appeared and deponed that he had delivered two horses of David McBriar, which were being kept by him until McBriar returned to the country and paid his outlays. Shortly after this, the McBriars appear as having an interest in Richerne, so that the fugitive may have to be owned as a parishioner of Urr. It is probable, also, that there were sufficient reasons for John Redik being ordained upon 29th December to bring in his runaways, and deliver them to the

Captains at Dumfries before the end of the year, under a penalty of 40 merks money for each man he failed to produce.

The campaigns which preceded and followed these operations of the Stewartry Committee eventuated in the downfall and execution of King Charles, and the establishment of the Commonwealth under Oliver Cromwell. In connection with them, the men of Galloway are frequently mentioned as playing an important part; and there is little doubt that representatives from Urr were usually included in their number. Some of the parishioners were probably present at Dunse Law in 1639, when the strength of the Presbyterian Army alarmed King Charles, and caused him to come to terms. Some of them must have fought in the Scottish wars against the Royalist forces led by Montrose, and shared in the signal honours won by the South Regiment at the victory of Philiphaugh on 13th September 1645. Some must have been in the English campaign, which continued for several years, and ended in 1647 with the surrender of Charles to the Scottish leader.

The period of Cromwell's rule was not without its commotions. After the execution of Charles, the hearts of the Scottish people began to turn again to their old royal House, and various intrigues and movements were set on foot to restore his exiled son. These the Protector promptly and rigorously suppressed. It was not till 1660, after Cromwell's death, that the Stewart Prince was brought back and crowned as Charles II., amid popular acclamation and joy. The event, which seemed to promise well to Scotland, was deeply disappointing in its results: instead of peace, it brought a sword: and Galloway in particular was soon engaged in a fierce and deadly struggle with the authorities for its civil and religious rights. Forgetful alike of his father's fate and his own promises, Charles II. renewed the old infatuated endeavours to foist the Episcopalian system upon Presbyterian Scotland; and, being met with a stubborn resistance, resorted to persecution and oppression. For five and twenty years, Galloway was subjected to martial law in its crudest form, and suffered ever-increasing severities. In Urr, the first overt action was the ousting of the minister, Mr Gledstaines, from his church and manse, and the installation of an Episcopalian "curate" in his place. The parishioners immediately began to manifest their antipathy to the "curate," by general abstention from his services, and indirect obstruction of him in his work. This he resented and retaliated upon them, by denouncing their offensive ways, and naming the more obnoxious to the authorities. The rancour between the "curate" and his opponents deepened; and on occasions they became so openly and positively hostile as not only to put personal affronts upon him, but to make attacks upon his house. For one of these attacks, a fine of six hundred pounds Scots was levied upon the parishioners. In time they combined to give an informal call to a minister of their own persuasion, and concealed or shielded him from the authorities, while he went about amongst them, confirming and encouraging them in their resistance, as well as ministering to them the Word. Even when the Revolution of 1688 had overthrown the Stewart dynasty, and again secured to Presbyterianism the ascendancy in Scotland, the people of Urr continued for years to harbour grievances against the State, and maintain an attitude of isolation and distrust. These matters, however, belong more closely to the ecclesiastical history of the parish, and will be considered more fully at a later stage: they are simply mentioned here, in order to indicate the mind and temper of the inhabitants, and account for the penal attentions they received. Standing firmly by the Presbyterian cause, they made no secret of their sentiments, but boldly braved the wrath of their unrighteous rulers, and took their share of the cruelties and privations of the time. The dragoons of Grierson and Claverhouse seem to have been frequently quartered upon them, with a roving commission to seek out and arrest the disaffected, whose punishment was fine, imprisonment, mutilation, or death. The curate, Mr John Lyon, like most of his brethren, aided the dragoons with information, and set them on the track of the most objectionable and rebellious; he was even said, on occasion, to have accompanied them on their visitation, and assisted them in their search. There is no record of the death sentence having been carried out upon any of the parishioners of Urr; but many of the poorer class were subjected to cruel hardships and deprivations, some of the people of means were fined, or suffered imprisonment and the spoiling of their goods, and all were terrorised and treated as rebels. In 1662, James Chalmers of Waterside was fined six hundred pounds; and, about the same time, John Macartney of Blaiket was subjected to a similar penalty. In June, 1680, George Macartney of Blaiket, the son of John, was declared to have forfeited both his life and his property, not merely for his adherence to the Presbyterian cause, but also for his active resistance of prelatical domination, in so far as he had been accessory to the armed rising that resulted in the Battle of Bothwell Bridge. His life was spared, but he was committed to prison, and left to languish there for over six years, while his estates passed into the possession of his persecutors, who ravaged them at their will.

These are the more outstanding cases of what, to a greater or less extent, was the common experience of the parishioners. Sir Robert Grierson of Lag, the arch-enemy of the covenanters, seems to have had a personal association with the parish, through the Lauries of Redcastle, which may have made him more intimate with its affairs, if it did not stimulate his desire to reduce it to subjection. One of his most notorious atrocities was perpetrated in the vicinity of Urr, and is kept in rueful memory by a tomb-stone and monument in the northernmost corner of the parish, over the hill behind Larglanglee, and just on the edge of Lochenkit Moor. Captain Bruce of Earlshall, a tempestuous man, only inferior in cruelty to those whom he served, had been appointed lieutenant to Claverhouse, and was co-operating zealously with Grierson in the suppression of the covenanters. On 11th February, 1685, he surprised and captured six of their number in a field at Lochenkit; and four of them, John Gordon, William Heron, William Stewart, and John Wallace, he ordered to be shot upon the spot. The remaining two, Edward Gordon, and Alexander McRobin or McCubbin, he carried prisoners to the Old Bridge of Urr, where Lag was holding an examination of the people, and administering the Abjuration Oath. Grierson would have sentenced them to death at once; but Bruce interceded for them, and insisted that a proper assize or jury should be called for their trial. Lag's reply was to swear " bloodily that he would seek no assizes;" but ultimately he agreed to leave the matter over to the following day. On the morrow, without any pretence of trial, they were hurried off to Irongray, and summarily hanged upon an oak tree near the church. McCubbin found means to send a pious message to his wife, to the effect that " he left her and the two babes upon the Lord, and to His promise." His last words were addressed to the hangman, who had begged his forgiveness: " Poor man, I forgive thee, and all men: thou hast a miserable calling upon earth." Both martyrs, we are told, " died with much composure and cheerfulness." In connection with their death, there is a tradition that the lady of Haughhill or Hallhill, a farm near the spot where they were hanged, gave her scarf or handkerchief to cover their eyes, and for this act of womanly commiseration was sentenced to seven years' banishment in the American plantations; but the ship in which she sailed was wrecked upon the Virginian coast, and she, having providentially escaped, was spared to return to Scotland after the Revolution.

McCubbin and Gordon were buried near the place of their martyrdom, about a quarter of a mile from Irongray churchyard. In 1832, the original tombstone which marks their graves was surrounded by a stone wall, as the result of a collection made after an impressive sermon preached at the spot by the Rev. George Burnside, then of Terregles, and afterwards of Urr. A further service of the same kind, leading to the addition of an iron railing and a new tombstone, was rendered some years ago by the Rev. J. McDermid, minister of the Reformed Presbyterian Church in Dumfries.

The martyrs' tombstone and monument in Urr, which are easily reached by the road which leads past Brooklands, mark the graves of the four men shot at Lochenkit. The tombstone was renewed in 1823, and has the following inscription upon it:—

> Here lyes
> Four Martyrs, John Wallace, William Heron, John Gordon, and William Stewart, found out and shot dead upon this place by Captain Bruce and Captain Lag for their adhearing to the Word of God, Christ's Kingly Government in his house and the Covenanted work of reformation against Tyranny, Perjury, Prelacy.
>
> 2 March MDCLXXXV.
> Rev. Chap. XII. ver. II.
>
> Behold
> Here in this wilderness we lie
> Four witnesses of hellish cruelty
> Our lives and blood could not their ire assuage
> But when we're dead they did against us rage
> That match the like we think ye scarcely can
> Except the Turk or Duke de Alva's men.

The monument, which is of grey granite and obelisk in form, was erected in 1843, and stands close at hand on the northern slope of Larghill. Both memorials were recently overhauled with the proceeds of a religious service held in the neighbourhood by the Rev. James Barr, B.D., minister of St. Mary's United Free Church, Govan. The scenery around them is romantic and imposing enough to be in perfect harmony with the sentiments and recollections they awaken.

The "killing times," as they were called, came to an end in 1688, with the flight of James VII., the brother and successor of Charles II., who maintained the tyrannical traditions of his family till they brought about his downfall. On the accession of William and Mary to the throne, the people of Urr were free to acknowledge publicly the minister they had secretly chosen, and to enjoy the pure covenanted doctrine in their own old parish church, "no man daring to make them afraid." Their time of suffering, however, had left its traces upon them; and for over a generation they were excited and unsettled, refusing to accept the new constitution of Church and State, and evincing a readiness to detect and resent grievances, that kept them in continual conflict with both.

One incident of the Revolution may be recalled, as possessing some local interest, though of little consequence in itself. A number of King William's troops, on their way to Ireland, shortly before the Battle of the Boyne, passed through Galloway; and one contingent of cavalry, at least, encamped for a night at the Haugh of Urr, in the little field beside the Spottes Burn, in front of the Laigh Row. This fact was remembered and attested in 1787, nearly a hundred years afterwards, by an old woman, Jean Walker, then living at Carlingwark. As a witness in a law case, she was asked if she had seen any of King William's cavalry on their way to Ireland in 1689, and replied that "she did not see them, but on coming to the Haugh of Urr soon after the dragoons had left it, she saw on a piece of the Holmland, near the spot where the bridge now stands, the place where war horses had been fed, and several poor people scraping up the remains of the black oats which the horses had left." The bridge referred to was removed many years ago, but traces of its supports may still be seen, at the side of Spottes Burn, a little way below the present bridge. Jean Walker, it may be added, died in 1790, in the 108th year of her age.

The eagerness of the poor people to obtain the horses' leavings is suggestive of the condition to which the district had been reduced by the dissensions and disturbances of the century. Ecclesiastical faction, political strife, and the consequent insecurity of life and property, had paralysed the activities of the people, and brought them to the verge of starvation. Hatred and oppression, too, had embittered their dispositions, and detracted from the amenities of life; the sufferings that concentrated their interests upon religion having served at the same time to obscure its finer qualities, and even impair its moral obligations. Time and wiser treatment alone could repair the injurious effects of the persecutions, in the characters as well as in the lives and homes of the people. With a few exceptions, such as Edingham, which is mentioned about the time of the Union of the Parliaments as a place of consequence, their houses remained hovels of rough stone and turf, which they shared with their cattle: their domestic utensils and furniture were of the rudest and most primitive kind: their food was coarse and badly cooked, consisting for the most part of brose or porridge and kail: their dress was simple and uncouth, and mostly made of woollen plaiding, an article of home manufacture: shoes were worn only upon occasions. Curiously enough, tobacco had come into general use, but tea was a rarity, and still cost thirty shillings a pound. Agriculture was conducted in the old clumsy, inefficient way: horses and oxen were yoked together to the cumbrous plough: there were no carts, as a rule, on the farms, and manure had to be carried in creels, hay and corn in trusses, tied to the women's or horses' backs. At the beginning of the year, the animals were lean and ill-conditioned, their subsistence during the winter having been reduced almost to the vanishing point.

Money was scarce, as is shown by the fact that, when the Union of the Scottish and English Parliaments took place in 1707, after bitter controversy, and amid the strongest opposition and discontent, the whole coin in the country, according to the most liberal calculation, did not amount to a million Sterling. The roads were ill-made and ill-kept, being in many places mere bridle-paths over the otherwise trackless wilds. The main road from Dumfries passed through Milton, where it diverged into three branches: one crossing Hoggans Hill, and going through the farm of Auchenreoch, almost straight to Kirkpatrick-Durham Church: the second leading by Glenarm, Barr of Spottes, and Grange, to the Old Bridge of Urr: and the third following very much the track of the present road to the Haugh, where the river was crossed by a ford. The last-mentioned was the nearest way to Carlingwark and Kirkcudbright, and was generally taken in preference to that by the Old Bridge of Urr, when the water was not too great, especially as it was the "most patent for coaches and carts." Traces of the other two roads, which seem to have been improved in later years, but are now almost disused, are still to be seen.

The experiences of the century had, of course, been adverse to the growth of education; still there must have been some little improvement since the days of Mr Alexander Robertson, when there was no school in the parish, as we find that, in the middle of the persecuting period, a school was kept at Kirkland by Mr John McAdam. The encouragement given to it, however, may be estimated from the relation in which the schoolmaster stood to the "curate" of the time, Mr John Lyon; who, as we shall see, vowed to have him out of Galloway. Mr McAdam's labours, and any others that are unrecorded, were probably on a scale quite inadequate to the wants of the parish; and the bulk of the people would depend for information of events, and intellectual guidance as well as religious instruction, upon the services of the minister.

One striking fact of the close of the century is the continued strength and prevalence of the old superstitions, especially the belief in witches and ghosts. Even the educated classes seem to have shared in this belief, which excited needless terrors among the people, and sometimes led to scenes of great cruelty. Disreputable and eccentric old women were still tried for witchcraft, with all legal formality and solemnity, and sentenced to banishment, torture, and death; while the laying of ghosts was regarded as a duty still pertaining to the clergy.

CHAPTER V

THE EIGHTEENTH CENTURY

WITH the Union of the Parliaments in 1707, a new era of our history begins. The event completed the incorporation of Scotland and England into a single kingdom, with common interests, institutions, and aims, and left them free to enter upon the course of mutual helpfulness and harmonious development which they have since pursued. Especially to the northern and poorer country was the Union fraught with solid and lasting advantages; though these, of course, could not appear till old animosities and jealousies had had time to subside.

In the circumstances, it is not surprising that the proposal for Union was vigorously resisted by a large proportion of the Scottish people, and narrowly escaped defeat from their perfervid and mistaken patriotism. The passing of the measure aroused a widespread irritation and discontent that seriously augmented the feeling in favour of the banished House of Stewart, and encouraged its partisans to prepare for an attempt upon the throne. To counteract this dangerous excitement, another Act was passed in 1712, restoring patronage in the Scottish Church. The object of this measure was to detach the ministers from popular and especially Jacobite influences, and secure their loyalty, by taking the right of appointing them from the people, and vesting it in the Crown or such of the nobility and gentry as were favourable to the reigning family. The result, however, was not only to create a fresh grievance, and precipitate rebellion, but to set a principle in operation which, until it was removed in 1874, proved a continual source of religious disunion and dispeace.

The minister of Urr, Mr John Hepburn, was violently opposed to both these measures, and the parishioners generally sympathised with him in his antagonism. He had also the support of a numerous and devoted body of followers, scattered over all the southern counties. Ever since the Revolution of 1688, the Hebronians, as they were called from the name of their leader, had deplored the shortcomings and backslidings of the times, and maintained a restless and bitter agitation against them. The prospect of Union in 1706 had awakened their alarm, and united them in a petition to Parliament against it, which was signed on their behalf by Mr Hepburn and other seven individuals. Its actual accomplishment aroused their resentment, and called forth their unsparing denunciations; while the further measure of 1712, interfering with the freedom of the Church in the election of its ministers, added fuel to the flame of their wrath. To their minds, the Union of the Parliaments was not only a surrender of national independence, but a sinful correspondence with an uncovenanted people: the restoration of patronage was a flagrant violation of the rights and privileges of the Scottish Church, supposed to have been secured and safeguarded in the Treaty of Union; both alike were defections from the principles of the Covenant, and insults to the Kingly Crown of Christ. Their feelings were pronounced enough, and their words and actions sufficiently threatening, to excite uneasiness among the civil authorities as well as the more moderate members of the Church.

Consequently, when Lord Kenmure and other Galloway gentlemen took up arms for the Pretender in 1715, there was considerable anxiety as to the course which Mr Hepburn would adopt. That he was a person to be reckoned with may be inferred from the fact that, while the ministers of the Synod of Galloway could only pledge themselves to contribute three pounds Sterling, or in lieu thereof provide a single armed man for warlike eventualities, he could bring into the field a force equal, if not superior, to that of any Galloway laird. Mr Hepburn was fully conscious of the value of his support, and for a time declined to declare himself; but, ultimately, he threw the weight of his influence upon the side of the Government, and stood forth in defence of the existing constitution. The part played by him, however, at this juncture, belongs more particularly to his own life, an account of which will be given in a later chapter; meantime it need only be mentioned, in order to maintain the connection of events. With a knowledge of military matters probably derived from some earlier experiences, he mustered 320 of his followers, equipped and drilled them, then marched at their head to Dumfries, with banner flying and drum beating, to assist in warding off a threatened rebel attack upon the town. No hostilities, however, occurred to test the valour of Mr Hepburn and his men; consequently, when the danger had passed, they returned quietly to Urr, and dispersed to their homes. The sword carried by the minister on this warlike expedition is described as " a very formidable claymore, the basket of the hilt being of polished steel, and lined with purple velvet." It and the drum used on the occasion, with other interesting relics of the redoubtable clerical warrior, are known to have been in the possession of his great-grandson, Dr. Mundell of Wallace Hall Academy, less than a century ago. His flag is still preserved in Urr Manse.

The Rebellion came to an end with the surrender of the Jacobite forces at Preston in November, when William Maxwell of Munches and his brother, George Maxwell, were amongst the prisoners taken by the Government troops. From this fact it may be inferred that some of Mr Hepburn's parishioners were engaged upon the side of the rebels. Then, as now, the Munches family possessed lands in the lower part of the parish; and it is highly probable that the brothers Maxwell would be followed in the rising by retainers from these lands. However that may be, the collapse of this

THE EIGHTEENTH CENTURY 41

disastrous undertaking is a noteworthy event in the history of Urr, as it brings the long-continued tale of its fighting days to a close. Never since then have the inhabitants been summoned to take up arms, and leave their hearths and homes for the risks and privations of the battle-field. The subsequent Rebellion of 1745 produced considerable excitement in Galloway, and instigated some general measures of defence, in both of which they shared; but it did not gain footing in their part of the country, nor involve them in any martial expedition. After 1715, they were free from the excursions and alarms of war, and could "beat their swords into ploughshares, and their spears into pruning-hooks."

Slowly, however, as Dr. Muirhead of Urr remarks in speaking of this period, does a nation recover of the wounds made by civil discord. Disturbing influences had been removed, but the people of Galloway could not at once settle down to sober pursuits, or reap the full advantages of the peaceful times that had been secured to them. Indications of the revival of the industrial spirit soon became apparent, but at least a generation had still to pass before there was any marked improvement in agriculture, or real amelioration of the conditions of life. In this period, the food, clothing, houses, and employments of the people, remained very much as they had been for centuries; grey corn was almost the only crop grown, and the old hand quern was still in use for grinding it; the principal industry was the raising of black cattle, which could be grazed for two shillings and sixpence a head, and fetched between two and three pounds in the market. Money was scarce, and wages low, the ordinary day-labourer being content with sixpence a day, and a good mason receiving a shilling, so that in 1749 the walls of Mollance House could be built for forty-nine pounds Sterling. The only baker of the district resided in Dumfries, and hawked his bawbee baps of coarse flour and bran at the fairs of Urr and Kirkpatrick-Durham.

The first attempts to utilise the land to greater advantage were made in 1723, and met with determined opposition from the common people, who regarded them as a subversion of their ancient rights, and an interference with their means of livelihood. Hitherto, as already indicated, the tenant of a farm, besides his dwelling-house and a small portion of cultivated land in its immediate vicinity, possessed the right of pasturage, in common with his fellow-tenants, over the whole of his landlord's estate. As the farms were small, and there were no enclosures, a vast number of people were employed upon the land, many of them in the capacity of herds. Wishing to improve their system of management upon lines that had been followed with success elsewhere, many of the Galloway proprietors began to divide and enclose their land, chiefly by means of dry-stone fences, with the result that many small tenants had to be dispossessed, and many herds and labourers lost their employment. Having no other resources, these unfortunate people were rendered desperate, and took to riot and retaliation. Banding themselves together in a kind of organised mob, with companies of fifty, and a captain or commander over each, they marched through the country side, levelling the newly built dykes, and sometimes lifting the cattle that came in their way. Armed with pitchforks, gavellocks, and spades, or simply long pieces of wood called kents, a company would range themselves along a dyke-side, each man at a set distance from his neighbour, with his weapon fixed at the same height from the foundation; then, when all were ready, the captain would give the word of command, "Ow'r wi't boys," and the dyke was overturned amid shouts that might be heard for miles. Among the first places visited by the Levellers, as they were called, were Barncailzie and Munches, and probably some of the intervening properties in the parish of Urr; afterwards they passed southwards and westwards through the Stewartry, leaving a trail of ruined fences behind them. The proprietors raised their servants and dependents, and endea-

GEORGE MAXWELL OF MUNCHES.
PHOTO. BY DAVID NEWALL, DALBEATTIE, FROM A
PAINTING AT MUNCHES.

THE EIGHTEENTH CENTURY 43

voured to disperse the mob, but without success, until they received the assistance of dragoons from Dumfries, Ayr, and Edinburgh. On the appearance of the military, most of the rioters withdrew from the movement; the rest surrendered soon afterwards at Duchrae in Balmaghie. The principal delinquents were marched to Kirkcudbright, and punished with fine, imprisonment, or transportation to the Plantations. Among the leaders is said to have been one William Marshall, a celebrated chief of the Gipsies, who at this time infested Galloway.

Simultaneously with the attempts to enclose the land, attention was directed in the south of Scotland to the state of the roads, and the need for more bridges. These matters were taken in hand by the Commissioners of Supply, who, for many years, carried on extensive operations, in the way of building bridges, and widening and levelling the roads, to make them suitable for wheel-carts and carriages. In their efforts they were encouraged and assisted by the ministers of the parishes, who took collections in their churches for the prosecution of these necessary public works. That Urr was not behindhand with its contributions, however small they might be, is witnessed by the fact that, on 6th March, 1734, the minister, Mr Wright, reported to Dumfries Presbytery that he had collected six shillings and eightpence from his congregation for the bridge over the Stinchar. Till 1722, there had been but one bridge over the Urr Water, the Old Bridge where the weekly markets and fairs were held; but in that year another was erected in the vicinity of Buittle Castle, connecting the parishes of Urr and Buittle. It was built by John Frew, mason in Edingham; but either from faulty engineering or deficient workmanship, it was unable to withstand the sudden rises of the river, and, according to the testimony of an eye-witness, Mr John Maxwell of Munches, "fell the succeeding summer." The remains of the old road which led to this bridge can still be traced through Meikle Dalbeattie

Cow-park, and at Hillhead near the golf course. The pool immediately above the ruins of Buittle Castle, where the bridge is supposed to have been situated, goes by the name of the " boat pool," and it is probable that a boat was used for passage when no bridge was available. The present bridge, at the foot of Craignair Hill, was built in 1797.

The roads in the parish shared in the general improvement; and, as the century advanced, were partially at least redeemed from their ancient reproach. In 1760, a new road was opened between Dumfries and Portpatrick, passing through the middle of the parish, from Milton to the Haugh of Urr, and crossing the river by a strong and picturesque bridge at the latter place. This road, commonly called the military road, like others constructed about the same time, is carried as straight as possible from point to point, over hill and dale, and consequently abounds in stiff and steep declivities. Those who have occasion to use it frequently will appreciate the remark made upon it by the Rev. Dr. Muirhead. While mentioning that it is the only benefit, up to his time, for which the parish stands indebted to public benevolence, he says it pursues " a line so preposterous, that mere Folly could hardly have stumbled upon it." In estimating that remark, however, it must be remembered that the military road was a vast improvement upon those previously existing, and doubtless was regarded as a great boon at the time it was constructed.

For the first advances in the art of husbandry, Galloway seems to have been indebted to Ireland. In 1725, a person from that country, called William Hyland, introduced potatoes into the Stewartry. For a time they were regarded as a luxury, and grown only in small quantities, Hyland carrying his whole crops to Edinburgh, and selling them in pounds and even ounces; by and by, however, they became a staple article of diet among the people. In 1730, some gentlemen from Galloway, on a visit to Ireland, observed the beneficial effects of shell marl as a manure, and employed an Irish

THE EIGHTEENTH CENTURY 45

farmer to prospect for it in their native province. Many of the Galloway bogs were found to contain it, and it was soon in general use among agriculturists, with the most satisfactory results. This substance, which is a mixture of clay and carbonate of lime, naturally deposited by water, has a tendency to exhaust the land by over-stimulation, when it is continuously applied; and so it was found that, though producing for a time the most abundant crops, it ultimately rendered the soil impoverished and infertile. Proprietors, consequently, had to lay down definite conditions for their tenants, by which they were not allowed to take more than three successive crops after the application of marl, or break up pasture lands until they had been six, or even nine years in grass. Where marl could not be found, sea shells and lime were brought into requisition, as containing the same fertilising ingredients in a more concentrated form. The lime, which was brought from Cumberland to the Water of Urr, and thence carried inland and diffused over a radius of fifteen miles, gradually took the place of marl, and effected a great improvement in the agriculture of the district. By its agency, not only were more plentiful crops raised upon the land already in a state of cultivation, but much waste land was cleared of heath, fern, and other natural growths, and made highly fertile. As time went on, expedients were adopted for preventing the periodical exhaustion of the soil by excessive cropping, and an intelligent system of tillage was developed, which stimulated a spirit of industry in the people, and vastly increased their prosperity and comfort. Moreover, causes and conditions were removed, which tended to discourage husbandry, and hamper or impede the general progress. Facilities of communication were increased by the improvement of the roads, and the building of bridges: the smuggling trade with the Isle of Man was suppressed about the year 1760: the capital necessary for the working of large farms was accumulated, and credit rendered available, by the foundation of banks: the droving trade, which in the days of the raising of black cattle upon the common pastures had been a great feature in the life of the people, was not so eagerly prosecuted. A backset was given to the progressive movement in 1773, by the failure of the Ayr Bank, which brought disaster upon many Galloway agriculturists, including Patrick Gordon of Kingsgrange and David Bean of Meikle Furthhead, each of whom held five hundred pounds' worth of stock, and was, with the other shareholders, personally responsible for its whole debts. The ground lost, however, was speedily regained: renewed efforts were put forth, and more theoretical knowledge was applied to the cultivation of the soil: so that, before the end of the century, the agriculture of Galloway was in a highly flourishing and prosperous condition.

The state of affairs in Urr about the year 1790 is given by the minister, Dr. Muirhead, in his Statistical Account of the parish. The rents of the farms had largely increased, in consequence of the more efficient and remunerative methods of agriculture. Holdings which, a hundred years before, had been offered at the church door to any tenant who would undertake to pay the land-tax, the minister's stipend, and other public burdens, were now let for over £200 per annum. Most of the farms within three miles of the church of Urr paid ten times the rent they had paid about the middle of the century. The general produce of these farms was oats, barley, wheat, potatoes, and black cattle. Much of it was transported to Greenock and the west of Scotland, as well as to Whitehaven, Liverpool, and other adjacent ports in England. The value of the oats and barley sold out of the parish in 1782 was not less than £4000. About 800 bullocks of two and a half years' age were annually sent to England: the best of them weighing from 30 to 35 stones, and fetching from £7 7s. to £8. The number of sheep in the parish was comparatively small, only about 900 in all, according to the best information. Those kept upon the moorland farms belonged to the black-faced variety; those upon the cultivated lowlands were of the

MICHAEL HERRIES OF SPOTTES.

English breed, with finer and more abundant wool. Dr. Muirhead discusses at considerable length the origin of the blackfaced sheep, and concludes that they are derived from cross breeding between the goats at one time abounding in Galloway, and the small, native, white-faced sheep, for which the province was formerly noted.

Marl was plentiful in the parish, as in most places within a radius of twelve miles of the Solway. That which lay nearest the surface having been exhausted, lime from England was in common use, as less troublesome and expensive to procure than the marl from the greater depths. From the marl pits and peat mosses, many large bones and heads of extinct animals had been obtained, chiefly of the urus and reindeer type. The scarcity of fuel was beginning to be felt, as most of the mosses had either been entirely worn away, or dug so deep that they stood covered over with water, and the proprietors were unwilling to drain them. Coals could be had from England, at a cost of 4d. per hundredweight, had they been admitted into Galloway duty free; but an iniquitous coal-tax, against which Dr. Muirhead inveighs, raised the price to the consumer to over a shilling. Some proprietors had taken to the planting of trees, and many more were likely to do so, in the event of the unpopular coal-tax being retained. The growth of wood, especially of Scotch fir, oak, ash, and elm, was exceedingly rapid in the district, and yielded a good return for the money expended upon it. In 1766, Mr Copland of Kingsgrange had planted a piece of waste ground, about sixty acres in extent, near the site of the present town of Dalbeattie; and, in the four years previous to Dr. Muirhead's writing, there had been sold from this plantation, to the owners of the coal mines in Cumberland, Scotch firs to the value of £150 per annum. Besides these, a good many had been disposed of locally, and a large number consumed by the accidental firing of the heath in 1781. This annual revenue, it was computed, would be continued for ten years to come, by which time the deciduous trees, which were so far unfit for cutting, would have matured.

The gross rental of Urr was £4446 Sterling, which Dr. Muirhead does not regard as extravagant, considering the peace and prosperity of the time. The valued rent, that is to say, the total of the rents as estimated in the reign of Charles I., for the payment of ministers' stipends, schoolmasters' salaries, and other parochial burdens, was something over 5000 pounds Scotch. As £1 Sterling is equal to 12 pounds Scotch, these figures indicate that the rents of the parish, on the average, had increased over tenfold, in the intervening century and a half; and this had been the case, Dr. Muirhead assures us, all over Galloway, a valued rent of 100 pounds Scotch implying a real rent of £100 Sterling, or thereabouts. This increase, of course, had taken place entirely during the preceding fifty years.

The population of the parish was 1354, of which number 997 were above ten years of age, and 357 below that period of life. The proportion of males and females was somewhat unequal, there being considerably more of the former than the latter. The reasons given for the preponderance of males are that labourers and gentlemen's servants were in great demand, and that many Irishmen, driven from their homes by tithes, had come into the district, attracted by the ease with which a living could be obtained. Dr. Muirhead admits that no records of burials were kept, and that those of marriages and baptisms were kept very carelessly, chiefly owing to the fact that hardly any marriages, and only ten baptisms, had been celebrated in church during his incumbency. This admission is amply corroborated by the state of the existing records in the General Register House in Edinburgh. On a comparison of the statistics given by him with those supplied to Dr. Webster in 1755, when he drew up his estimate of the population of Scotland, it is found that the number of people in the parish had increased by 161 from that date, the figure given to Dr. Webster having been 1193. In the interval, Dr.

Muirhead says, the population of Urr had gone down considerably, possibly as low as 900; but this is little more than a conjecture, suggested by the recollections of a veteran precentor. The main cause of the increase in his time was the greater scarcity of fuel in other parishes as compared with Urr, caused by the operation of the coal-tax, which he vehemently denounces, as not only producing depopulation in many parts of Galloway, but indirectly bringing troubles and diseases upon the poorer people everywhere, through the cold and privation it entailed upon them.

Most of the inhabitants were employed upon the land, either, as may be presumed, in the ordinary work of the farms, or in building dykes for fences, making roads, or cutting and cleaning ditches, which were the only means of draining at the time. Not a few, however, followed subsidiary occupations, as masons, joiners, smiths, shoemakers, and tailors, as might be expected from the size of the population, and the general activity consequent upon the improvements in the houses and ways of living. There were hardly any idle or dissipated characters in the parish, and only two or three of the natives had enlisted in the army during the whole period of Dr. Muirhead's ministry. These two facts are conjoined by Dr. Muirhead, as if both alike reflected credit upon the parish. Agriculture being so prosperous as to provide a sufficiency of labour, little more than a beginning had been made in the establishment of manufactures. A few years previously, a paper mill had been erected at Dalbeattie, on the estate of Mr Alexander Copland; which, being personally managed by the proprietor, and duly equipped with the necessary machinery and storehouses, had been abundantly successful. So also had a lint mill established in the same vicinity; though, in Dr Muirhead's opinion, the district was better adapted for the rearing and feeding of cattle than for the growing of flax, owing to the alternations of heavy rains and severe droughts to which it was liable. What he calls

" the absurd custom of fixing a rate of wages at which servants and other labourers are obliged to work " was not thought of in the neighbourhood, and masters and servants were free to make their own terms with each other. The remuneration of all kinds of work was good, in comparison with other counties in Scotland; and the working classes, having no real ground for complaint, were comfortable and contented. Mechanics in general employment were paid by the piece, so that no accurate return of their daily gains could be given. Tailors were mostly paid by the day, at the rate of 8d., with their victuals in addition. An ordinary labourer could earn from 1s to 1s. 6d. per day. Men servants had from £4 4s. to £4 10s. and even £5 in the half year: women servants from £1 2s. to £1 15s. or £2 for a similar term. The cottar, or regular farm servant, was paid by the year, and had as follows:

1. 60 bushels of corn, valued at 20d. per bushel, £5 0 0
2. A house and yard, at - - - - - 1 0 0
3. A cow, kept summer and winter, - - 3 10 0
4. 3 pecks of potatoes, set with the master's, - 1 10 0
5. A sheep at Martinmas, or in lieu, a swine grazed 0 10 0
6. Wages for the year, in money, - - - 2 0 0

£13 10 0

These wages indicate the progress that had taken place during the latter half of the century, though they are still comparatively small from the point of view of the present day. The prices of provisions, of course, such as grain, beef, and mutton, were correspondingly lower than they are now, as may be seen from the values put upon the commodities in which the cottars were partly paid. They were generally estimated in Urr at the rates prevailing in the Dumfries market.

There was still a good deal of waste ground in the parish, which has since been inclosed and brought under cultivation. The population, which worked out at a very small average per acre or square mile, was somewhat unequally distributed, so that while some parts were thickly enough peopled, others had but a few inhabitants. The occupations of the people, as well as the air and climate, being conducive to health, there was not much sickness among them; what there was arose chiefly from exposure to cold, hard labour, and the debilitating effects of old age; consequently one surgeon sufficed for Urr and several neighbouring parishes. Since the houses of the farmers and labourers had been built of better materials, and rendered more comfortable and convenient, there had been a great improvement in the health of the parish, and a surprising decrease in the rate of infant mortality. Some remarkable instances of longevity are adduced by Dr. Muirhead, in evidence of the healthiness of the parish, and the wholesomeness of the lives of the people. Within the previous 15 years, several persons had died at the age of 100, or above it. Most notable of all, one Peter Buchanan had died ten years before in the village of Dalbeattie, who, though his age could not be exactly fixed, was certainly over 115 years. To the day of his death, which took place after half an hour's illness, he enjoyed remarkable health, and showed a surprising degree of activity. At the time of writing, there were two or three people in the parish over 90 years of age, and several others who had reached four score. With the exception of a few, who were quite incapacitated for work, every poor person made some exertion to maintain himself; it being nothing unusual for a man of 70, or even above it, to continue his usual employment, and receive an ordinary day's wage. The travelling beggar, that is to say, the pauper authorised to go from house to house and solicit doles, had become practically extinct; nor had there been more than three such persons during the preceding twenty years, and these had been strictly confined to the limts of the parish. As a whole, the character of the inhabitants was good: their behaviour sober, inoffensive and dutiful. With an independence of spirit and acuteness of judgment, fostered by the free institutions under which they lived, they had taken the measure of the seditious language and literature of the time, particularly of a pamphlet called the Patriot, and remained unaffected in their loyalty to the existing government. Indeed, in the opinion of Dr. Muirhead, there was not a man in the parish, who would not risk his life for the support of the King's authority, and the defence of the British constitution, as established at the Revolution of 1688. In the matter of religion, the bulk of the inhabitants adhered to the National Church; the Dissenters numbering 270 persons, divided between 30 families of Antiburgher Seceders, and 28 families of Roman Catholics. Old animosities, however, had been so far forgotten, that no bitterness or misunderstanding was occasioned by the differences of religious opinion.

In this comparatively satisfactory condition of parochial affairs, it is a disappointment to find the state of education so backward and neglected as to call forth an indignant protest from Dr. Muirhead, and a strong plea for its amelioration. His trenchant criticism of the illiberal and ineffective system in vogue, for the most part, is couched in general terms; in order, on the one hand, to avoid personalities, and on the other hand, to attract popular attention to the widespread nature of the disabilities and discouragements under which the teaching profession laboured. To his mind, there was no proper appreciation of the value and importance of education; and the means provided for its support were quite insufficient even for its most elementary requirements. The better classes were not favourably inclined to popular education, and argued against the necessity of teaching their tenants and cottars anything more than to read their Bibles and subscribe their names. The salaries of the schoolmasters were the merest pittances; which, when occasion demanded, the heritors had no scruple in subdividing, for the support of additional teachers. Appointments were made at random, and often from year to year, without the ministers being consulted, or even allowed a vote. "The

THE EIGHTEENTH CENTURY

consequence is," as Dr. Muirhead puts it in his characteristically sarcastic style, "a parish school is now a momentary, or at least a temporary employment, for some necessitous person of ability; or a perpetual employment for some languid insignificant mortal, hardly deserving the shelter of a charity workhouse. Learning and literature are out of the question. In order to be popular, the parson finds it indispensable to propagate a dangerous enthusiasm, or to declare himself retainer to a contemptible superstition."

The salary of the schoolmaster in Urr was 200 merks Scotch, or £11 2s. 2¾d. Sterling; and, even from this inadequate allowance, the sum of £3 was subtracted for the maintenance of a subsidiary school in the moorish part of the parish. Dr. Muirhead is careful to abstain from characterising the contemporary holders of these shadowy scholastic benefices; but his opinion of them may be inferred from his naive comment, that "for such an encouragement, it is not to be expected that teachers of very respectable qualifications can be found." When his plea for the establishment of more schools in the parish is conjoined with this remark, no doubt is left in the mind of the inferior and inadequate character of the education of the time. It is quite evident that the youth of Urr were in no danger of realising the fears of the affluent, that they would be over-educated, and come to think themselves better men than their fathers.

Among the changes taking place during his ministry, Dr. Muirhead notes the beginning of several new villages in the parish. This was a natural result from the increased attention to agriculture, and the general improvements going forward, which necessitated provision being made for a considerable number of people not engaged as hired servants on the farms. Dalbeattie seems to have made the fairest start; but it has since grown into a town of such dimensions, that its rise and development must be relegated to a separate chapter. The villages in the other parts of the parish are not named: they are simply mentioned, as having been recently commenced, and so far having made but little progress. The reference is probably to Haugh-of-Urr and Hardgate, which had begun to appear on the sides of the old military road, as it dipped down to cross the valley of the Urr.

The close of the century was marked by the appearance and settlement in the parish of a strange sect of religious enthusiasts, called Buchanites, from their founder and leader, an illiterate and fanatical, but apparently clever, woman. There is an old story which connects them with Dr. Muirhead, at the very outset of their romantic career in the district. Some of the fraternity had been engaged by the minister of Urr for the harvest of 1787, and in September of that year were working quietly at his corn, along with other harvesters, who, though they had learned of their peculiar opinions, had so far observed nothing uncommon in their conversation or behaviour. Towards the afternoon, as the work was proceeding briskly, a woman arrived upon the scene, when the strangers immediately fell into a state of excitement and commotion. Desisting from their work, they threw down their implements, and embraced each other; then, forming themselves into a body, they advanced slowly and reverentially to meet her. Gathering round her in the field, with hats off, and hands uplifted as if in prayer, they sang together as follows:

"Let no one imagine we here mean to tarry,
Although to the parish of Urr we have come;
By us Auchengibbert has only been taken
To rest in, as onward we march to our home."

The woman was about fifty years of age, and had nothing exceptional in her appearance to account for the strange power she wielded over her simple followers. She was born at Banff in 1738, and her maiden name was Elspeth Simpson; but she had been married and settled for a time in the neighbourhood of Glasgow, and was known throughout her erratic career as Mrs or Luckie Buchan.

THE EIGHTEENTH CENTURY 55

With her was associated in the movement the Rev. Hugh White, who had previously been the minister of the Relief Kirk in Irvine. Happening to hear him preach in Glasgow, at an administration of the Sacrament, in December 1782, she had professed herself profoundly moved and benefited by his discourse; and, after some correspondence, he had invited her to Irvine, with a view to giving her further instruction. There she began to make pretensions of divine origin, which Mr White was induced to believe and aid her in imposing upon members of his congregation. His vagaries soon attracted the notice of his Presbytery, who promptly deposed him; but many, even of the wealthier members of his flock, adhered to him, and formed themselves into a sect of Buchanite believers, who met mostly at night, and listened to the blasphemous ravings of their pretended prophetess. Her assertions were of a somewhat mixed description: she was made from the blood that flowed from Christ on the Cross; she was the Spirit of God incarnate, or the third Person in the Trinity: she was the woman spoken of in the 12th chapter of Revelation: Mr White was the man child she had brought forth, who was to rule the nations with a rod of iron: her followers would not taste of death, but would be translated directly to heaven: meantime they were to live together in a separate community, give up their private property, and have all things in common. The promulgation of these tenets was violently resented in Irvine, and the magistrates had to expel Mrs Buchan from the town to save her from the fury of the populace. At Kilmaurs, she was joined by Mr White and forty of her adherents, when the whole party set out upon their pilgrimage " to the New Jerusalem," as they expressed it, singing hymns upon the way, and causing considerable wonderment in the country districts through which they passed. After various wanderings they arrived at Closeburn in Dumfriesshire, where they settled for nearly three years, and built themselves a small house, at a place since called Buchan Hall, on the farm of New Cample.

Two attempts were made, after elaborate and solemn preparation, to accomplish the ascent to heaven; the failure in each case being readily excused by Mrs Buchan, as the consequence of their want of faith. Afterwards a fast of forty days was decreed among them, evidently with a view to the diminution of the weight of the body as well as the discipline of the soul; but this ordeal proved too much for many of them, whose health or endurance broke down under its severity. The people of Closeburn rose in anger and disgust, and compelled the authorities of Dumfriesshire to eject them from the county.

In March 1787, they appeared at Tarbreoch in Kirkpatrick-Durham, where they were allowed the use of an old house for a time, and held open-air meetings under the presidency of Friend or Father White, as he was called by his flock. At first the country people were widely interested in their doings, and frequented their gatherings; but they soon grew tired of them, and left them severely alone. Indeed, all the time of their sojourn in Galloway, they do not seem to have made a single convert.

In May of the same year, they removed to the farm of Auchengibbert; where, with all their peculiarities of practice and belief, they proved themselves capable agriculturists, and led a frugal and industrious life. Some of them were employed in the erection of stables, byres, and fences; others attended to the stock, and worked the farm; one man made spinning wheels of an improved type; a few practised as joiners, tinsmiths, and such like, among the neighbouring inhabitants; while the women spun yarn, and worked it up into woollen goods, which became popular throughout the south of Scotland. The general verdict upon them was happily summed up by a farmer of the time: "their heids may be a wee bit aff, but they're gran' wi' their hauns."

Miracles were ascribed to Mrs Buchan by her followers; but the great miracle which she again essayed at Auchen-

THE EIGHTEENTH CENTURY 57

gibbert—that of raising herself and them to heaven—was more than she could perform. Platforms were raised on the top of the hill upon the farm, on which the whole company gathered themselves together, in trembling expectation of the glorious consummation; but the day passed without anything exceptional occurring, and they were forced to descend, crestfallen and disappointed, from their elevated station. The faith of some was shaken: a few spoke of retiring from the community: even Mr White is said to have lost confidence in "Mother" Buchan, and heaped reproaches upon her in private; but her death, on 29th March 1791, anticipated the coming storm, and at least restored her to her old place in their affections. Before her departure, she enjoined them to continue in the faith she had delivered to them, and assured them she was only going to sleep for a time, and would return again to accompany them to heaven. She might take on the appearance of death, but would not really die, as she had received indisputable evidence of her divine origin and nature. The time of her return would depend upon the strength of their faith: it might take place within six days, or it might be delayed for ten, and even fifty, years.

The demise of the leader was the signal for the disruption of the infatuated party. Shortly afterwards, Mr White and other thirty of the Buchanites, abandoning the hope of ever seeing Mrs Buchan again, if not indeed entirely undeceived in regard to her pretensions, emigrated to America. The more credulous remnant, numbering only 12 persons, determined to remain in the neighbourhood, which was destined, as they believed, to be the scene of her reappearance, and rented the farm of Larghill, whither they betook themselves. There they followed the same pursuits, and led the same quiet industrious lives, as they had done at Auchengibbert. They continued to hold their property in common, and came to be held in great respect by their neighbours, not only for their staid and inoffensive manners, but for their uniform kindness to the distressed, for which, as a matter of principle, they refused even to be thanked. Their carts were known in the district by the inscription upon them "Mercy's property," or as it afterwards read: "The people of Larghill." As time went on, they grew fairly prosperous; so that, in 1800, they were able to purchase five acres of land at Crocketford, and build several houses, which became the nucleus of a thriving and populous village. Their first house was ready in 1802, and received the name of Newhouse: it still stands on the New Galloway road. In the rear of this house, they established a little cemetery for themselves, so as to be together at the expected advent of Mrs Buchan. In 1808, all that were left of them removed from Larghill to Crocketford; where, as marriage was discouraged among them, they eventually died out. To the last, though by no means holding aloof from the social life around them, they retained their peculiar ceremonies and beliefs.

The final survivor of the community, and the most interesting of its members, was Andrew Innes. He was a comparatively young man when he joined the Buchanite movement, and he was spared for nearly fifty-five years after the death of its founder. Throughout that time, the remains of Mrs Buchan were carefully preserved by her devoted followers, and carried about with them in their various changes of abode, apparently on the chance of her requiring them again. Immediately after her death, they were secretly buried in Kirkgunzeon Churchyard; but, a few nights later, they were disinterred as secretly, and brought back to Auchengibbert, where they were concealed under the kitchen hearthstone. Probably a dispute had arisen as to their disposal, between the faithful remnant and those who afterwards went to America. From Auchengibbert they were removed to Larghill; and, after sojourning there for a time, were brought down to Crocketford at the establishment of the village. Eventually they fell to the sole charge of Andrew Innes, who kept them on the premises at Newhouse,

THE NINETEENTH CENTURY 59

and anxiously watched and tended them to his dying day. When he passed away, in January 1846, they were laid to rest beside him, in the little Buchanite cemetery.

CHAPTER VI

THE NINETEENTH CENTURY

GENERAL AND AGRICULTURAL MATTERS

DURING this century an unprecedented development of social and industrial life took place throughout the country. At the same time various influences came into operation that broke down the comparative isolation of rural districts, and brought them into closer touch with the outside world. So far as its circumstances and resources admitted, Urr participated in the general movement, and exhibited at the close of the century a very different condition of affairs from that which obtained at its beginning. Greater changes accordingly fall to be recorded in the parish during this period than in any previous stage of its history. It will be convenient to deal with these in sections, and to begin with those relating more directly to the general conditions of life upon the land.

The opening years of the century found the country in the throes of the war with France. The consequence was that a decided though artificial impetus was given to agriculture, by the creation of abnormal demands, and the rapid inflation of prices. In Galloway, grain and cattle rose in value to points which had never previously been touched: the sale of swine became so lucrative that large quantities of them were raised for the market: and, as rents for the time were by no means excessive, some of the leases having only recently been renewed, the working of the farms left a considerable margin of profit. Under these favourable circumstances exertion was stimulated, and encouragement given to carry out improvements upon the land. With a view to united intelligent action, a Society of Agriculturists was formed in the Stewartry—the first in the county—on 20th March 1809. Its membership included all the leading farmers and proprietors in the district: it offered prizes to the amount of 41½ guineas for Galloway cattle, sheep, horses, ploughing, and servants of various qualifications: papers upon relative subjects were read at its meetings and occasionally published, one of the earliest and best being contributed by the Rev. Alexander Murray of Urr.

The parishioners of Mr Murray seem to have entered with earnestness into the spirit of the time: emulating their neighbours in bringing waste land into cultivation: importing lime and judiciously applying it: enlarging their patches of potatoes, which, with meal and milk, were the staple diet of the peasantry, and were also used for feeding the pigs: improving the breeds of cattle and sheep: making fresh divisions of the fields, and erecting better fences, for the proper rotation of crops. Besides the bulk of the villages, many of the steadings in Urr were built at this time, and others had extensive renovations carried out upon them. Some of these, like Holehouse which stood a little to the south of Halmyre farm, and Corsehill which was situated on the edge of the wood so-called, have since entirely disappeared; others, though still standing, and occupied as dwelling-houses, have lost their distinctive consequence; the result in both cases of smaller farms and crofts being absorbed into larger holdings. About this time, also, the roads of the parish received exceptional attention, and had a large amount of labour and money expended upon them. With the doubtful exception of the old military road, they were found quite unsuitable for the new forms of traffic, and improvements were made of which the benefit is reaped to the present day. Some of the old roads were entirely given up: others were reconstructed: new ones were made, such as the port road from Dalbeattie to Kirkpatrick-Durham, for the transit up-country of the goods and materials that came by sea, and the fine coach road passing through the villages of Crocketford and Springholm, which brought the district into touch with other parts of the country. The latter was opened from Dumfries to Castle-Douglas in 1800, and was extended to Portpatrick in 1807. The result of these operations was that, before the century was far advanced, the lines of traffic through the parish followed practically the existing routes. The condition of these roads, of course, has been improved, and some minor changes have been made upon them, in later times. For instance, the road which connects the Haugh-of-Urr with the coach road was straightened and broadened, partly about eighty years ago by Mr W. Y. Herries of Spottes, and partly about forty years ago by Mr Thomas Biggar of Chapelton, at the points where it passes their respective properties. Still later, the bridge which carries it over the Spottes Burn was widened, and had its direction slightly altered, without disturbing the original arch.

Some idea of the progress of the early years of the century may be gained from the consideration of such parochial statistics as are now accessible. The population, which had been given by Dr. Muirhead about 1790 as 1354, rose in 1801 to 1719, and increased even more rapidly afterwards, being 2329 in 1811, and 2862 in 1821, the females now considerably outnumbering the males. In the same interval the valuation more than trebled itself, approaching at the end of the period fifteen thousand pounds. Considerable room, however, must have remained for improvement, when ploughs drawn by oxen were still to be seen in some parts of Galloway, and, even where horses were used, the harness and implements were largely of home manufacture.

The close of the wars with France in 1815, though affording a welcome relief to the country, put an end to the fictitious rates prevailing for farm products, and was so far fraught with adverse results to agriculture. A period of depression succeeded which, except for some years of alleviation between 1830 and 1840, lasted almost to the middle of the century. Prices were reduced to such an extent that the profits of the agriculturist disappeared: bad seasons were encountered: rents fell into arrears: disaster overtook many of the tenants, and was only averted from others by the liberal behaviour of the landlords. In spite of these untoward circumstances, or possibly in consequence of them, the art of farming continued to progress, and some of the changes instituted during this period have proved themselves of lasting value. Turnips began to displace potatoes as the principal green crop, and were advantageously used in the feeding of sheep. Greater energy was thrown into the raising of black cattle, the fattening of swine, and the improvement of farm implements and graith. The sickle had long reigned alone in the harvest-field: the scythe now appeared in competition with it, and soon passed into general use, as a more convenient and effective instrument. A beginning was made with the laying of tile-drains; and in 1842 the movement received impetus and guidance from the grant of a Government subsidy, on condition that certain rules and directions were observed. The greatest advance, however, was perhaps inaugurated by the introduction in 1825 of bone-dust, the first of those artificial manures which have since been scientifically tested and compounded, and are now practically a necessity to the agriculture of Galloway. About the same time increased facilities began to be provided for exporting the produce of the farms to populous places, chiefly by the institution of a small steamship service between the ports of Galloway and Liverpool, Glasgow, and other places. The best-known steamer engaged in the trade was the Countess of Selkirk, which was built in 1835, and plied for many years between Liverpool, Wigtown, and Kirkcudbright. Another small steamer, called the St. Andrew, sailed every second Thursday for a time from Palnackie, with passengers, stock, and goods, for Whitehaven and Liverpool, and intermediate ports.

That Urr was not behindhand in the development of its resources may be inferred from the condition of things in the parish in 1845, when the New Statistical Account was published. According to it, the farmers were industrious and skilful, and not only imported lime from Cumberland and bone-dust for the turnip-crop from Liverpool, but exported considerable quantities of grain, chiefly to the latter place. The crops were even more varied than they are now, consisting largely of barley and wheat, as well as oats, turnips, and potatoes. The system of sheep feeding was greatly on the increase, owing to the facilities afforded of raising turnips by the recent use of bone manure, and of conveying fat sheep to Liverpool and other English markets, by means of steam-vessels. The raising of pigs and feeding them for the market had long been pursued with profit; while a fair share of attention was also given to the breeding of horses and black cattle. Besides a paper manufactory in the village of Dalbeattie, there were corn, flax, and saw mills in different parts of the parish. Owing to the less favourable conditions, however, under which agriculture had been carried on during the preceding quarter of a century, the annual rents of the farms showed no appreciable increase, being practically the same as they had been in 1815, or a total of £16,000. The population had risen slightly, being 3098 in 1831, and 3096 in 1841; but this addition was no sign of well-being in the community, for it is stated that "the villages of Dalbeattie and Springholm contain a population (a great proportion of which is Irish), which the state of the surrounding country is unable to support by lawful industry. Hence poverty with its generally accompanying evils greatly prevails in these two villages." The land-owners numbered 34, the principal being John Herries Maxwell of Munches, William Copland of Colliston, John Sinclair of Redcastle, William Maitland of Achlane, William Stothert of Cargen, William Young-Herries of Spottes, and John Hyndman of Milton. Of the other proprietors in the second quarter of the century, it is sufficient to mention two whose descendants still retain possession of their lands: Alexander Blair of Upper Auchenreoch, and Sir David Maxwell of Cardoness. Another

JOHN HERRIES MAXWELL OF MUNCHES.

THE NINETEENTH CENTURY

proprietor of the time was Thomas Gibson of Little Cocklick: his family have parted with the possession of the lands, but one of them still continues to farm them. In this connection it is interesting to notice that, of the tenant-farmers whose names appear in 1835, the following have left descendants who still hold farms in the parish: James Biggar in Kingsgrange, Maxwell Clark in Little Culmain, Thomas Dinwoodie in Auchenreoch, and James Hyslop in Nether Auchenreoch.

About the middle of the century the prospects of agriculture began to brighten, and a period of increasing prosperity set in, which lasted with occasional interruptions for nearly thirty years. The general effect was to raise the valuation of parishes about fifty per cent.; double the wages of servants; enable the more active and enterprising farmers to increase their stocks and holdings, or retire upon a modest competence; and largely improve the manner of living in country districts. In the latter years of the century, however, a different condition of affairs was experienced, the briskness and prosperity of former days disappearing gradually, until about 1896 a depth of depression was reached, from which so far only a partial recovery has been made. The profits of farming were reduced to vanishing point, and rents had to be lowered to such an extent that the valuations of agricultural subjects fell practically to the figures of fifty years before. Indeed it is no uncommon thing for farms to be held at the present time at very much the same rents as were paid for them in the first quarter of the century. Servants' wages, on the whole, have remained stationary, being the same at the end of the century as in 1875, except in the case of those of women, which show a slight increase. They may be taken to be as follows:

Married ploughmen, with house and garden, and fuel carted - - - - - - £38 to £42
Single ploughmen, with board and lodging, per six months - - - - - - - £12 to £14

Women, with board and lodging, per six months £8 to £10
Men's harvest wage, with victuals - - - £4 10 to £5
Women's harvest wage, with victuals - - £3 10 to £4
Labourers, per day - - - - - - 3/
Women, per day - - - - - - 1/6

The fluctuations of agricultural prosperity in the latter half of the century were largely due to general causes, and simply reflected the prevailing state of trade in the country, and the new conditions under which agricultural pursuits were carried on. At first the rise and progress of industrial communities enlarged the demand for agricultural products and raised the prices: the development of the railway system increased the facilities of transit: the improvement of farm implements, and the invention of machines for tilling, sowing, and thrashing, economised labour and conduced to better results. On the other hand, the industrial slackness of the country in recent times, and the competition forced upon the farmers with the produce of other lands, have operated to the disadvantage of their occupation, and diminished their profits. Through all, however, there has been no abatement of agricultural progress in Galloway; on the contrary, the agriculturists of the province have enhanced their position in the farming world, by their readiness to adapt themselves to new conditions and adopt new methods and machinery. The breed of horses has been greatly improved, some of the best Clydesdales now hailing from this part of the country: the fattening of sheep and cattle for the butcher has taken the place of the old system of raising them for the store market: dairies have been instituted in many places with successful results: farms have been equipped with a full complement of machinery, including the reaper introduced about 1860, and the self-binder some thirty years later: seeds, manures, and feeding materials have been subjected to such theoretical and practical investigation as has helped to put the whole business of the farmer upon more scientific lines.

THE NINETEENTH CENTURY

While sharing the common vicissitudes of the second half of the century, the farmers and land-owners of Urr were quick to move with the times, and in several instances took a conspicuous part in promoting agricultural interests and improvements. Among the most noted agriculturists of his day was the late Mr Wellwood Herries Maxwell of Munches, a leading proprietor of the parish, whose name will long be remembered for the enlightened zeal and ungrudging energy with which he devoted himself to public affairs. Besides presiding for lengthened terms over most of the local bodies, Mr Maxwell represented the Stewartry of Kirkcudbright in Parliament from 1868 to 1874, and occupied the position of Convener of the county for forty years; his services in the last-mentioned connection being recognised in 1890 by the public presentation of a portrait to him, the work of Sir George Reid. As superior of the larger part of Dalbeattie, Mr Maxwell gave every encouragement to the rising town, and spared no efforts to advance its development and prosperity. In agricultural matters he took a lifelong and widespread interest, not only giving patronage and support to local agricultural societies, and stimulating improvements upon his own and neighbouring lands, but directing his attention to the larger questions of national agricultural progress, and participating in the work of the Highland and Agricultural Society of Scotland. In 1895, when the Highland Society paid one of its periodical visits to Dumfries, Mr Maxwell, who was one of its vice-presidents for the year, acted as Convener of the local committee, and was largely responsible for the success of the show. In the passing of a vote of thanks to him for his services on the occasion, notice was taken of the fact that Mr Maxwell's association with the Society had existed for sixty-five years, during which time he had been present at all the shows, eight in number, which had been held in Dumfries. Induced to put on record his reminiscences of these shows, as well as of the progress of agriculture in the interval covered by them, he contributed a paper to the Transactions of the Society for the following year, which is full of interesting and valuable information. The present Laird of Munches, Mr William Jardine Herries Maxwell, who was Parliamentary representative of Dumfriesshire for a time, inherits much of his father's public spirit, and fills many of his offices, including that of Convener of the Stewartry of Kirkcudbright.

Of the other agriculturists of the parish the most prominent were the Biggars of Chapelton, the descendants of an old Irongray family, who came from Skinford, Dunscore, in 1829, and settled in Urr as tenants of Kingsgrange. So early as 1842, Mr Thomas Biggar, a man of strong character and great natural gifts, commenced a business in farm seeds and artificial manures, which attained considerable proportions in his hands, and was still further extended under the management of his sons. At the same time, by his practical skill and enterprise in farming, first at Kingsgrange and afterwards also at Chapelton, and the success of the herd of Galloway cattle which he established at the latter place, he became widely known as an able agriculturist and breeder of stock. The younger of the two sons who became associated with him in business, Mr William Biggar, now resident in Corbieton, Buittle, devoted himself more particularly to the manufacturing department of the firm, while the elder, Mr James Biggar, attended to its commercial affairs, and managed Kingsgrange and other farms. The latter took a keen interest in everything relating to agriculture, and early in life established a reputation for himself, by his exceptional grasp of agricultural matters, and his conspicuous ability in dealing with them. Before he was thirty years old, he had written and published a series of able articles upon the agriculture of Galloway, which demonstrated his acuteness of mind and powers of observation, as well as his possession of an easy and accurate style. In 1876, these articles, which attracted considerable attention at the time,

THOMAS BIGGAR OF CHAPELTON.

THE NINETEENTH CENTURY

and still make most interesting reading, were reproduced in pamphlet form and presented as a report to the Highland Society. Three years afterwards, Mr James Biggar was selected as the representative of the Stewartry upon the deputation appointed to visit Canada and report upon its agricultural resources. This was the first of a series of visits to Canada and the United States; which, while helping to enlarge his ideas of agricultural practice, and make him a warm advocate of agricultural education, secured him a position as an authority upon these subjects on both sides of the Atlantic. Besides privately advising upon matters of practical farming, he was much employed as an arbiter in the settlement of disputed questions, and filled many offices in connection with agricultural societies and institutions. For many years he took an active part in the work of the Galloway Cattle Society, and ultimately succeeded Mr Maxwell of Munches as chairman of the council. He was a governor of the Glasgow and West of Scotland Agricultural College from the start: an examiner for agricultural diplomas, first under the Highland Society, and afterwards under the joint scheme of the two national societies of Scotland and England: a member of Mr Joseph Chamberlain's commission on the fiscal question: a member of the Scottish Chamber of Agriculture; and in 1906, the year of his death, the chairman of that body. In 1903 he was invited across the Atlantic to award the champion and other leading prizes at the great International Live Stock Exhibition at Chicago. In addition to the activities imposed upon him by these offices and the exactions of his private business, Mr Biggar found time to take an active interest in the affairs of his native parish; being a member of Urr School Board for a time, County Councillor from the first, and a devoted elder, like his father before him, of the parish church. Immediately after his death a movement was started to commemorate his work as one of the most active, useful, and enterprising men of his generation; and a sum of over £700 was speedily raised, with which a bursary was founded and called by his name in the Glasgow and West of Scotland Agricultural College, an institution in which he had always taken the liveliest interest.

These examples of outstanding ability and enterprise may be regarded as indications of a general spirit of agricultural progress in the parish. A further indication of the same spirit is afforded by the formation in 1855 of the Agricultural Society of Dalbeattie, for the purpose of promoting an annual exhibition of the farm stock and produce of the neighbourhood. This society continues in existence, and has maintained its annual show with great regularity, only giving way every five years to the Dumfries Union, and at longer intervals to the Highland Society, when their exhibitions were held at Dumfries. Its influence in raising the quality of farm products in the surrounding districts, to which it is open, may be inferred from the high character of the exhibits annually presented at its gatherings. In the opinion of competent judges these have usually reached a standard, especially in the classes of Galloway cattle and horses, that would have reflected credit on an exhibition drawing upon a much more extensive area. The meeting at which the society was inaugurated was held in the Maxwell Arms Hotel, Dalbeattie, on 11th May, 1855, and the following names appear upon the sederunt: Messrs. Wellwood H. Maxwell of Munches, Carswell, Rawline, Brown (draper), George Wilson, Paterson (baker), Grieve (banker), McLaurin, Burnie (banker), and George Nisbet, all of Dalbeattie; Messrs Hyslop, Meikle Firthhead; Marchbank, Buittle Mains; Wilson, Corsock; Carson, Laggan; Clark, Cowar; Dickson, Uppertown; Biggar, Kingsgrange; Loudon, Orchardton; Thomson, Chapelton; Graham, Meikle Culloch; Thomson, Blaiket; Gordon, Barsyard; Brown, Meikle Dalbeattie; Steel, Millbank; Muirhead, Barchain; and Loudon of Clonyard. Mr Maxwell, who had been the prime instigator of the meeting, was appointed chairman, and subsequently president of the society, an office he continued to hold for forty-five years. At a meeting held

JAMES BIGGAR OF CHAPELTON.

on 18th March, 1901, shortly after his death, Mr James Biggar, one of the vice-presidents, paid a fitting tribute to him for his life-long services to the society, and it was resolved to appoint his son, Mr W. J. H. Maxwell, to succeed him in the presidentship. The first secretary was Mr James Grieve, agent of the Union Bank, Dalbeattie. He held office for twenty-two years, and was succeeded in 1877 by Mr R. W. Macnab, his successor also in the agency of the bank. Mr Macnab fulfilled the duties of the office almost for the same length of time as his predecessor, resigning on 8th March, 1898, when Mr William Milligan, land steward on the Munches estate, took his place. On the resignation of Mr William Milligan in April 1901, Mr J. E. Milligan, solicitor, was appointed; and he has since conducted the affairs of the society, and carried through its shows, with conspicuous success. The shows of the society have usually been held on the first Tuesday of October, and the progress achieved by it during the fifty years of its existence may be estimated from the fact that, at the first show held in 1855, the premiums awarded amounted only to £47, and the receipts from all sources to £112 4s. 8d., while at the jubilee show of 1905 over £160 was given in prizes, and the total income, including subscriptions and donations, reached the sum of £260 19s. 9d.

Three years after the institution of the Dalbeattie Agricultural Society, another stimulus was given to the agriculture of the parish by the opening of the railway line between Dumfries and Castle-Douglas, with a suitable station at Dalbeattie. This, again, was largely the result of the efforts of Mr Maxwell of Munches, who not only interested himself warmly in the undertaking from the beginning, but acted for eleven years as chairman of the company that promoted it. Extensions were afterwards made to Portpatrick and Kirkcudbright, which brought the whole of the south of Scotland into direct and easy communication with other parts of the kingdom. To the farmers of the district this railway has been of incalculable service, by affording them a quick and economical method of exporting their produce to the centres of population, and importing lime, tiles, implements, and artificial manures, for the culture and improvement of their land. Previous to its introduction in 1858, traffic was dependent on horse-carriage; and the only means of travel available, apart from private vehicles which were few, and horseback which was mostly favoured by the farmers, was the comparatively slow-going stage-coach, a heavy, covered conveyance, with some outside seats behind and above. One of these coaches used to run upon the old military road between Dumfries and Castle-Douglas, passing through the Haugh-of-Urr, and connecting the main routes of the country with Portpatrick and Ireland. After the opening of the new road in 1800, the coach was transferred to it, and travelled backward and forward daily through the parish, taking the villages of Crocketford and Springholm by the way. Another coach from Dalbeattie passed twice a day for a time through the Haugh-of-Urr, depositing and lifting passengers and letters at the house now occupied as the post-office. The arrival and departure of the coach, with its sound of horn and gleaming accoutrements, were the great excitements of the villages in those by-gone days, and linger still in the memories of the older inhabitants. The system no doubt was a great convenience, and served a useful purpose in its day; but the installation of the railway revolutionised the means of travel, and initiated a new development in the conveyance of stock and goods. The only semblances of the old coaching system that persist are the buses that ply two or three times a week between the villages of Kirkpatrick-Durham and Hardgate and the market towns of Castle-Douglas and Dumfries, and the postal conveyances that leave Dumfries and Dalbeattie every morning, the one with the mails for Crocketford, and the other with the mails, and any passengers that may be forthcoming, for Corsock and intermediate villages.

The details of agricultural life in the parish during the last

THE NINETEENTH CENTURY

fifty years range themselves generally along the same lines of progress as were followed in other parts of the Stewartry. The use of artificial manures increased so rapidly that in 1875 the quantity required to meet the demand was about five times as great as it had been in 1850, and in consequence a great extension had taken place in the growing of those green crops on which the farmers now largely depend. It is no small tribute to the progressive spirit of the farmers of Urr that they were quick to recognise the value of these new fertilisers, and that some of their number were among the first to engage in the business of preparing and selling them, as well as mixing and dealing in farm seeds. At the Highland Society's show held at Dumfries in 1845, Mr Thomas Biggar, then in Kingsgrange, was awarded medals for "perennial ryegrass seed" and "a new variety of grass seed." This was only the beginning of many similar successes gained by him, and the firm which he afterwards established in conjunction with his sons. Before his removal to Chapelton in 1864, the tenant of that farm, Mr Alexander Thomson, was also carrying on a considerable trade in manures, which was continued by his son, Mr James Thomson, Barr of Spottes, for a time. In later years a similar business was taken up by several traders in Dalbeattie; and, as lectures upon the treatment of the land have been given at intervals under the direction of the County Council, and the various machines for lightening and improving upon hand-labour have been generally adopted upon the farms so soon as they proved themselves effective, the result has been to modernise the system of tillage in the parish, and bring it into a condition that compares favourably with that of other places.

In the maintenance and improvement of the breed of Galloway cattle, the agriculturists of Urr have taken a creditable part, some of the more noted breeders among them, such as Biggar of Chapelton, Thomson of Blaiket, and Clark of Culmain, achieving more than a local fame. At the Dumfries

Union Show of 1867, Thomson and Biggar both obtained a number of prizes: at the Highland Society's Show in 1869, Biggar was first for cows with "Clara": at Dumfries in 1870, Thomson had the best two-year old, and Biggar got first place with a bull stirk bred by himself, at the same time carrying off the prize for yearlings with "Lallah Rookh." These were only the forerunners of further successes won for the parish by the breeders named; and, although the Blaiket and Culmain herds have been dispersed, the Chapelton cattle continue to give a good account of themselves at the leading shows, and in recent years have frequently carried off the highest honours. This attention to Galloways, it may be noted, has had no injurious effect upon other classes of stock; for, at many of the larger farms, the raising of sheep and cattle of other kinds, and the fattening of them for the market, have been carried on with great vigour, and form one of the staple activities of the parish. On the other hand, a considerable number of farms in recent years have been turned into dairies, with stocks of Ayrshire cows ranging from twenty or thirty to more than three score, the total number of cows in the parish at present being 396. The dairy system of farming is practically a development of the last fifty years in Kirkcudbrightshire, though it had established itself in the neighbouring county of Wigtown about the beginning of the nineteenth century. It was stimulated for a time by the incoming of Ayrshire farmers with the methods and experience of their native county; but it is now fairly represented all over the Stewartry, and is recognised as one of the most remunerative systems of farming. The following farms in Urr have large dairies attached to them, either worked by the farmer himself, or conducted on the bowing or kaneing principle: Meikle Dalbeattie, Waterside, Auchengibbert, Blaiket, Torcatrine, Burnside, and Edingham. At some seasons of the year a considerable quantity of the milk is sent to the creameries and the large towns: at other seasons, it is mostly turned into cheese, which is made upon the Cheddar system, and commands a good price in the market. The parish is well suited for dairy farming; which, as it can be conjoined with sheep feeding, is calculated to yield a less fluctuating return than that derived from the keeping of store or fat cattle, and seems consequently to be growing in favour. In this connection it may be noted that fewer pigs are reared now than formerly, and none of the farmers take a prominent place in the breeding of horses; though it is still remembered that a two-year old colt, bred by Thomson of Blaiket, headed a class of 41 entries at the Highland Society's Show in 1873.

As in other places, the rents of the farms, after increasing considerably in the third quarter of the century, had to be reduced towards its close, and now stand about the figures of fifty years ago. In 1900 the gross rental of the landward division of the parish was £15,388. Since then it has fallen still further, and is now £14,536. In contrast to this decline in agricultural subjects, the rental of the burgh of Dalbeattie, which had reached the sum of £9994 in 1900, continues to rise, and is now £11,354, making the total valuation of the parish at the present time £25,890. The population has fluctuated in a similar manner, falling off considerably in the landward division during the last few decades, but continuing to show an increase in the town. In 1891, the population of the landward division was 1440, and that of Dalbeattie 3149: in 1901, the former had decreased to 1267, while the latter had risen to 3469. A comparison of these figures with those of the early part of the nineteenth century, when Dalbeattie was only a rising village, and the total population of the parish was nearly three thousand, reveals a striking diminution in the number of rural parishioners.

During the period under review, many of the farms have had new houses and offices provided for them, or their old ones reconstructed and enlarged. About fifty years ago Mr Thomas Rawline, Dalbeattie, having acquired the lands of Little

Firthhead, enlarged the farm-house, and made it into a comfortable country residence, commanding a beautiful view of the lower reaches of the Urr valley. In 1857 Mr Thomas Biggar purchased the farm of Chapelton; and a few years afterwards, he erected a large and handsome dwelling-house upon it, with extensive offices and stores, into which the original farm-house and steading were worked. In 1878, a large addition was made to the farm-house of Hermitage for Mr Joseph Brown, a well-known figure in the agricultural world, and now proprietor of the Brae Estate, who continues in occupation of it. The old farm-house of Kingsgrange may still be seen in the grounds of the mansion-house, in close proximity to the garden, and is still used as a dwelling by the servants on the estate. This having been vacated by Mr Thomas Biggar on his removal to Chapelton in 1864, the present fine steading was provided for Kingsgrange farm, the tenancy of which he retained, with that of some smaller farms that were attached to it; and in 1874, when the management of them was taken up by Mr James Biggar, a new and commodious house was built for him, which he occupied till within a few years of his death. Thirty years ago, Mr James Affleck erected a large new residence upon his farm of Auchengibbert; and, quite recently, the steading and old farm-house, originally built by the Buchanites, have been renewed and extended by the present proprietor, Mr J. Harold Hacking. Amongst other farms, on which new building or reconstruction has been done of late years, may be mentioned Barfill, Brandedleys, Burnside, Burnfell, Fell, Newark, Crochmore, Larglanglee, Barbey, Little Cocklick, and Little Kirkland. The latest is Meikle Cocklick, which has just been renovated, enlarged, and renamed Broadlea, by the new proprietor, Mr William Reid. In the case of Redcastle, the necessity for a new farm-house was avoided, by transferring the tenant to what was formerly the mansion of the estate, and leaving the old farm-house to the servants.

WILLIAM YOUNG-HERRIES OF SPOTTES.
FROM A PORTRAIT BY SIR JOHN WATSON GORDON,
P.R.S.A., R.A., 1850.

The two most important houses in the parish are the mansions of Spottes and Kingsgrange. They occupy the sites of very ancient residences, which are marked on Timothy Pont's map; where, however, their positions are interchanged, possibly through confusion of names, as the Grange seems also to have been known as Spottes or Little Spottes in the sixteenth century. Besides the home-farm, the estate of Spottes comprises Old Hermitage Croft and the farms of Hermitage, Midtown, Hall, and Barr of Spottes. The present Hall of Spottes was built by Mr Michael Herries, soon after his acquisition of the property in 1784; but considerable improvements have been made upon it since, particularly in 1873 and 1887, when the two wings were rebuilt. It is a fine old place, with beautifully wooded grounds, a large ornamental lake, some striking yew and beech hedges, and an antique garden, standing close to the Haugh-of-Urr, in the angle formed by the junction of the river with the Spottes Burn. A footpath from the lodge gate passes up the burnside to the Glen of Spottes, with its picturesque mill and waterfall, forming one of the prettiest walks in the neighbourhood. The present family has been in possession of the property since 1823, when Mr William Young, born on 3rd July 1794, the only son of Mr Alexander Young of Harburn, Midlothian, the descendant of an old Dumfriesshire family, came into it, as second in succession, under a deed of entail executed by Mr Michael Herries, and assumed the Herries name and arms. His occupancy lasted for nearly fifty years, during which time he not only exerted himself to develop the estate, and instituted extensive improvements upon the house and grounds, but also, being a man of keen and active mind, took a warm practical interest in local affairs, and exhibited a public spirit and thoughtfulness for the well-being of the community, which have passed into a tradition of the district. His wife, whom he married on 3rd September 1822, was the Honourable Amelia, fourth daughter of James, first Lord De Saumarez, of the Island of Guernsey, a distinguished admiral in the time of the French wars, who was associated with Nelson as second-in-command at the Battle of the Nile on 1st August 1798, and for his services on that and other notable occasions, especially between the years 1808 and 1813, when he had command of the Baltic Fleet, was ultimately raised to the peerage.

Mr William Young-Herries died on 12th February 1872, and was succeeded by his only son Alexander, who was born on 15th December 1827, and is the present Laird of Spottes. He qualified as an advocate, but did not practise; and, on 21st August 1850, he married Miss Harriet Gore, only daughter of Captain Charles Chepmell, 53rd Foot, De Beauvoir, Guernsey. Throughout his life, Mr Alexander Young-Herries has been the steady friend and supporter of every good object in the district, and in a quiet unobtrusive way has conferred many benefits upon it. All local movements and societies have been indebted to him, not only for the financial support he has always accorded them, but for the personal concern he has shown in their success, and the facilities he has freely put at their disposal. Accessible to any of his humbler neighbours, he has particularly interested himself in those in any kind of trouble; and it goes without saying that a feeling of deepest respect and regard for him prevails throughout all classes of the community. The recent attainment of his eightieth birthday afforded an opportunity for the expression of this feeling, and the people of the neighbourhood surprised him with the presentation of a handsome silver love-cup, suitably engraved, while the tenants and servants on the estate offered their congratulations in the form of a beautifully inscribed address. The heir to the estate is again an only son, Mr William Dobrée Herries, born on 12th July 1866, who continues the family interest in local affairs, and has not only been Chairman of the Landward Committee of the Parish Council since its institution, but representative of the parish on the County Council since the death of Mr James Biggar. Like his father, he

ALEXANDER YOUNG-HERRIES OF SPOTTES.
PHOTO. BY ELLIOTT AND FRY, LONDON.

qualified as an advocate. For twenty-three years he has served in the 3rd Battalion of the King's Own Scottish Borderers, and is now an Honorary Major of the regiment. On 15th April 1891, he married Bethia Marion, the younger daughter of Sir Joseph Fayrer, Bart., a distinguished Indian official, who was Residency surgeon in Lucknow during the siege, and ultimately retired from service with the rank of Surgeon-General. He has one child, Alexander Dobrée Herries, born on 1st March, 1892.

The mansion-house of Kingsgrange occupies a good position about two miles up the river from Spottes. It stands on a slight elevation, between the Water of Urr and the Corsock road, and is surrounded by spacious, well-planned grounds, one of the features of which is the beautiful flower-garden lying at the foot of the sloping lawns. This flower-garden is the site of the previous residence of Kingsgrange, which was still habitable when the estate was purchased by Mr Thomas Rainson Gray in 1863. The present house had been built before his time, but he was the first to occupy it, after making some additions. In 1874, the estate, which includes the farms of Kingsgrange, Bushabield, Nethertoun, and Townhead, was sold to Mr Thomas Gladstone, a prominent Birmingham gentleman, whose family had long been connected with the parish of Kelton. He still further enlarged the mansion-house, and made it his summer residence during the remainder of his life. Though absent from the parish for the greater part of the year, Mr Gladstone, who was a man of active sympathies as well as exceptional shrewdness and ability, took a most benevolent interest in its concerns, and was always anxious to promote its well-being. His death occurring at Kingsgrange on 9th November 1904, he was laid to rest in Urr Churchyard, amid general expressions of regret. Since then, Mrs Gladstone, to whom the property now belongs, has continued to occupy the house during the summer months.

CHAPTER VII

THE VILLAGES

WITH the exception of Milton, the villages of the parish are modern growths, and have little or no history beyond the last hundred years. They came into existence with the revival of agriculture that marked the transition from the eighteenth to the nineteenth century; and, under the stimulus of the development that followed, they speedily attained proportions which they have scarcely since been able to maintain. During the first half of the nineteenth century they enjoyed a fair measure of prosperity, and were centres of varied and active life; but the changed conditions of later years put a check upon their progress, and in some respects reduced them to the shadows of their former selves. New works were at a minimum: the introduction of machinery lessened the demand for hand-labour on the farms: and the increased facilities of communication with the larger towns opened up channels of supply that seriously affected the business of the country shopkeeper and tradesman. To some extent, also, the prosperity of the villages suffered by the alterations made from time to time in the trade route through the parish. The transference of the traffic from the old military road to the new coach road in 1800 was a severe blow to the consequence of Milton, though the making of Crocketford and Springholm; and these two villages, again, lost a considerable part of their means of support in 1858, when the line of commerce was once more changed by the opening of the railway through Dalbeattie. Of all the villages, perhaps, Haugh-of-Urr has suffered least deterioration, owing to its situation in the centre of the parish and other advantages; but

THE VILLAGES

even its condition and population compare unfavourably with those of former years.

MILTON

This village, as noted in Chapter IV., was a place of some importance in the first half of the seventeenth century, being a Burgh of Barony with a market cross, and a meeting-place of the War Committee and their forces. The site of the soldiers' encampment is said to be the piece of ground lying on the northern side of the road that passes Milton Mill, which at that time was used as a common; and it may be of some significance in this connection that a farm in the immediate vicinity is called Courthill. For a hundred and fifty years thereafter, no precise information regarding the history of the village is forthcoming, though its favourable situation on what was then the main road to Dumfries enabled it to maintain its existence. The probability is that the size of the village varied considerably during this period, the number of its inhabitants diminishing in the troubled times of the persecutions and the Jacobite uprisings, and increasing with the revival of prosperity that followed these disturbances, and the opening of the old military road in 1758. Twice only is it mentioned in the Minute Books of the Presbytery, and on both occasions in connection with matters of witchcraft. On 22nd April 1656, John McKerohan of Milton confessed that he had gone to a witch woman at Dundrennan for medicine for his wife, and Janet Shennan admitted resorting to the same person for medicine for her mother, both being admonished and rebuked. On 3rd March 1703, Marion McWilliam from Milton appeared before the Presbytery and complained that Janet Little, spouse to John McKinnell, had called her a witch, and that Mr John Hepburn, the minister of Urr, had obtained a warrant from the Laird of Milton to put her out of the parish, without any trial or evidence of her guilt. The Presbytery appointed two of their number to see the Stewart-Depute about the case, and instructed the kirk-officer of Kirkpatrick-Durham to cite Janet Little.

In 1794, according to the Old Statistical Account, the total population of the villages of Urr, which at that time comprised the new villages of Haugh-of-Urr and Dalbeattie as well as Milton, did not exceed 400. As the larger proportion of this number is to be ascribed to Dalbeattie, it is probably a liberal computation that allows to Milton a population of something between 50 and 100. Most of the inhabitants followed agricultural pursuits, though there were amongst them the usual admixture of weavers, joiners, masons, blacksmiths, and shoemakers. One name has come down from the closing years of the eighteenth century which deserves to be recorded, as that of a prominent elder in the parish church, a descendant of whom is still living in the village. In the Kirk Session Minutes from 17th May 1797 onward for five and twenty years, the name of John Coltart of Milton appears occasionally upon the sederunt. His only daughter, Janet Coltart, married Robert Smith, joiner in the village, and was the grandmother of Janet C. Smith, who continues to reside there.

In the early part of the nineteenth century, the large number of farms in the immediate vicinity of Milton, some of the steadings of which are almost within the village, gave plentiful employment to the different classes of workers it contained, so that a considerable degree of activity prevailed, and the number of the inhabitants was well maintained, in spite of the fact that the bulk of the through traffic had been withdrawn from the old military road. Maxwell was the name of the blacksmith, and McEwen that of the tenant of the Mill which, after passing through six different hands, was lately occupied by Matthew McKean. About the middle of the century, a large trade was done in joiner work and the cutting and sawing of timber, some of which was exported from Dalbeattie, while the remainder was utilised in the parish. This necessitated the employment of a number of horses as well as men, and

THE VILLAGES 83

was the means of keeping up for a time the prosperity of the village. Amongst others engaged in this occupation were the Smiths, who had a sawmill upon Newark farm, a few hundred yards down from the front of the house, and who, besides keeping horses and giving employment to carters and others, had usually five or six journeyman joiners in their service. Their mill has been removed, and the only reminder of the extensive wood trade of the village is the sawing and joinering carried on at Milton Mill in conjunction with the grinding of grain. The business done there, however, in both branches is small in comparison with that of former times. In recent years the village has dwindled down to nine or ten inhabited houses, exclusive of the farms that abut upon it, with a population of about a score, most of whom are now past active work. Besides the Mill, the only other trade or shop is that of the blacksmith; though the school, being utilised both for secular and religious meetings, continues to make the village the social centre of the district. The oldest farm tenants in the neighbourhood are the Wilsons of Burnfell, who have held their land for nearly seventy years; but the Johnstones of Barbey, when the last of them died some years ago, had been quite as long in the occupation of their farm. The Hendersons of Newark and the Thomsons of Milton Mains have both been about forty years in possession of their respective properties, and resident upon them.

Haugh-of-Urr and Hardgate

These villages, being within half a mile of each other, and both situated upon the estate of Redcastle, may be conveniently treated together. They originated in the closing decades of the eighteenth century, and doubtless had their site suggested by the vicinity of the old military bridge; for it is a common tendency, in countries that are being opened up, to plant houses near the passage of an important water. The first houses were built on either side of the old military road, as it rises gradually, but sometimes very steeply, from the north end of the bridge to the high lands of Hardgate. It can only be to these houses that Dr. Muirhead refers in the Old Statistical Account of 1794 when he says that, in other parts of Urr besides Dalbeattie, villages are begun, but advance slowly; for Milton, as we have seen, had been long in existence, and Crocketford and Springholm did not appear till later. Some of these original domiciles have entirely disappeared; in particular, one that stood upon the piece of vacant ground lying opposite the Laigh Row, between the Spottes Burn and the Mill lade. Here about a century ago lived a family of Morrisons, one of the daughters of which married the late James Ireland, blacksmith, and was the mother of the present occupant of the smithy by the Catlick Burn. Below this house, on the same side of the road, was another occupied by the widow of Joseph McWhae, blacksmith; but it was of much later date, as some of the present inhabitants remember its erection as well as its demolition. Others, however, of the houses that arose before the end of the eighteenth century, continue in existence; for some of the feu-charters in the villages, which were originally granted for a term of 99 years, ran out and were renewed ten and fifteen years ago. The Laird of Redcastle, who began the process of feuing that resulted in the villages of Haugh-of-Urr and Hardgate, was Mr Walter Sloan Laurie, whose name appears in connection with a decreet of stipend in 1788, and in the valuation roll of 1799. One family at least in the village of Haugh-of-Urr, that of Montgomery, can show a continuous residence in it almost from the start. The house in which they live was built in 1796, and was inhabited by their great-grandfather John Garmory or Montgomery, whose wife was Betty Coltart, a daughter of the tenant of Stepend. Their grandfather, John Montgomery, who married Sarah Conchar or McConnochie, belonging to a family in Haugh-of-Urr, and died in 1859, and their father, Robert Montgomery, who married Jessie Welsh

OLD COTTAGE BY SPOTTES BURN.

from Town of Urr, and died in 1896, continued the occupation of the house, in which the daughters of the family now reside; their brother, John Montgomery, having added to it separate accommodation for himself. An interesting fact regarding this family is that the last three male representatives have all been masons, and have left their mark upon many of the buildings in the neighbourhood; while the great-grandfather, John Garmory or Montgomery, was a joiner, and worked at the erection of the old mansion-house of Spottes.

Another old Haugh-of-Urr family is that of Johnstone, Millbank. The grandfather of the present representatives, John Johnstone, was tenant of the mill and farm attached to it at the beginning of the nineteenth century. On his retiral from active work in 1813, he built the house of Millbank for himself, and lived there till his death. He was a well-known man in his time, when milling was a much more lucrative and important business than it is now.

Before the rise of the villages, and for some time after, there were two small farms in the immediate neighbourhood, one of which has since been taken into the hands of the proprietor, the Laird of Spottes, and the other absorbed in the larger farms of Redcastle estate. The former was called Bridge-hall, and had its steading where Bridge-end house now stands; indeed, the lower half of this house formed the farm dwelling, before it was raised a story by Mr William Young-Herries of Spottes, about fifty-five years ago, after being given over to his servants. The farm of Bridge-hall consisted of 53½ acres of good arable land, and was tenanted between 1779 and 1783 by Joseph Graham, at a rent of £18 per annum, with 3 hens at 8d. each, and 6 chickens at 4d., or £18 4s. in all. Attached to the farm were two cottages and yards at the bottom of the Laigh Row of a yearly value of £1 10s. each, one of which was occupied by John Thomson, grocer, and the other by Joseph McWhae, blacksmith, whose sons John and Joseph retained the house and carried on the business well into the nineteenth century.

The other farm went under the name of Howcroft, and is mentioned in records of the seventeenth century. The lands lay between Haugh-of-Urr and Hardgate, and the houses stood almost on the site of the present public school. In later times the three houses standing on this spot were known as Gillhole, which means Hole of the Leeches, and is supposed to have been originally a nickname applied to them by a well-known local worthy, William Haining of Threemerkland, humorously characterising the number of mischievous children with which they swarmed. However that may be, the name Howcroft seems to have been transferred to one of the earliest houses in Haugh-of-Urr—that now occupied by David McGill, the representative of another old village family. This house was built by Mr McGill's grandfather, occupied by his father, and raised a story by himself a good many years ago.

At Kirkstyle and Causey, in close proximity to the church, there were several houses, of which the only remains are some ruins in the vicinity of the manse gate. The tenant of Kirkstyle was Margaret Blair, who looked after the mending of the mort-cloth, a black pall generally used at funerals to cover the coffin. She was probably a relation of George Blair, the leader of the church praise in Dr. Muirhead's time, who is frequently noted in the Session Minute Book as receiving his allowance of £1 6s. for reading or presenting the psalms. This house was afterwards occupied by James Thomson and his family, one of whom, Jean Thomson, conducted a small school in it. The fashion in those days and long afterwards was to address women, married and single alike, as well as men, by their Christian names, unless their superiority was decided enough to warrant the courtesy titles of Mr and Mrs, or laird and leddy.

There is a mention of Hardgate in the Kirk Session minute of 29th July 1790, where it is recorded that Agnes Stewart, a poor woman of that place, had received a small donation or "compliment" from the church funds. A number of the

JOHN JOHNSTONE, MILLBANK.
FROM AN OLD PAINTING.

THE VILLAGES

older houses still existing, and some of those that have fallen into ruins, had arisen by this time; and others, including the Church of the Associate congregation, were added before the end of the eighteenth century.

The opening of the nineteenth century marked the beginning of a period of growing prosperity and rapid extension for both the villages. Till 1823, the proprietor of Redcastle estate was Mr William Bigham Laurie, and he and his successors gave every encouragement to the feuing and building in progress. The increased demand for labour, occasioned by the public works going on in the district, and the impetus that had been given to agriculture by the French wars, brought many people to the villages, even all the way from Ireland, for whom accommodation had to be found, and other necessaries of life provided. The result was that, in five and thirty years, Haugh-of-Urr and Hardgate expanded to their present limits, and increased their population to nearly 400 souls. About 1835, when Langbank was built by James McCaig, the grandfather of the present occupant, the housing of the villages was practically completed as it now appears, only three or four additional houses, such as that at the top of the hill on the right hand side of the military road in Haugh-of-Urr, and the manse and school at Hardgate, having been erected since. So far, however, many of the houses were roofed with thatch, and this in later years was replaced by slates; in several cases, also, an upper flat or attic story was added to houses which had originally been of one floor. The largest and most prominent house in Haugh-of-Urr was that which stands at the cross, and is now owned and occupied by William Gibson. This is said to have been the only hotel between Portpatrick and Dumfries, in the days when the mail-coaches still plied upon the old military road. In the early years of last century it certainly was an inn, called the Dog and Duck, the proprietor of which was a man of the name of Burgess. His daughter married William Wright, who is still remembered in the village, and who continued to occupy the property, though not as a licensed house, till it was acquired by the father of the present owner about fifty years ago, when the wooden sign was converted by James McLeod into a tailor's board. Other three houses in the village were used for the sale of alcoholic liquors in those free and easy days before the passing of the Forbes Mackenzie Act. One of these was the first house on the right hand side of the road leading up to Hardgate, and was kept first by a man called Smith, afterwards by John Dempster. On the other side of the road, in what is now the post-office, James Lowden carried on the business which he had commenced in the Fish Inn, the house in the middle of the Laigh Row now used by John Dalziel as a smithy. He was the father of the late John Lowden, who succeeded him in the occupancy of the house, but not in the business, and died there in 1897. The latter was a prominent official of the parish for over fifty years, and achieved the unique distinction of acting as clerk to the Parochial Board during the whole term of its existence. Besides holding this office, John Lowden was Heritors' clerk for almost the same length of time, and clerk of School Board from its institution in 1873 till shortly before his death. A methodical, painstaking, and thoroughly reliable man, he served his native parish in these places of trust with a rare fidelity and zeal. The other place of public entertainment was the original of the present Laurie Arms Hotel, and was kept by William McGowan, whose descendants in the female line still reside in the parish. He was followed by James Charteris; and, about thirty years ago, the house was renovated and enlarged into the present commodious and comfortable building, since which time it has been occupied by Mrs Begg, Thomas Gibson, and now David Scott.

In Hardgate, the most outstanding building, apart from the church and school premises, which are noticed elsewhere, is the residence of Summerhill, standing back amongst the trees, with its fine old garden in front. This house was built by the

THE VILLAGES

Rev. James Biggar in 1813, on his withdrawal from the ministry of Hardgate church, and was occupied by him until his death in 1820. It is now the residence of his grandson, Dr. James Johnston, a retired Naval surgeon, who saw active service during the Crimean War, and was afterwards engaged on the Chinese and other foreign stations. A tragic event is associated with the early days of Summerhill. A bright young girl of the family, the granddaughter of Mr Biggar, and sister of the present occupant, was engaged with the children of the Rev. John McWhir making sweetmeats at the kitchen fire of Urr Manse, when her dress was accidentally ignited, and she received such injuries that she died shortly afterwards. In the early days of the century, there were a number of small crofts in the Hardgate locality, with houses and offices upon them. One of these was at Blackford, and was rented by William Heughan: another was worked from the nearest house in the village to Blackford, that occupied by the late Margaret Robinson, and was tenanted by her step-father, James Thomson: another stood on the top of the hill, where Miss Margaret McKimm at present lives, and was occupied by her grandfather, George McKimm, and afterwards by James McKimm, her father: while two were situated further down the village, and were held respectively by James Rae and John Slater. With the exception of a few fields now in the occupation of Robert Slater, the lands of these crofts were combined in later years to form the small farm of Hardgate, of which Alexander McKie is the present tenant. The Slaters, it may be noted, are a very old Hardgate family, the great-grandfather of the present bearer of the name having been a resident of the village. His name was Andrew Slater, and he is said to have lived at Sowerhill, the house that still stands between the present school and the schoolhouse.

Besides field-labourers, dykers, drainers, and roadmakers, for whose services there was an abundant demand in the early, more prosperous years of the century, the inhabitants of the villages included two blacksmiths, several joiners, masons, tailors, shoemakers, weavers, shopkeepers, and other tradesmen. A considerable business was done in carting goods and materials, chiefly between Dumfries and Haugh-of-Urr or Hardgate, most of the crofters having horses and carts which could be requisitioned on occasion, and there being also some regularly established carriers. For a while the principal Hardgate carrier was John Craig, whose son now resides at Burnside, in Kirkpatrick-Durham. In the middle of the century a miniature painter of no mean talent, by name Alexander, resided in Haugh-of-Urr, and many of the people in the neighbourhood had their portraits taken by him. These miniatures are not only well-executed, but of great present-day interest as records of the features of worthies who passed away before the age of photography had fully dawned.

One of the great industries of the time, and the source of considerable profit to the villagers, was the collecting and slaughtering of pigs. These animals were obtained, for the most part, in Wigtownshire, and either carried to Dalbeattie by boat and brought thence to Haugh-of-Urr by road, or made to travel all the way at the risk of having to send out vehicles to bring in the lame ones. It was the great excitement of the youths and small boys of the time to go out along the roads to meet the drovers, and assist them with their intractable charge. Every second Monday during the season a strong force of men and women was mustered, who set to work to slaughter the pigs that had come to hand, and clean and pack their carcases in carts, to be sent off early on Wednesday morning for sale to the pork-curers of Dumfries. The number disposed of at one killing was seldom less than 80 or more than 150; but a great occasion is remembered when the record of 200 was reached, twelve men being occupied in dispatching them from the early hours of Monday morning well into the following night. On the days when the killing took place, the gutters of Haugh-of-Urr literally ran with blood,

THE VILLAGES

and an array of carts, containing from eight to ten pigs each, and varying with the number of the slain, might be seen halfway up the slope leading to Hardgate. The trimmings of the carcases, such as heads, trotters, and similar parts, were afterwards hawked around the villages, or sold upon the spot, at popular prices. The business was originally conducted at the second house behind the present post-office, but was subsequently transferred to the fifth house on the other side of the street, where it reached its greatest dimensions. The leading men in the trade were Joseph Welsh and two of his four sons, Alexander and William. The introduction of the railway probably had a detrimental effect upon it, so far as the Haugh-of-Urr was concerned; at any rate it was entirely given up when the Welshes relinquished it about forty years ago.

The appalling hurricane that swept over Galloway on 7th January 1839 is still a tradition in Haugh-of-Urr, as considerable damage was done both in the village and the adjoining Spottes woods. David McGill's father used to tell how he stood with some of his neighbours in a sheltered garden and listened to the continuous crash of falling trees, the only remark passed being, "there goes another, boys." The cholera visitation of 1848-49 also left its impression on the district, several of the villagers, such as John Morrison and Thomas Forsyth, succumbing to the disease. This time of trouble and alarm is still associated in the recollection of the inhabitants with an incident that occurred in connection with the coming of age of Mr Alexander Young-Herries, the Laird of Spottes, which happened to fall about the same time. A complimentary dinner was arranged for the occasion, to be held in Castle-Douglas, but it never came off, as some of the principal persons interested were seriously indisposed, and one of the prime movers in the matter, Mr Clark McMichan of Corbieton, was carried off by the cholera, on the very night preceding the day fixed for the event.

From an early date an annual fair was held in Haugh-of-Urr, when everybody went on holiday, and a good deal of business was transacted, not only in farm stock and produce, but in articles imported by travelling merchants. The exact date of its discontinuance is uncertain; but it was still in full swing in 1829, when mention is made of it in the Kirk Session minutes as having taken place about the end of May or beginning of June.

Interwoven with the memories of the villages are the names of several of those harmless, irresponsible individuals, usually denominated half-witted, whose eccentricities of speech and behaviour excite the mingled pity and amusement of their neighbours. Jock Gordon is said to have frequented the manse kitchen, and on one communion Sunday, when he was left alone for a short time, to have slipped a cat into the pot of broth intended for the dinner of the officiating clergy. William Payne is remembered in Hardgate: William Harrison in Haugh-of-Urr, where his portrait, done by Alexander, is still preserved: Johnny Tait only died two years ago. For the greater part of his life the last-mentioned, who was intelligent enough in some respects and a voracious reader, was scarcely ever absent from the services of the parish church, in which there was no more interested and reverent worshipper. Thither he might be seen wending his way every Sunday, dressed in an old-fashioned top-hat and surtout coat, with his large bible wrapped in a red handkerchief in one hand, and his alpaca umbrella in the other. The only occasion on which he ever interrupted the service was a communion evening, towards the end of his life, when a strange minister was preaching, and Johnny, whose hearing had become very hard, could not follow the unfamiliar voice. Anxious to hear, yet baffled in all his efforts, he bore patiently for a time; but at last he turned to his neighbours with an appealing look, and called loudly for some one to " tell him what the man was saying; as he couldna hear a word, and micht as weel hae steyed at hame."

WILLIAM HARRISON.
FROM A PAINTING BY JOHN ALEXANDER.

THE VILLAGES 93

In 1845, the post-office at Haugh-of-Urr was a mere receiving-house, not under Dalbeattie as it now is, but like Dalbeattie itself and Crocketford, under the post-office at Castle-Douglas, from which it had a daily runner. After the railway was opened, this arrangement was altered; and within the last twelve years, the post-office at Haugh-of-Urr has been fully equipped with a money-order and telegraph service, while quite recently it has been connected by telephone with the rest of the kingdom. For many years under the management of the late Alexander Gunn, it is now in charge of his widow and family.

The last forty years, as already indicated and explained, have witnessed a gradual diminution of the prosperity of Haugh-of-Urr and Hardgate. Most of the houses continue in use, but few of them are in thorough repair, or contain the number of inhabitants they once contrived to lodge; many of them, indeed, with ample accommodation for a family, are occupied only by one or two persons. The total population of the two villages consequently is only slightly over 200. There are still two blacksmiths plying their trade, but shopkeepers, tailors, and masons, who were formerly more numerous are now reduced to the same number, and there is only one joiner, while other tradesmen, such as weavers and shoemakers, have entirely disappeared. Scarcely a score of persons of both sexes find work upon the farms in the neighbourhood, and a still smaller number are employed upon the roads and adjacent gentlemen's estates. About a dozen of the inhabitants are old-age pensioners, but only two or three are in receipt of parochial relief.

It is no symptom of returning prosperity, but only of the tendencies of the time, that recently a public hall and library have been erected in Haugh-of-Urr. In early days the public meetings and social entertainments of the district were generally held in some commodious and convenient barn; and one such gathering is commemorated in a poem composed on the occasion by Robert Kerr of Redcastle. It took place in 1839,

"That vera year we had the muckle wun'
Which levelled trees and houses to the grun."

It was in the form of a dramatic entertainment, some of the young people of the district giving a representation of Allan Ramsay's play of the "Gentle Shepherd" for the benefit of the poor of the neighbourhood. As Robert Kerr puts it—

"Doun Spottes' burn street there was an auld laigh raw,
And at the end o't leeved ane John McWha,
A dacent chiel at this time kept a smiddie
Wha gave his barn, and sune it was made ready.
Some country lads that doffed the sock and pleuch
Donn'd sock an' buskin' an' did weel eneuch."

In later years the want of a more suitable meeting-place began to be felt; and, the School Board being always willing to grant the use of Hardgate School for large gatherings, Mr Herries of Spottes fitted up and maintained for five and twenty years a house in the village, as a reading and recreation room. Three years ago a movement was inaugurated to provide a building specially for public and social purposes, and a large and representative committee was appointed, with Major Herries, younger of Spottes as convener, the Rev. David Frew as vice-convener, and Quintin Aird, schoolmaster, as secretary and treasurer. The movement has been completely successful, and the new buildings, erected at a cost of over £500, and comprising a large hall for public gatherings, a comfortable reading-room, and other conveniences, were opened for use on 5th March 1909. In the reading-room is deposited the parish library, which was instituted about fifty years ago, chiefly by the efforts of the late Rev. John M. Sandilands, and is a trust of the Kirk Session. The memorial stone, placed over the main window of the hall, was laid by Master Gordon Birney of Redcastle, in the summer of 1908; and the opening ceremony was

HAUGH-OF-URR.

PHOTO. BY J. AND J. BROWN, CASTLE-DOUGLAS.

entrusted to Master Alexander D. Herries of Spottes, but in his unavoidable absence was performed on his behalf by the parish minister.

Springholm

This village is situated on the new coach road, almost exactly in the middle of the section of it which passes through the parish. It consists of one irregular street, which extends to the greater part of a mile and has most of its houses on its eastern side, with a single row of seven or eight houses running at right angles to it along the road to Kirkpatrick-Durham. There was practically no village upon this site before the beginning of the nineteenth century; there were only a few rough-stone and mud hovels with thatched roofs, which stood about the corner of the road leading down from Auchenreoch. One of these primitive dwellings stood upon the site now occupied by the Grapes Hotel, and belonged to the grandfather of its present owner, Thomas Donaldson. It had a number of spring-fed pools around it, in which the lint was steeped that was afterwards to be spun into yarn; and from this circumstance the name of the village is popularly supposed to be derived. About the year 1800, when the new coach road was constructed, a better style of building was introduced, which gradually displaced the older type of houses; and in five and thirty years the present village arose, and attained its full-grown proportions, chiefly in consequence of the large amount of traffic passing through it, and the agricultural activity and improvement going on in the district. Some of the houses were erected on the lands of Millhall, but most of them on those of Nether Auchenreoch, the proprietor of which properties at the time was the Rev. David Lamont, D.D., minister of Kirkpatrick-Durham, and afterwards Moderator of the General Assembly, who afforded feuars every facility for building, and granted leases for a term of nine hundred and ninety-nine years. Only a few additions, such as the school and schoolhouse, have been made to the village during the last seventy-five years; but many of the houses have undergone extensive repairs, and had roofs of slates substituted for their original covering of thatch.

Three quarters of a century ago, the population of Springholm exceeded 200, and the general condition of things was such as to mark the high-water level of prosperity. The men found plentiful employment, not only in ordinary farm labour, but in draining, fencing, building drystone dykes, cutting wood, and planting trees, in connection with the various improvements undertaken on the neighbouring estates; while many of the women were occupied upon the fields, sowing seeds and manures, hoeing turnips, haymaking, and harvesting, according to the season of the year. A considerable trade in ham and bacon curing was done by the brothers William and Peter McMorrine; there was also some pig-killing by them and other inhabitants; but this business never grew to anything like the extent it attained in Haugh-of-Urr. A few crofts existed at both ends of the village, the occupants of which usually acted as carriers; but the most outstanding industry was the milling of various kinds carried on at its southern extremity. On the lands of Millhall, above the bridge where the stream crosses the coach road, the ruins may still be seen of the corn and meal mill conducted by John Bell. On the other side of the bridge, the sawmill, now occupied by William Reid in succession to his father, James Reid, was in full working order, and employed a number of hands, under the management of Mr Willett of Dumfries, who did an extensive trade in the cutting and preparing of wood for railway purposes. A little further down the stream, John McMillan had possession of Newbank Woollen Mill, where carding and spinning were done upon a considerable scale, and the wool of the district was manufactured into blankets and tweed. Probably for convenience to the mills, the blacksmith's business of John McClune, senior, was also established at Millhall, in the premises now occupied as a joiner's shop.

THE VILLAGES

The population and trade of the time gave scope to the merchant's calling, and a fair proportion of the inhabitants subsisted by dealing in the necessaries of life, either in shops in the village, or by means of carts sent round the outlying houses. One old woman is still remembered, who lived with her son, and kept a shop, on the spot on which the post-office is now situated. Her name was Jeanie McGeorge, but she was affectionately termed, in accordance with the prevalent custom, Granny McGeorge; and she is said to have attained almost the age of a hundred. Her wisdom and experience were supposed to have enabled her to acquire a minute acquaintance with the healing art, and she was largely consulted on behalf of the sick, for whom she had no hesitation in prescribing medicines and pills. Another old woman, Elizabeth Murray, perambulated the district, accompanied by an ancient pony of diminutive stature, with side-creels fastened on his back. Her chief business was the collecting of eggs, which she transported on Wednesday to Dumfries, and retailed in the market.

Two mail coaches passed through the village daily, Sundays excepted; the one going towards Dumfries, the other coming from it. Besides passengers, they carried letters and newspapers, which in the days before the introduction of penny postage were not transmitted in very large quantities. The post-office was kept by William Alexander, who disposed of most of the correspondence across his shopcounter, but employed a male runner for the delivery of packets addressed to persons residing at a distance of over five miles. Another public official of the time was the resident constable and sheriff-officer; the person best remembered as acting in these capacities being Allan Burgess, the grandfather of James Burgess, now residing in the village. That his office was no sinecure may be inferred from the fact that there were several public-houses in Springholm, as in other country villages at that time, and that these seem to have been extensively patronised, not only by the inhabitants, but by numerous carters, carriers, and drovers, that passed along the road. One of these public-houses was the forerunner of the present Grapes Hotel: another occupied the house at the cross in which the post-office is now established, and was called, from the representation on its sign-board, the Coach and Horses: another stood at the northern extremity of the village, and went under the name, still borne by the house, of the Bacon Ham. With respect to some of them, at least, there is an illuminating minute in the Kirk Session books of date 18th January 1818, to the effect that " sundry gross irregularities had been reported from Springholm," and that two members of Session, John Roddick and Robert McMillan, had been ordained to make inquiry into them. It is also noted in the minute of 21st September 1828 that some of the lodging-houses are conducted in such a manner as to be a nuisance to the parish, large numbers of sturdy vagrants and strolling beggars being accommodated in them, and sometimes remaining for weeks together in a continued state of drunkenness and debauch. Evidently, throughout the parish at this time, there was a good deal of loose behaviour and excessive drinking; for in the minute of 19th April 1830 the Kirk Session deeply deplore the prevalent drunkenness and vice, and call upon the civil authorities to lessen the number of licensed houses, and take stronger measures to suppress disorders. A copy of this minute was directed to be laid before the Justices of the Peace at their next meeting for the renewal of licences.

Amongst the names associated with the village in the days of its prosperity may be mentioned those of William Halliday, blacksmith; David Wilson and George Fergusson, carriers; John Fisher, proprietor of one of the small holdings; John Wood, father of Alexander Wood now resident in Dumfries; James Donaldson; John Dempster; Samuel Fergusson; and the family of Faulds. In those days, notwithstanding the rougher elements in the population, there was a considerable

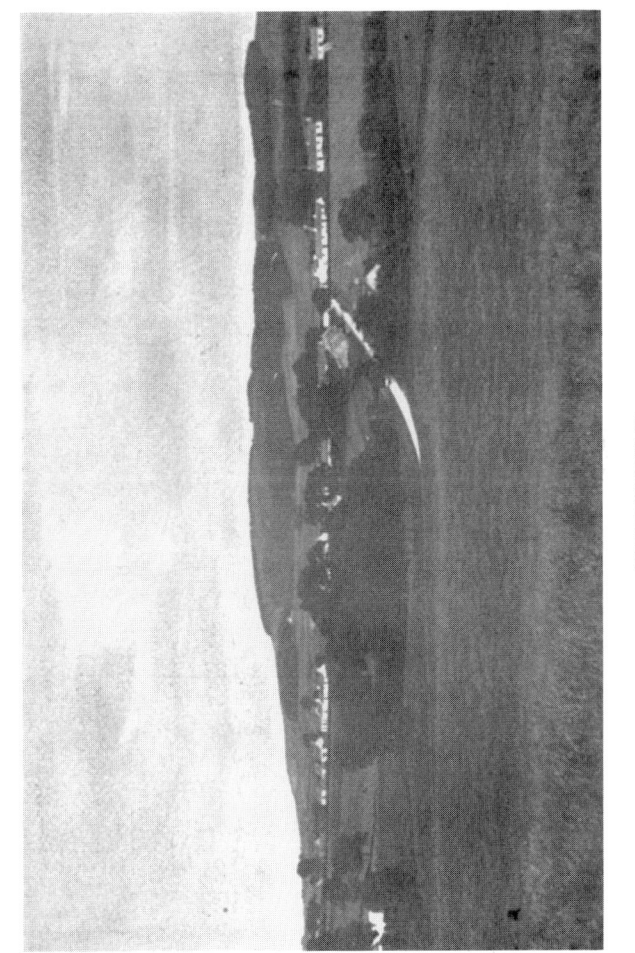

SPRINGHOLM.

PHOTO. BY J. AND J. BROWN, CASTLE-DOUGLAS.

religious life among the inhabitants, many of whom were attached to the various places of worship in the neighbourhood. Besides those attending the Associate Church at Hardgate, there were in 1835 twice as many members of the Establishment in Springholm as in Haugh-of-Urr, which was quite as large, and situated much nearer the church. At the same time the village had a neat little church of its own, belonging to the Cameronian denomination, with which a proportion of the inhabitants were connected. For many years there had been a number of people in the neighbourhood devoted to the old covenanting principles upheld by McMillan of Balmaghie and Hepburn of Urr; these had been in the habit of holding meetings in Springholm, which had drawn together people of like mind from an extensive area; and the rapid increase of the population in the beginning of the nineteenth century seemed to offer a favourable opportunity for erecting a place of worship for themselves. A feu was obtained from Dr. David Lamont in February 1816, the representatives of the congregation who signed the charter and undertook its obligations being John McMorrine, mason in Culshan, John Ewart in Shenrick, James Douglas in Auchendolly, and John McWilliam in Whitecairn, while the witnesses to their signatures were John McWhae and James Thomson, both servants of Dr. Lamont. The lease was granted for a term of 999 years at an annual rent of £1 17s. 6d., with an additional payment of one shilling in lieu of all public and parochial burdens. On the site thus secured to them, the promoters of the movement erected a comfortable little church, with a short, square spire, and a suitable manse for the minister.

This result was largely due to the efforts of the Rev. James Thomson, an able and energetic man, the son of a joiner in Kilsyth, Stirlingshire, who had been called to the pastoral charge of the Cameronian congregation at Quarrelwood, in the parish of Kirkmahoe, and had been given a general oversight of all the members of the denomination, as far south as the

Water of Urr. In the course of his ministrations he preached and held fellowship meetings at Haugh-of-Urr and Dalbeattie as well as Springholm; and before his death in 1810 regular congregations had been formed at the two latter places, which soon erected places of worship for themselves, that at Dalbeattie being the old church afterwards acquired by the Establishment, and now used as an Armoury, that at Springholm being the picturesque ruin now to be seen at the north end of the village. The first minister over the double charge on the Water of Urr was the Rev. Mr Allan, who held office till 1816, and under whom accordingly the church and manse of Springholm were built. He was succeeded by the Rev. John Osborne, a man of great power as a preacher, but of somewhat uncertain reputation, regarding whom there was great difference of opinion in his lifetime, and round whose name many questionable stories have since gathered. Deposed in 1825 by the Cameronian body, he continued for five years to minister to a few faithful followers in Dalbeattie, but afterwards went to America, where he died. The Rev. Mr McLauchlan followed Mr Osborne in the Cameronian Churches of Urr; and after him, the church at Dalbeattie having been sold to the Church of Scotland, that at Springholm was worked as a station by the Reformed Presbyterian ministers of Castle-Douglas. In later times it was opened for service to ministers of other denominations, and about thirty years ago was entirely given up, the last sermon having been preached in it by the Rev. George Laurie of Castle-Douglas. In the days of its popularity it is said to have been attended by great crowds of people from a widely extended district; at some of the Communions, in particular, which were celebrated in the open air, on the grass plot lying to the south of the church, as many as five hundred are asserted to have been present; but it is now a crumbling, ivy-covered ruin, with grass growing thick upon the walks once trodden bare by the feet of many worshippers. A certain reverence, however, still pertains to it from the holy uses to

THE VILLAGES

which it has been put, and only a thoughtless mind can regard with indifference the place which was to several generations of sincere believers the very House of God, the Gate of Heaven.

The decay of the church was in great part the consequence of the gradual diminution of the prosperity of the village, though other causes may have assisted in it. During the last fifty years Springholm has suffered severely from the changes passing over the country-side, and the adverse conditions affecting country villages. Some of the houses have almost disappeared: others stand roofless and dilapidated: the smithy has been closed for some time: shops of all kinds are reduced to two or three: the grain mill is a thing of the past: the saw mill does little business: the population has decreased to about a hundred, many of them old, and in not very easy circumstances. Some of the men still carry on the trade of dykers, though they have frequently to travel far afield for work: others make a living as travelling merchants: many are employed on the roads: and some of the women find work upon the farms. Newbank Woollen Mill, after being suspended for a time, has again been started by Mr Frank O'Brien; but there is no general industry on which the villagers can depend, and little hope of any renewal of prosperity.

Crocketford

Two miles north of Springholm the coach road is joined by the road from New Galloway, and round the point of junction clusters the village of Crocketford, with its venerable toll-house occupying the sharper angle of the roads, and its irregular, double lines of houses radiating from it in three directions. In the days of its usefulness the toll-house, with its bar or gate to stay the passage of the traveller and secure the levying of the legal impost upon him, had the honour of conferring a secondary name upon the village, by which it is still widely known. It happened to stand almost midway between Castle-Douglas and Dumfries, the distance from either place being about nine miles; and from this circumstance the village with which it was associated acquired the name of the Nine-mile Bar. Most of the houses, especially along the main thoroughfare of the coach road, are of two-story height and commodious appearance—a fact which communicates a certain distinctiveness of feature to the village, and witnesses to its former prosperity. The boundary line between the parishes of Urr and Kirkpatrick-Durham passes through the middle of it, dividing it into fairly equal parts; but the unity of its life is not sufficiently affected thereby to prevent the treatment of its history as a whole.

The origin of Crocketford is to be traced to the Buchanite sect, who were resident in Larghill at the time the coach road was constructed. Anticipating an enforced removal from their farm, and perceiving the advantages of the situation offered by the junction of the two roads, they hastened to secure a site for houses and gardens, and in 1800, the very year in which the new road was opened, purchased five acres of land from the proprietor of Crocketford. Here they built several dwellings for themselves, the first of which was Newhouse, erected in 1802; and to these their whole community was transferred in 1808, when their connection with Larghill ceased. People from other parts were attracted to the spot, by the possibilities of trade and employment which it presented, with the result that a good-sized and growing village was soon established.

About the end of the first quarter of the century, Crocketford had practically assumed the proportions which it continues to exhibit; for, although repairs and alterations have since been effected from time to time, the additions made have been of small account. The condition of things, as it appeared in 1825, was prosperous and thriving; abundant employment being available for the inhabitants, and a continuous stream of traffic passing their doors, which could not fail to be of substantial benefit to them. So numerous and varied were the callings practised, that the community was able to provide most things for itself, and was largely independent of extraneous sources of supply. Besides the ordinary field-workers of both sexes, there were four shoemakers with plenty to do, and a corresponding proportion of joiners, wheelwrights, masons, tailors, and blacksmiths. As might have been expected in a village founded by the Buchanites, to whom was due the introduction of the two-handed wheel into Galloway, and whose make of linen was in great demand among the nobility and gentry of the Stewartry, spinning and weaving occupied the attention of a number of the inhabitants. The lint and wool were grown upon the neighbouring farms, and all the processes of their manufacture into linen and woollen goods were carried through in the district, from the preparation of the raw materials—the transformation of the lint into "heids" for the spinner, and the wool into "rowins" for the weaver—to the production of the finished article. The schoolmaster attended to the education of the young, the constable or sheriff-officer to the behaviour of the more mature; there were several grocers doing a good trade, a few busy bacon-curing establishments, and a number of public-houses with no lack of patrons. The names of the following inns are remembered as existing simultaneously, though only the first-mentioned has survived: The New Inn, The George, The Plough, and The Commercial. It was not only in keeping with the spirit of the time, but to some extent a consequence of the circumstances of life in the village, that drinking with its inevitable evils should be tolerably rife; and the public houses of Crocketford were doubtless included among those on which the Kirk Session found it necessary to animadvert in their communication of 19th April 1830 to the Justices of the Peace. There was a ceaseless coming and going of strangers, many of them of a type likely to encourage the consumption of alcoholic liquors. There was no coach service on the New Galloway road, but the through-mail on the coach road called twice a day on its journey between Portpatrick and

Dumfries, when postboys as well as passengers were generally ready for a refreshment, in which their friends might be invited to join. At intervals large droves of cattle, with their more or less thirsty attendants, appeared in the village, on their way to Dumfries and the markets of the South. Carriers also were much in evidence, especially about the middle of the week, when they journeyed to Dumfries for the Wednesday market, with the produce of the country in their carts—sometimes also with considerable sums of money in their pockets, entrusted to them for deposit in the Dumfries banks—or made their way home, with the merchandise of the town for the country shop-keepers and gentry. On Tuesday night and Wednesday morning the stir and excitement were at their height, as a crowd of twenty or more carts halted in the Toll-bar close, and many others passed in slow succession through the village, some of them filled with the carcases of the pigs slain at Haugh-of-Urr and other places. The traffic of a wide extent of country thus converging upon Crocketford, a number of the villagers, as a matter of course, took to the road, as drovers, carriers, post-boys, and such like; many of whom, it is to be feared, succumbed to the temptations incidental to an itinerating life.

The health of the inhabitants seems to have been remarkably good, partly no doubt in consequence of the situation of the village upon a bracing elevation, nearly 400 feet above the level of the sea. What cases of sickness there were received treatment from two persons of the Buchanite persuasion, who were permitted to bleed, drug, and diet at their discretion. Only one regular doctor is known to have lived in Crocketford until recent years, when Dr. Archibald Chalmers took up his residence in it; but the ailments of the village did not absorb his attentions, any more than they do those of his successor, which are distributed over the surrounding district. A testimony to its exceptional healthiness was afforded in 1832, during one of the dreaded visitations of cholera that happened periodically in olden times. The farmers and stock-dealers became so alarmed at the virulence of the epidemic in Dumfries, that on Wednesday, 10th October, not a bullock was presented for sale upon the Sands, and the proposal was made to transfer the market for a time to the Nine-mile Bar. One death, indeed, occurred in the village from the disease, but it was that of a stranger newly arrived in it; and in 1849, when the epidemic renewed its ravages in the South, it seems again to have passed by the inhabitants of Crocketford.

Though not possessed of a church of its own, like Springholm, Crocketford has not been without a fairly regular supply of religious ordinances, a preaching station upon undenominational lines having been established in the village school, so far back as 1839. The services have been maintained ever since, and are still carried on by the various ministers of the district, under the direction of a committee appointed by the inhabitants.

Towards the middle of the century the prosperity of the village reached its limit, and thereafter signs began to appear of the decadence which has since overtaken it. The total population was over two hundred, of which number the houses within the parish of Urr contained about a hundred and twenty. For a time the briskness of the old days seemed to be sustained by the extensive drainage operations undertaken upon the farms in the neighbourhood. Besides affording increased employment to the inhabitants, these operations attracted a number of strangers to the village, whose presence served to quicken its life and enhance its material prosperity, if it did not improve its social harmony and moral tone. Most of the incomers hailed from Ireland, and according to the traditions of the district were endowed more liberally with the vices than the virtues of their nation. Their sudden influx into the village taxed its accommodation to the utmost; and, in default of plentiful lodging, a goodly number of Clare and Connaught men were herded together in one of the old Buchanite houses, where they were compelled at night by limitations of sleeping space to lie "heids an' thraws." Here many a rowdy and drunken scene is said to have occurred, especially on Saturday nights, when the disorder occasionally developed into a regular Donnybrook fair. One evening a pitched battle took place between the men of the different counties, with the result that the Connaught men suffered ignominious defeat, and were ejected from the house. As they retired in wrathful disgust from the scene of the fight, one of them was heard to declare that he would never light a pipe again in the "Clare Lodge"; and the name was immediately affixed to the house, which is still popularly known as Clare Lodge or Castle Clare.

An earlier instance of the acquisition of a by-name in an incidental way is presented by Castle Hardships, a collection of three or four houses at the extreme end of the village on the road to Dumfries. Though now ruined and tenantless, these houses at one time contained their full complement of inhabitants, and were the scene of a busy, prosperous life. Even in those days, when there was no great pretence of strictness and decorum, they had a somewhat unenviable reputation for the conviviality of their occupants, and the amount of ardent liquor they consumed. So many bottles of whiskey are said to have been required in the tenement, that a pail or watering-can was sometimes used for their conveyance, in order to screen them from the observation of the neighbours. On one occasion a Scotch wool merchant of Wigan, called William Hyslop, a grand-uncle of Mr Joseph. H. Brown of Hermitage, paid a visit to a weaver in the tenement, with whom he had some business to transact. Being himself a believer in total abstinence, he was considerably shocked by some of the things he saw; and, on his return to Wigan, he addressed a newspaper to the weaver at "The Orphan's Home, The Drunkard's Den, Castle Hardships, near Starvation Point, Crocketford." Under the quaintness of the humour was probably concealed a serious and deliberate purpose; at any rate the newspaper was safely delivered, and was the means of

CROCKETFORD.

PHOTO. BY J. AND J. BROWN, CASTLE-DOUGLAS.

giving a name to the tenement, which seemed to foreshadow its ultimate fate.

With the conclusion of the drainage operations, and the withdrawal of the coaches and through-traffic upon the opening of the railway, the symptoms of decline became more pronounced. The history of Crocketford during the last fifty years has simply been a repetition of that of the other villages in the parish. Besides Castle Hardships, other houses have fallen into disrepair: the population has dwindled down to less than a hundred, or scarcely a half of what it was in more prosperous days: there are still three grocer's shops, but only one of the inns remains: all the old trades have disappeared except that of the blacksmith: and the only employment now to be had is ordinary labouring work. In 1891 a common lodging-house still existed in the village, but it was removed shortly afterwards, a smart epidemic of typhus having appeared in it, which was the means of causing three deaths. With this exception the health record has been well maintained, even the ordinary forms of sickness and disease having been comparatively rare.

There are few representatives of the old inhabitants now resident in the district; but, within recent years, some improvements have been introduced, and conveniences obtained, which attest the existence of a public spirit among their successors, and add materially to the amenity of the village. In 1898, at the instigation of the inhabitants, Crocketford was formed by the County Council into a special water supply district, and the old well and hand-pump water system was replaced by a gravitation supply. A public lamp was provided in 1906 by the proceeds of an entertainment in the village, and brightens up the vicinity of the old Toll-house on the long winter nights. Into the post-office, long in charge of the McCriries, but now managed by David C. G. Johnston, the telegraph was brought in 1902, under local guarantee; and, similarly, in 1907 the additional facilities of a money-order office and post-office savings bank were secured to the inhabitants. Such symptoms of reviving interest suggest that Crocketford may still have a future before it; but the hope of a full return to the bustle and prosperity of former days is scarcely to be entertained.

DALBEATTIE BURGH ARMS.

CHAPTER VIII

Dalbeattie

THE rise of the town of Dalbeattie has been an outstanding feature of the development of the parish in modern times. Scarcely of earlier date or more promising beginning than Haugh-of-Urr, Springholm, or Crocketford, Dalbeattie has had a more uniformly progressive career, and is now a place of considerable size and importance—the largest town, indeed, in the Stewartry of Kirkcudbright, if Maxwelltown be left out of account, as practically a suburb of Dumfries. It occupies a fine situation, on the banks of the stream which bears its name, at the point where the Vale of Urr begins to broaden out towards the Solway Firth, and is built almost entirely of the fine grey granite which abounds in the neighbourhood and has been the principal source of its prosperity. Its neat and attractive appearance, with its tasteful though unpretentious style of building, its well-ordered streets, its pleasant little public parks, and many recently effected improvements, is not unbecoming the picturesqueness of its surroundings, and witnesses to the enterprise and public spirit of the inhabitants, as well as their pride in "the granite burgh."

According to McKerlie, the name Dalbeattie may be a corruption of the Norse words dalr and beita, and may mean the dale or glen in which the sheep or cattle graze. More generally and probably it is held to be derived from the Gaelic dal, a field or portion of land, and beith, a birch tree, and to have the significance of the Field of the Birches. The popular rendering of the Vale or Valley of the Birches seems to be a combination of the two derivations.

Originally the name was applied, with a variableness of spelling characteristic of former days, to the land on which the town now stands, and others in the immediate neighbourhood. So far back as the fifteenth century, these were mostly in the possession of a family called Redik, who continued to be associated with them for at least two hundred years. Under the date of 4th January, 1488, the name of John Redik of Dalbatye appears as witness to a charter granted by Herbert, Lord Herries, to Sir Gilbert Anderson, perpetual chaplain of Chappelzaird in Terregles. Thereafter many references to the family occur in ancient documents, including that in the Talbot Papers already given in Chapter III, and those in the Minute Book of the War Committee of the Stewartry which have been cited in Chapter IV. There is no mention of the Rediks after the end of the seventeenth century, about which time the property passed away from them. Another family of the name of Cairns seems also to have possessed land in the neighbourhood of Dalbeattie at an early date; for in a deed executed at Kirkcudbright in February, 1491, " John Carnys of Dalbaty " appears as one of the witnesses. Though there is no further evidence of the connection of the Cairnses with Dalbeattie, proprietors of the same name are found in several of the surrounding parishes during the following centuries.

In the Statistical Account of Urr drawn up by the Rev. Alexander Robertson in 1627, the lands are divided into the "rooms" or farms of Mekle and Litle Dalbetie, of which the usual details are given. " Mekle Dalbetie is twa myll distant frae the kirk. It pays in present rent thrie and threttie bollis off meill, that is four chalder and twa bollis. The stock is fywe scoir bollis off small korne, that is twelff chalder and ane halff. The personage teind is twell bollis, that is ane chalder and ane halff. The vicarage is sextein merk. Litle Dalbetie is twa myll distant frae the kirk. It pays in rent presentlie twontie bollis off meill, that is twa chalder and ane halff. The stock is fywe scoir bollis, that is twell chalder and ane halff off small korne. The personage teind is fywe bollis, that is ane halff chalder and twa bollis. The vicarage is ten merk." This agrees with Timothy Pont's map, which is dated seven years previously, though it only appeared in 1654 in the atlas of Jan Blaeu. On it two farms are marked in close vicinity to the present site of the town: " M. Dalbety " on the southern bank of the Dalbeattie Burn, and " L. Dalbety " on its northern bank; while further up the stream on the southern side, the " Mill of Dalbety " is shown. The ancient Valuation Roll of the Stewartry, made up in 1642, contains the following entries: " Dalbeatie's Waterside, and the rest of McBrair's lands, two hundred and twenty pound; Little Dalbeatie, one hundred and twenty pound; Meikle Dalbeatie, one hundred and fifty pound." The modern Valuation Roll of 1777 reproduces these entries, but adds, with a curious change of spelling, " Park of Dalbatty, twenty five pound." There are other references in deeds of infeftment or sasine, all of which go to show that, before the existence of the present town, the estate on which it stands was divided into several farms, into the names of which the word Dalbeattie entered.

The occasional notices of Dalbeattie in the minutes of the Presbytery of Dumfries are not without significance. On 10th August, 1658, it is resolved that Robert Herries in Dalbeattie should be dealt with for popery and refusing to subscribe the covenant; and on 15th September, 1747, Mr McKinnel, the minister of Urr, is instructed to apply to James Copland in Dalbeattie, the popish master of Helen Conchar, in whose house she has been corrupted, to put her away, and in the event of his refusal to apply to the judge ordinary to remove her as law directs. The use of the general name Dalbeattie, instead of a more distinctive appellation, appears to indicate that neither Herries nor Copland was connected with any of the farms. In the latter case especially it might be taken to imply the existence of a small township or clachan in the neighbourhood of the Dalbeattie Burn. That there was such a township, at least about the middle of the eighteenth century, is made almost certain by the further minute of 5th July, 1751, which refers to a report upon the stenting of the parish laid before the Presbytery by James Martin, schoolmaster in Dalbeattie. It would be no more, however, than a little row or cluster of cottages, built in the rough and ready fashion of the time, with walls of unhewn stones, and a roofing of heather or thatch. A similar collection of houses is said to have been situated on what is now known as Barrhill, and to have gone under the name of the village of Cunningham.

These houses, of course, have all disappeared. Even the oldest erections in the present town of Dalbeattie do not date back before the year 1780. About that time, the process of feuing was begun on both sides of the Dalbeattie Burn—on the north, by Mr George Maxwell of Munches, and, on the south, by Mr Alexander Copland of Kingsgrange. To each feuar was granted, besides a plot of land for house and garden, an allotment for perpetuity in one of the adjacent peat mosses. This provision, according to Dr. Muirhead in the Old Statistical Account, was rendered necessary by the scarcity of fuel occasioned by the heavy tax upon coals imported from England, and had a stimulating effect upon the growth of the new village. From the outset, there was a sharp demand for feus, people coming considerable distances to build a home for themselves on the banks of the Dalbeattie Burn. The village increased with such rapidity that in twelve or thirteen years it contained over 200 inhabitants. Besides its convenient fuel, it possessed a further advantage in the suitability of its situation for milling and manufacturing establishments, at a time when these continued to be worked by water power. The " Mill of Dalbety " mentioned in Pont's map was, of course, a grain mill, and was still in existence. To this was added, soon after the rise of the village, a lint mill which, as Dr. Muirhead informs us, was well conducted, and had its full

DALBEATTIE

share of what business the country afforded in that branch. About the same time, a paper manufactory was started which, we are told, was conducted by a prudent, intelligent, and sober person, and prospered accordingly. This was probably a man called Wilson, who was very early in the paper manufacturing line, and has a descendant still living in Dalbeattie. It is significant of the increasing size and activity of the place that, in 1797, a new and commodious bridge was built over the Urr Water, at the foot of Craignair Hill. This is the bridge that still connects the town with the southern and western divisions of the county. Strangely enough, the stones for its erection were brought all the way from Kirkgunzeon, to the neglect of the granite supplies in the immediate neighbourhood, which have since been so largely exploited. An interesting notice of the town, at the end of the eighteenth century, is given in Robert Heron's " Journey through Scotland," published in 1799. According to Heron, there were a few cottages at the Craignair bridge, with a dyeing house and a corn mill. Dalbeattie was a small but thriving village, with some mills and the beginnings of a coasting trade, the chief imports being lime and coal, and the chief exports grain and potatoes. To Heron's mind, it was " surprising that a situation so favourable had not before this time been occupied by a town or village of considerable magnitude "; and he expected, " if some suitable manufactory could be established at Dalbeattie, to see it rise to rival the most considerable towns in this part of Galloway." The acuteness of these observations, it is almost unnecessary to remark, has been strikingly demonstrated by the subsequent history of "the granite burgh."

In the early years of the nineteenth century the development of Dalbeattie proceeded very much upon the lines already described in the cases of Haugh-of-Urr, Crocketford, and Springholm. It was simply one among the villages of the parish, though rapidly outstripping the others in population, and beginning to show signs of its future industrial importance.

The main spring of its progress was the agricultural activity stimulated by the French war, which brought the usual influx of field-workers and labourers into the district, and provided increased employment for masons, joiners, and other tradesmen. To supply the wants of the rising community, a number of shops were opened in due course, which gradually increased with the rise of the population. At one time, there were only two or three grocers, two or three drapers, one butcher, and one baker in the place. Among the earliest of the grocers was a man called Nisbet; and others who took up the same calling at an early date were Merchant Copeland and John Milligan. The first drapery establishment of any pretensions was opened in 1832 by Thomas Rawline, in the shop between the Commercial and the Maxwell Arms Hotels. Mr Rawline lived almost to the end of the century; and, though he purchased the estate of Little Firthhead in 1861, and removed to it shortly afterwards, he maintained his interest in the town, and was practically associated with its progress, throughout his life. A Justice of the Peace for the Stewartry, and an original proprietor of the Dumfries and Galloway Standard, he was also one of the members of the first Police Commission of Dalbeattie, after it became a burgh. The butcher's shop at one time was in the hands of a man named Porter; but John McCormick is better remembered as carrying on the business in the corner property opposite the site of the present Union Bank, which was then unbuilt upon, and was popularly known as "Jennie Robinson's field." The baker's shop was in the same vicinity, and so early as 1840 was occupied by David Paterson, whose son still continues in the trade.

According to the rule in those days, the wants of the people in the way of liquids needed somewhat plentiful provision, and public-houses were in evidence to an extent that would now be regarded as out of all proportion to the requirements of the population. The Plough Inn and the Brown Cow faced each other at opposite corners of the Cross; and between the

THOMAS RAWLINE OF LITTLE FIRTHHEAD.
FROM AN EARLY PORTRAIT.

Cross and the Burn stood quite a number of houses of the same kind. On the other side of the Burn, the King's Arms, now known as the Commercial Hotel, and the Maxwell Arms did a busy trade in their present premises, remodelled of course and considerably enlarged in later years. McGarvie and Muir were the names of two successive tenants of the former of these hotels, and David Murray was the landlord of the latter. The daughter of Murray, it may be mentioned, was married to the Rev. John Osborne, the Reformed Presbyterian minister of Dalbeattie and Springholm. In those days the correspondence of the town cannot have been large, as the postal business was conducted by the landlord of the Maxwell Arms and his wife in a room of the hotel, Dalbeattie being only a receiving and delivery office under Castle-Douglas, with a daily runner to and from that town. The circumstances and conditions under which the liquor trade was conducted in the early years of the century were very different from those which now obtain, and excessive drinking and riotous behaviour were much more common. These regrettable features of the life of the time were probably accentuated by the large number of incomers of the labouring class, and the thriftless wanderers who found their way to the village. According to the minutes of the Kirk Session, especially those dated 21st September, 1828, and 19th April, 1830, the public-houses of Dalbeattie, like those in the other villages of the parish, were responsible for much vice and drunkenness prevailing in the district, and required not only to be reduced in number but to be much more strictly supervised by the authorities. The Kirk Session, indeed, found it necessary to make some strong representations regarding them to the proprietors and the Justices of the Peace.

Another source of trouble at the time was the number and character of the lodging-houses in the town. These were largely occupied by sturdy beggars or vagrants of a dangerous type, who infested the parish, and annoyed the inhabitants.

Complaints regarding them were laid before the Kirk Session, who commissioned three of their number to inquire into the way in which they were conducted. The elders appointed to this duty were: James Copland, the master of the parish school in Dalbeattie: James Heron, who held the farm of Edingham in the neighbourhood of the town: and Hugh Lindsay, who carried on a dyeing mill at Islecroft, and whose son, it is interesting to notice, still survives at the age of 94. On 23rd August, 1829, these commissioners gave in their report to the Kirk Session, and it fully confirmed the bad reputation of the lodging-houses. This report throws such light upon the characteristics of the time that part of it may be quoted. " Some of these houses are kept in a most disorderly and profligate manner: each and all of them are the receptacle of drunkards and vagabonds, the very offscourings of society: drink is brought into these houses (for they are below the character of obtaining licences) when the poor unthinking wretches get abominably intoxicate, and every species of sin and wretchedness is committed, even the Lord's Day, that sacred day, not excepted, to the great hurt and annoyance of every sober and well disposed Christian." The Session directed their clerk to furnish Mr David Armstrong, factor on the estate on which these houses were situated, with a copy of this report, " that if possible, according to the laudable proposal of Mr Copland of Collieston, a stop might be put to such sinful practices."

So soon as it had attained sufficient dimensions, Dalbeattie, like other country villages, had its established Fair-day, which for a long time was celebrated twice a year. Showmen and travelling merchants of all descriptions gathered to the town, to minister to the popular amusement, and dispose of their wares. The day was observed as a holiday for miles around, and the inhabitants of the town and district assembled in crowds in the High Street, to see the sights, and buy fairings for their sweethearts and friends. Hilarity prevailed on every

DAVID PATERSON, DALBEATTIE.

hand; some dissipation also took place, as might well be expected from the conveniences provided in the way of public-houses. Apart from the abuses, however, to which it was liable, there are sufficient reasons in the altered conditions of modern life to account for the discontinuance of the Fair between forty and fifty years ago.

The year 1835 may be taken as a convenient halting-place for a closer look at the town. About that time, it consisted almost entirely of four streets: High Street, Copland Street, William Street, and Maxwell Street. There were the beginnings of several other streets, but so far they had not advanced much. John Street and Station Road had not been started, and the only house in what is now Craignair Street was a small self-contained cottage, with a garden in front, which was called Dykeside, and was occupied by the Misses Carnan. It stood almost on the site of what is now No. 4 Craignair Street. Travelling was done on foot or by the stage coaches, several of which passed daily through the town from Castle-Douglas and Dumfries, and did not often extend beyond short distances. A journey to Edinburgh or across the border to an English town, so lightly undertaken nowadays, was a rare and important event. The Perseverance was the favourite coach; and when, after the commencement of the reign of Queen Victoria, a coach called by her name took the road in competition with it, the townspeople took no pains to conceal their partiality. Besides retaining the patronage of the travelling public, the Perseverance was met daily on the Dumfries road by the boys of Dalbeattie, and escorted to the town with cheers, while the Victoria was saluted with general hisses and groans. To Dumfries and other towns in the vicinity, there were regular carriers, who not only conveyed goods in their carts, but frequently also carried money in their bags for deposit in the banks, as so far no such institutions existed in Dalbeattie. Among the leading carriers was Nathan Major, who lived to a ripe old age, and used in his later years to recall the fact of his presence at the funeral of Jean Armour, the widow of Robert Burns. He is said to have written some elegiac verses on her death. Others who followed the same avocation were the Milligans, a family of four brothers, of whom one, Hugh, left a daughter, Mrs Gilchrist, who died at Blaiket Farm a short time ago. Besides their carrying business, the Milligans had the woollen mill for a number of years; but, disagreeing amongst themselves, they ultimately broke up their firm, and the site of the woollen mill was turned into a granite polishing yard. Five other mills were at this time in operation in Dalbeattie: the paper mill, called by the name of Mount Pleasant, which was in the hands of a man named Cochtrie, and which, after being conducted for a period by William Lewis, and afterwards for 37 years by John Forsyth, has recently been acquired by Andrew Wright, and is now carried on under the business style of Forsyth and Wright: a grain mill occupied by Anthony Broadfoot, whose dwelling-house may still be seen beside the timber yard in Craignair Street: the waulk mill of Hugh Lindsay, established by his father of the same name in 1801 at Islecroft: and two mills for sawing wood, which has always been an industry of Dalbeattie. There was also a bacon curing establishment, which was carried on by James McLaurin in conjunction with the grocery business long associated with the family, and was only given up about five and thirty years ago. Mr McLaurin was a leading and popular citizen in his time, and is gratefully remembered for the active part he took in public affairs, especially in connection with the inauguration of the burgh. His father, Dugald McLaurin, was in business in Dalbeattie early in the century, and in 1830 was appointed a deacon in the parish church. His son, who bears his grandfather's name, maintains the civic traditions of the family, and does not spare himself in the public service of the town.

Already, in 1835, the sea-going trade of Dalbeattie had attained to some dimensions, and a number of small vessels

JAMES M'LAURIN, DALBEATTIE.

plied regularly between it and places on the English coast. As some of these vessels were built on the Dalbeattie Burn, a short distance from its junction with the Urr, the construction as well as the sailing of them increased the opportunities of employment afforded by the town. It was about this time that Charles Riddick built his vessel, the "John and Sarah," which he continued to own and sail for nearly forty years. Then or in the immediately succeeding years, various well-remembered inhabitants of the town were associated with the shipping industry, either as skippers or owners. Nathan Copland was one of the most famous skippers of the Water of Urr. David Clark was another: he sailed the "Jessie Maxwell" which, as well as the "Heart of Oak," was owned by John Shaw, a retired blacksmith who lived in Water Street. Charles Clachrie was the master of the "Jane Elizabeth" or the "Elizabeth and Ann," a vessel which, from an incident in its early days, had earned the nickname of "the Curse." It was built at Dalbeattie; and, at the launching ceremony, the gentleman who was performing the principal part slipped his foot and dropped the bottle with which the christening should have been done. Instead of the name of the vessel he emitted a hearty curse; and from this fact popular humour conferred upon it the designation by which it was afterwards known. The "Importer" belonged to Thomas Rawline, but was afterwards sold to the Messrs Newall; and there were other vessels, such as the "Good Intent," and the "Tom Green," belonging to Captain George Wilson, which were frequent visitors to Dalbeattie port. In those days it was no unusual thing to see a line of donkey carts on the Haugh road, filled with coals and other merchandise for Haugh-of-Urr, Springholm, and Kirkpatrick-Durham.

So far there are no available returns for determining the population of the town, as the inhabitants continued to be reckoned in the census reports among the parishioners of Urr; but it is possible to arrive by inference at a fairly accurate estimate of the number of people it contained. In the roll of members of the parish church in 1835, exactly one-third of the communicants are given as belonging to Dalbeattie; and, as the ecclesiastical conditions in the town were very much the same at that time as in the country division of the parish, it may be safely concluded that Dalbeattie contained at least one-third of the entire population, or something over 1000 souls. Other indications, which need not be enumerated, point to the correctness of this figure.

During the following fifteen years, the progress of Dalbeattie was so well-sustained that it gradually outgrew the limits of a country village, and began to take full rank as a town. Its importance and promise seem both to have escaped the notice of the writer of the New Statistical Account of 1845. By no means so communicative as his predecessor regarding the general condition of the parish, he is particularly meagre in the information he affords of Dalbeattie. In his principal reference to it he conjoins it with Springholm, as a place in which there was a considerable Irish population whom the state of the surrounding country was unable to support by lawful industry, and in which accordingly poverty with its generally accompanying evils greatly prevailed. From other sources, however, we learn that the town was not only growing steadily in size, but was also developing some new and important lines of industry. Apart from the granite business, the foundations of which were being securely laid, other industries were being established which have proved of permanent benefit to the town. The business of grain millers and merchants, now carried on by James Carswell and Son at Barr-Bridge Mills, was established in 1837. In recent years, under the management of John Carswell, a continuously successful business has been greatly extended, and the premises repeatedly enlarged. Three years later Thomas Biggar commenced to lay the foundations of the trade in farm seeds and artificial manures, in which he was subsequently joined by his sons, and which has since grown to large proportions. By 1845, also, the Messrs Helme had established themselves on the banks of the Dalbeattie Burn, as wood merchants and bobbin turners. Their business was afterwards transferred to Messrs Jackson, who still carry it on at Islecroft. A similar business, it may be mentioned, was started in the year of Queen Victoria's Jubilee by Messrs Lawson and Henderson, who at one time were connected with the mill of Messrs Helme. Their works were burned down a few years ago; but soon afterwards they erected new and larger premises, with improved machinery, in which they continue to do a good business.

Though the population of Dalbeattie in 1850 is again a matter of inference, it is possible to determine it with tolerable exactness from the number of inhabited houses the town is known to have contained. Besides the streets already mentioned, which had been considerably increased, substantial progress had been made with Water Street, Burn Street, Mill Street, Alpine Street, Port Street, Union Street, Craignair Street, and Southwick Road. These streets contained from six to twelve houses each; and in addition to them a beginning had been made with John Street and Blair Street. Altogether it is computed that there were over 300 inhabited houses in the town; and a reasonable allocation of dwellers to each house would give a total population of at least 1500.

Some of these dwellers were individuals of sufficient enterprise, or interesting enough personality, to deserve special notice. John Denniston, the grandfather of Mr James Tait, builder, occupied the farm of Flatts, and was distinguished among other things for the fact that he had served with the poet Burns at Ellisland, and was one of his warmest admirers. James Kerr, clogmaker in High Street, was a noted player of draughts, and claimed to have initiated Thomas Carlyle into the game. Mrs Kirkpatrick and Miss Herries were two sisters who kept a small shop on the site of the present establishment of Mr R. Blyth, ironmonger, and were noted for their old-fashioned gentility, their keenness of intellect, and interest in political matters, as well as their claim to be of Huguenot extraction. Some veterans who had served in the Peninsular war, some who had been at Trafalgar, and one at least who had been with Sir Ralph Abercromby in Egypt in 1801, still lingered in the town. The last was William Wilkinson, who had enlisted in 1811, and was still hale and active so late as the sixties, when he departed to Australia. William Elliot had been in business as a blacksmith and forge-master at Islecroft from 1821. About the year 1835, his son, John Elliot, built a forge at Maidenholm for the manufacture of reaping-hooks; and, later on, when the scythe began to supersede the reaping-hook in the harvest-field, he effected such changes in his work as enabled him to produce forgings of a larger kind, for which he soon established a reputation among the country blacksmiths. Among his productions were sock plates, coulters, plough beams, grubber frames, cart axles, ship knees, spades, and shovels, in the making of which ten or twelve men were usually employed. After his retiral, the work was carried on for a time by his son, also called John, but he ultimately gave it up, and went to America. Among others engaged in business, and not otherwise mentioned, were the following: joiners, John Rigg, Mill Bush, Robert Wilson, High Street, and James Heughan, Union Street; carriers, James Watson, Water Street, and James Hyslop, High Street; grocers, John Milligan, Craignair Street, and Samuel Kirkpatrick, Maxwell Street; nailmakers, James Halliday and William Houston, High Street; blacksmiths, William Heughan, Water Street, and Peter Clark, High Street; weaver, Samuel Copland, Maxwell Street; shoemaker, Wellwood McGowan, Maxwell Street; and drapers, Lawson Hodson, Maxwell Street, and Samuel Brown, High Street. Thorniethwaite was the name of the landlord of the Maxwell Arms; McGarvie, that of the landlord of the King's Arms, and Carmont, that of the landlord of the Brown Cow.

DALBEATTIE

The middle of the century, which saw the tide of prosperity begin to turn in the villages in the upper division of the parish, was the commencement of a fresh chapter in the progress of Dalbeattie. The subsequent developments of the town, however, have been so closely associated with the exploitation of its granite resources, that the story of them must be prefaced by a short account of what is justly entitled to be called the staple industry.

Not long after the building of Craignair Bridge with Kirkgunzeon stone, the possibilities of remunerative enterprise that lay concealed in the neighbouring hills appear to have dawned on Andrew Newall, the founder of the family that has ever since been identified with the granite trade. The date of his first prospecting for the stone is not quite clear, but certainly falls among the earliest years of the nineteenth century. By 1820 he seems to have been quite established in the granite business, with quarries at Craignair, the Barrhill, and other places. A transaction is recorded, of date 17th March, 1828, in which he purchased $26\frac{1}{2}$ tons of granite at one shilling per ton; but so far his business does not seem to have been very extensive. Some time in the early twenties the attention of the Mersey Dock and Harbour Boards was called to the Dalbeattie stone as suitable for their purposes; and, in 1825, they opened a quarry at Craignair, which they continued to work till 1831, when considerations of easier shipment induced them to transfer their operations to Creetown, where they secured a quarry close to the sea front. Andrew Newall worked away at Craignair, and in course of time was succeeded in his business by his two sons, David and Homer, while another son, Charles, opened a quarry on his own account. Two of these pioneers of the industry, Charles and Homer Newall, were destined to be among its victims, each meeting his death in his quarry during blasting operations.

Till 1841 the stones of Craignair were used entirely for building purposes; but in that year a beginning was made with the polishing process, which has since become a distinctive feature of the industry. The first polished stone to be ordered —the forerunner of many highly-finished and ornate productions of the Dalbeattie workmen—was a memorial stone. In the absence of suitable tools and expert knowledge, it would scarcely have borne comparison with later specimens of the polishing art; but, such as it was, it was a further revelation of the possibilities of Dalbeattie granite, and did distinct credit to the workmen employed upon it — Thomas Copeland and John Kirk. The next important sample of polished Dalbeattie granite was a stone sent to the great International Exhibition at London in 1851. It was the production of David and Homer Newall, and had a Scotch thistle incised upon it. Special appliances not being available at that time, all the work upon it was laboriously done by hand; but the result was eminently satisfactory, and gave assured promise of better things.

Following upon this venture, there set in for the granite industry a period of great activity, which gradually assumed the character of a boom. Hewing and polishing departments were added to the original quarrying business, and an increasing demand arose for dressed and ornamental, as well as unhewn stones. While the Newall family continued to be largely interested in the trade, others were induced to enter it by the promising conditions of the time. The first polishing yard was established by the firm of D. H. and J. Newall on the site of the old woollen mill: this was afterwards given up for the more convenient and commodious situation now occupied by them on what was formerly called, after the miller already mentioned, "Anthony Broadfoot's field." The hewing sheds and polishing works erected by them on this site have since been largely altered and increased, new appliances and machinery being added as the methods of dealing with granite were improved, so that now they are as fully equipped places of the kind as are anywhere to be found. This firm also has quarries at Peterhead, Aberdeenshire, and Westerley, Rhode

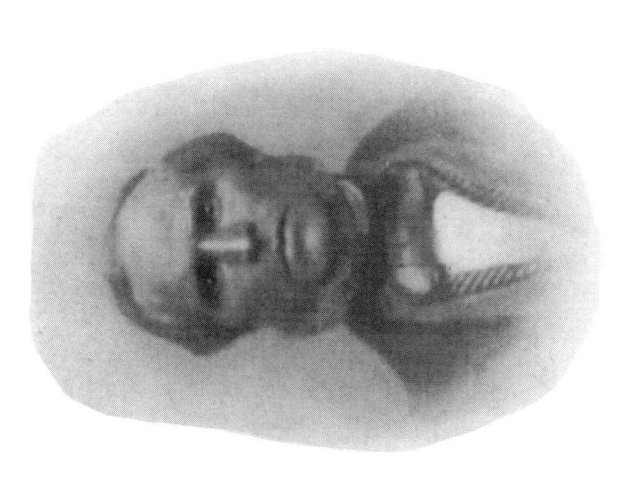

HOMER NEWALL, DALBEATTIE.

JOSEPH NEWALL, DALBEATTIE.

Island, America, from which they obtain supplies of the red and blue speckled granite respectively, which they work up at the mill in Dalbeattie into beautiful and effective designs, in combination with the local grey stone. In 1865, Messrs D. H. and J. Newall had already entered upon the occupation of their present premises, and were operating upon a very extensive scale: Charles Newall had started a polishing business in their former yard, and was carrying it on in conjunction with a quarry of his own at Craignair: and another firm, Shearer, Curteis and Company, were engaged in quarrying both at Craignair and the Old Lands. The polishing mill of Charles Newall was afterwards taken up by Shearer, Field, and Company, but finally abandoned in 1883, when this firm ceased operations. About that time the prosperity of the granite trade began to wane, and a new condition of things was appearing, which has continued ever since, and under which occasional briskness has alternated with spells of more or less prolonged depression.

In recent years a further development of the industry has taken place, in the production of crushed granite for the making of concrete and other purposes. By means of appropriate plant, the smaller and less shapely stones, which might otherwise be discarded as refuse, are ground down to various useful sizes, from that of road metal to the finest gravel for garden walks. This is now an important branch of the business of D. H. and J. Newall, who have a mill with the requisite crushing machinery in the vicinity of their quarries at Craignair, and an aerial ropeway, fully half a mile in length, connecting the mill with a loading bank upon the railway, and affording a rapid and economical means of conveying the products to the trucks. On this ropeway, buckets of a carrying capacity of six hundredweights each pass and repass at such a speed that something like 200 tons of crushed granite can be transported in a day. A large trade in the crushing of granite is done by the firm of Fraser and Young, who make it the chief feature of their business. This firm was established in 1888, since which time they have worked quarries at Old Lands, Stedstone, Howlet, and Spycraig. At the first-mentioned place they have a crushing machine; but the bulk of their work is done at a mill beside the railway line, in the vicinity of the station, where they have two crushers at work and every facility for the despatch of the output. In 1901, the total weight of crushed granite manufactured at Dalbeattie was 50,000 tons: in 1907, it had risen to 70,000 tons.

At the present time, in addition to the two firms last mentioned, David Newall carries on a quarry at Craignair and a polishing mill at Maidenholm, from which some excellent specimens of granite work are annually produced. There are also some smaller granite businesses, which work quarries, the stone from which is regarded as quite serviceable for setts and kerbs, though not so suitable for the higher uses to which that from other quarries has been put. The importance of the granite industry to Dalbeattie may be estimated from the fact that over 400 of the male inhabitants are usually employed in connection with it. On the other hand, the quality of its products may be inferred from the large and varied demand they have created, and the numerous places at home and abroad to which they have found their way. Dalbeattie granite was used in the building of Eddystone Lighthouse, the Thames Embankment, and the docks of Liverpool, Belfast, Silloth, and Greenock: in the form of basal blocks or polished ornaments, it has been wrought into the structure of some of the finest public buildings in London, Liverpool, Manchester, Glasgow, and other cities: as paving setts and kerbs, it has gone to the making of streets all over the kingdom: large quantities of it have been sent abroad to be utilised in various ways: and numberless memorials have been constructed of it, most of them for erection in town and country churchyards, but not a few of them to perpetuate the memory of the illustrious dead in public places, or mark the graves of those

DALBEATTIE

who have died in distant lands. It is no exaggeration to say that, besides affording employment and gain to the inhabitants, the granite resources of Dalbeattie have carried the name of the town to the remotest corners of the world.

The vicissitudes of the staple industry are reflected in the variations of the population from the middle of the nineteenth century to the present day. So long as the granite boom lasted, it rapidly increased; being 1736 in 1861, and rising to 3865, the highest point it has so far reached, in 1881. The period of depression which ensued between 1881 and 1891 saw the population fall to 3149; but since then there has been a considerable recovery, the census returns of 1901 revealing a figure of 3469, which is brought up to 3721 in the medical officer's estimate for 1908. The area occupied by the town is now 424 acres; and on the basis of the estimated population this would give a density of 8·775 persons to the acre.

One of the first symptoms of the new life infused into the town by the development of the granite industry was the institution, in 1851, of a subscription and circulating library. The movement, which was started by some of the more intelligent inhabitants, had the sympathy and encouragement of Mr Maxwell of Munches; and in the following year, when it was decided to form a Mechanics' Institute in connection with the library, he agreed to become its president. A room for reading purposes was afterwards secured by the Institute and carried on successfully in the premises of the Town Hall; but when these had been taken over by the Town Council, the reading-room had to be given up, and operations confined to the lending of books, and occasional courses of public lectures. At present, the library is located in the lesser Town Hall, and consists of 3000 volumes of well-selected general literature, to which the people of the town and district have ample opportunities of access. A few years ago, however, a bazaar was held for the purpose of raising money to provide a separate building for the Institute, and the erection of suitable premises is now well advanced. The new home of the Institute will be a commodious and unpretentious building of native granite, erected on a site at the Mill Isles, granted by Mr W. J. H. Maxwell of Munches on nominal terms.

Previous to 1852, there was no bank in Dalbeattie; but in that year this necessity of a growing industrial community was met by the establishment of a branch of the Union Bank of Scotland. The office was opened in a shop on the west side of High Street, four doors northward from the Cross. Some six years later, the handsome corner building now occupied by the Bank was erected, on what had been formerly known as "Jennie Robinson's field." The first manager, Mr Burnie, was soon succeeded by his brother-in-law, Mr James Grieve, who for many years took a lively, helpful interest in the affairs of the town; since his death the business of the Bank has been conducted successively by Messrs R. W. McNab, John Smith, Henry Moir, and John Simpson, the present agent.

By the time Dalbeattie came to have a bank, its postal correspondence had largely increased from the days when it could be manipulated in a room of the Maxwell Arms Hotel. No doubt this was partly the result of the rise of the local industries and the population; but it was still more due, in all probability, to the establishment of the penny postal system in 1840. In view of the cost of the transmission of letters, it may well be believed that there would be no great strain on the services of the post office in the earlier days. Isabella Watson, in the story of her life, a local pamphlet published in 1835, informs us that she paid a pound sterling to John McNish, postmaster in Dalbeattie, for some letters she received from him, one of them alone, a rather bulky packet, costing her eight and ninepence. By the middle of the century, however, all this was changed, and the business of the post-office had grown to such dimensions that separate premises had to be secured for it. For a time it was carried on in the second shop from the Burn on the west side of

High Street: thereafter it was removed to a house on the opposite side of the street from the Maxwell Arms; again it was transferred to the corner premises below the Town Clock: and finally it was accommodated in the fine, commodious building recently erected for it beside the Town Bridge. Miss Currie, the daughter of Dr. James Currie, a medical practitioner in the town, is still remembered as an active and efficient postmistress: so also is Miss Gillespie, who only retired lately, after many years of faithful service: the charge of affairs is now in the capable hands of Mr David H. Braid. The office is become an important centre in the postal system of the south, with telephone as well as telegraph connections, and various sub-offices in the surrounding district.

In 1858, a most important step in the progress of the town was taken by the formation of it into a Police Burgh. The movement towards this end was the natural outcome of the increasing consequence of the town; but it was directly stimulated by the pressing necessity of more effective control over local affairs, and closer attention to sanitary and kindred matters. Between 1840 and 1850, some alarm had been caused by cholera, typhoid, smallpox, and other epidemics; but so far the only collective attempt to deal with matters of public health had been the appointment of a voluntary committee to inspect public nuisances, and take what measures they could for their removal. Having no expert knowledge of sanitation, and no authority to enforce their recommendations, the committee found themselves unable to effect any considerable improvement; consequently it was deemed desirable to have the town declared a burgh, and put under the regulations of the General Police Act. The meeting at which this resolution was formally adopted was held in the Maxwell Arms Hotel on 17th April, 1858; and there were present at it, besides the Steward-substitute of the county, Mr William Hyacinth Dunbar, and the Steward Clerk Depute, Mr William Nicholson, the following householders of Dalbeattie: Thomas

McKnight, surgeon; Samuel Brown, draper; John Kirk, grocer; John Muir, innkeeper; John McGowan Lowden, chemist and grocer; Alexander Lindsay, draper; William Wilson, grocer; James Fowlis, John Elliot, Thomas Rawline, John Patterson Lewis, M.D., Alexander McCroskrie, George Nisbet, James McLaurin, David Paterson, John Carswell, James McMorrine, Andrew Newall, William Lewis, and James Grieve. Dr. Lewis moved, and James McLaurin seconded the resolution for the adoption of the Police Act, which was unanimously carried. The first Council of the new burgh was constituted on the 7th June following, and consisted of the following members: Robert Clark, John Carswell, John Elliot, Thomas Helme, Alexander Lindsay, Thomas Maxwell, James McLaurin, David Paterson, and Thomas Rawline. At a meeting held subsequently in the Commercial Hotel, Thomas Maxwell was elected chief commissioner or provost of the burgh, and James McLaurin and David Paterson were appointed junior magistrates. Except by courtesy, it may be noted, the title "provost" did not pertain to the chief commissioner, till it was conferred by an Act of Parliament about 35 years afterwards.

Dalbeattie was particularly fortunate in the selection of its first provost. Mr Maxwell was a man of liberal education, high principle, and sound business capacity, who was held in great esteem among his fellow-townsmen, and had already rendered notable public service. He had studied at Glasgow University, and afterwards for a few years conducted an adventure school in Dalbeattie; but an early change in his circumstances had enabled him to give up this employment, and devote himself more freely to the affairs of the town. During the three years of his provostship, he exerted himself with great public spirit to consolidate and organise the new municipality, and start it fairly on its career; and the success that attended it in its earlier stages may be ascribed in great part to the sagacity and judgment he brought to bear upon its affairs.

THOMAS MAXWELL.
FIRST PROVOST OF DALBEATTIE.

DALBEATTIE

To the end of his life he continued his interest in social and municipal matters, acting amongst other capacities as secretary of the Savings Bank, an institution which did a large amount of good in Dalbeattie, as a member of the Parochial Board, convener of the cemetery committee, and an elder in the United Presbyterian Church. In November, 1873, two years before his death, at a largely-attended public meeting in the Town Hall, which was presided over by Mr Maxwell of Munches, he received from the inhabitants of the town a gratifying proof of the esteem in which he was held, and their appreciation of his public usefulness, in the presentation of a handsome service of silver plate. Mrs Newall, Broomlands, it may be mentioned, is a daughter of Mr Maxwell.

In the first year of Mr Maxwell's provostship, a great improvement was effected in the condition of things in the town by the institution of a coal gas supply for illumining purposes, in place of the candles, oil lamps, and lanterns, formerly employed. After fifty years' working, the Dalbeattie Gas Light Company is still in a prosperous state, not yet having had its operations curtailed by the introduction of electricity; and the progress it has made in the interval, not only in the manufacture and supply of the illuminant, but also in efficient and economical management, is attested by the gradual reduction of the price of gas, from 12s. 6d. per 1000 cubic feet in 1858 to 5s. at the present day. Mr Dugald McLaurin has been chairman of the Company in recent years; and to his judgment and close attention to its interests, much of its success has been due. In November 1859, as already noted, a further boon was conferred upon the inhabitants of the town by the opening of a line of railway to Dumfries and Castle-Douglas, connecting it with the general railway system of the country. In celebration of the event, a public banquet was held, at which Provost Maxwell made an eloquent speech, forecasting the benefits that would accrue from it to the social life and industries of the town. His anticipations have been largely fulfilled in the part which the railway has played in the development of Dalbeattie during the last fifty years. Mr Maxwell of Munches, it may be added, was chairman of the company that constructed the line, and on the completion of the undertaking gave a free run to Glasgow to the workmen who had been employed upon it. So crude were the notions in those days of the conveniences provided by the railway, at least among the less intelligent section of the community, that one of the excursionists is said to have refused to leave the station in Glasgow to see the sights, in case the train would set off on the return journey to Dalbeattie without him. On the coming of the railway to the town, the widening of the bridge in High Street, which had been in prospect for a time, could no longer be delayed. This important work was undertaken in 1860, and added greatly to the conveniences of the town, as well as to the appearance of its principal street.

On Mr Maxwell's retiral in 1861, John Carswell, the founder of the business of James Carswell and Son, grain merchants and millers at Barrhill, who had originally been a farmer at Torkirra in Kirkgunzeon, succeeded to the civic chair. After a short occupancy of three weeks, he was followed by Thomas McKnight, surgeon, who continued in office for the full term of three years. Dr. McKnight had taken up the practice of Dr. James Currie in Dalbeattie, but he relinquished it, and removed to Ayr, soon after the termination of his provostship in 1864. He was succeeded by John Muir, the landlord of the Commercial Hotel, who remained in office till 1867. Mr Muir had been a farmer at one time in the neighbourhood of Castle-Douglas, and had afterwards been in business in England, before coming to Dalbeattie to take up the management of the hotel. Previous to his advent, there had been no regular posting establishment in the town, and only one horse was available for hire; but he instituted a service of conveyances twice a week to Castle-Douglas and Dumfries, and also carried passengers and parcels regularly to Colvend. He was a well-known public character, who had taken an interest in the affairs of the town from the time of its formation into a burgh.

The next provost was John Patterson Lewis, M.D. He served for two periods of twelve and five years respectively, with an interval of three years between, and thus established a record of seventeen years' tenure of office, which has not yet been passed. A native of Newabbey, and a graduate of Edinburgh University, Dr. Lewis had practised for a short time in Auchencairn before settling in Dalbeattie. He came to the town in 1856, and soon afterwards received the appointment of medical officer to the parish under the Parochial Board, whom he served in that capacity with rare ability and faithfulness till their function was taken over by the Parish Council in 1895. During the forty years of his professional life, he was a prominent personage in Dalbeattie, whose characteristic candour and thoroughness of method inspired respect and confidence among all classes of the community. Unsparing of prejudice and dereliction of duty, he was a terror to evildoers, no less in the sick-room than on the bench of the burgh court. His work as a physician was painstaking and skilful, and gained him a high reputation in the district; at the same time, his public services to the town, given at considerable sacrifice to himself, were of the most intelligent and beneficial kind, and still keep his name in grateful remembrance.

Until the accession of Dr. Lewis to the provostship, no great improvement had been effected in the general appearance of the town, or the sanitary conditions under which the inhabitants lived. The new powers conferred by the adoption of the Police Act had not been pressed to any extent, and things remained very much as they had been before the formation of the burgh. The old nuisances associated with piggeries, cowsheds, and the thoughtless disposal of refuse, continued to threaten the public health, and cause recurring epidemic troubles, through the pollution of the household wells which, in the absence of a gravitation water supply, were all the people had to depend upon. The streets were irregularly lined, unduly narrow in places, and not very clean, as there was no regular system of drainage, and very little scavenging was done. At the same time the population was increasing at such a rate, owing to the boom in the granite trade, that the evils of the old order were accentuated by the serious overcrowding that occurred in many of the houses. Dr. Lewis set himself from the first to stir up popular interest in these matters, and have a new order of things introduced. To some extent the way was cleared for him by the disappearance of many of the piggeries, owing to the fact that the rearing of swine had become a less profitable industry than it had been. On the other hand, he was much discouraged in his efforts by the stolid indifference of many of the inhabitants, and seriously obstructed by the active opposition of others, who either did not realise the necessity of the changes he proposed, or had a personal interest in preventing them. With patient determination, however, he pressed forward his municipal policy, and such support was accorded him by the more public-spirited and foreseeing section of the community that, in a few years, some considerable improvements were effected, such as the widening and straightening of the streets, the abolition of overcrowding, and the removal of the more clamant nuisances. At the same time progress was made with the discussion and maturing of the two great schemes which he believed to be essential to the health and well-being of the town—the introduction of a gravitation water supply, and a general drainage system. The actual completion of these undertakings took place in the interval between his two terms of office; but the origination of them was due to him, and it had practically been decided to proceed with them before he withdrew from the provost's chair for the first time in 1879.

JOHN PATTERSON LEWIS, M.D.
PROVOST OF DALBEATTIE.

During the period of Dr Lewis's retirement, which lasted from 1879 to 1882, the affairs of the burgh were presided over by Thomas Helme, the originator of the bobbin-making industry in the town. Mr Helme was a native of Cumberland, and had settled in Dalbeattie so early as 1840, since which time he had taken an active part in its social as well as its industrial life. To him was reserved the satisfaction of carrying through the two schemes of municipal enterprise initiated by Dr. Lewis, which aimed at the abolition of the old, unsatisfactory system of household wells, and the placing of the sanitary condition of the town on a proper, permanent footing. The institution of the gravitation water supply occasioned considerable discussion, not only upon the preliminary point of its necessity, but upon the feasibility of the various plans suggested for carrying it out. Dr. Lewis indeed was opposed to the scheme ultimately adopted, and the growing feeling in favour of it is said to have been the chief cause of his withdrawal from the Commission. The surrounding district offered a plentiful choice of sources, nine of which were examined and considered: the reservoir at Isles, Kirkgunzeon, the collecting ground between Buittle High School and Knoxhill, Dalbeattie Loch, Auchensheen, Barean, Clonyard and White Lochs of Colvend, Loch Arthur, Edingham, Auchenreoch and Milton Lochs. The Milton Loch scheme was favoured for a time; but, in consequence of the cost of it, and difficulties with the shore proprietors, it was ultimately abandoned, in favour of that which proposed to bring the water from the farm of New Buittle. The latter scheme was estimated to cost only a third of that of Milton Loch; and, as it embraced the formation of a collecting area of 136 acres, on which there were several streams and springs of remarkably pure water, it was recommended by the engineers as likely to meet all the requirements of the burgh. On 22nd October, 1879, the commissioners decided to adopt the New Buittle scheme, and formed themselves into a committee, with full powers, to see it carried out as expeditiously as possible, the estimated cost being £4598. The result was eminently satisfactory, and provided the town with a plentiful supply of good, pure water from the Buittle hills. So soon as the water scheme had become an accomplished fact, it was decided to proceed with the introduction of the drainage system. No particular difficulties were involved in the execution of this supplementary work, as the town so far had been without drainage, and there were no old systems to be cleared away or repaired; while the vicinity of the river Urr, tidal up to Dalbeattie, offered a convenient outlet for the disposal of the burgh sewage. The completion of the two undertakings raised Dalbeattie to a unique position among the towns of Galloway, none of which as yet had ventured upon such municipal enterprises. Nor was it long till the benefits accruing from them were markedly felt in the burgh, in the disappearance or diminution of fever and other epidemics and a general improvement of public health. The effect of the introduction of the water and drainage systems, with other changes rendered possible by them, has been to transform the sanitary condition of Dalbeattie, so that it has since become one of the healthiest places of its size in Scotland. The latest returns of the medical officer show a death rate for the burgh of only 15 per 1000.

After three years of important service in the provostship, Mr Helme, in 1882, gave place to Dr. Lewis, who resumed the reigns of office, and held them till 1887. His exertions during this period were chiefly confined to routine work, and the elaboration of the schemes projected during his first term of authority. Retiring finally from municipal affairs in the last-mentioned year, he continued to practise his profession in the town till the beginning of 1896, when he disposed of his business to Dr. S. A. D. Gillespie, and went to reside in Dumfries. Here he lived only two years, dying in December, 1898, and being buried in the churchyard of his native parish.

Dr. Lewis having retired in the middle of the municipal year, the interim of six months was filled up by the appointment of Joseph Heughan, a native of the district, who had been in business as a blacksmith at Caulkerbush, Southwick. At the close of the year—November, 1887—David McNish, a builder in the town, who had previously taken a prominent part in municipal affairs, was called to the provost's chair, which he continued to occupy with acceptance till his death in 1890. Mr McNish was followed by George Shaw, who retained the provostship for twelve years, and only retired in 1902, after the second longest term of office in the history of the burgh. Mr Shaw was a native of Glasgow, and had come to Dalbeattie in 1862, at the age of twenty-three, to take up the business of manufacturing bricks and tiles on the estate of Mr Maxwell of Munches. For twelve years he was in partnership with Mr Andrew McEwan, who worked the clay in the neighbourhood of Dalbeattie port, but afterwards he became the sole proprietor of the business, which is still carried on by him at the old works. Having entered the Town Council in 1880, he had already completed ten years of public service before he was promoted to the civic chair; and, as his time and business abilities were freely put at the disposal of the community during all the years of his association with its affairs, his record of public work is one of the most honourable in the career of the " granite burgh."

Mr Shaw's tenure of the provostship was marked by some outstanding improvements, which have gone far to render the town the comfortable and attractive place of residence which it is at the present day. One of the earliest of these was the renovation and enlargement of the town hall. This useful public building had its origin in a hall provided some years before by Mr Maxwell of Munches in a property erected by him at the northern extremity of High Street. For a time, Mr Maxwell retained the ownership in his own hands, but left the management of the hall under certain conditions to the town. Ultimately, however, an arrangement was made by which the hall and the property connected with it were transferred to the Town Council upon easy terms; and in Provost Shaw's time the whole building was reconstructed and arranged to meet the growing requirements of the town, with the result now seen in the handsome and commodious premises available for public use. The principal feature of the building is a large upstairs hall, capable of accommodating any likely gathering of the inhabitants: to this a Council chamber, committee room, and waiting rooms are attached: while on the ground floor there are a smaller hall for less important meetings, two shops, an office, and a dwelling house, from which a considerable revenue is obtained. At the most prominent corner, and giving character to the whole, is a neat, square tower, with a large clock in it, which is illuminated at night by gas. Another work of some consequence undertaken during the provostship of Mr Shaw was the formation of concrete pavements, with kerb and channelling borders, along the principal streets. Previously there were few regularly formed footpaths in the burgh; but in his time the Town Council applied itself so energetically to remedy this defect that most of the streets were provided with comfortable and convenient pavements. Till 1896, the streets and roads within the burgh had been under the charge of the County Road Trustees, but in that year the management of them was transferred to the commissioners of the town, who have since effected considerable improvements upon them. Two fine samples of ornamental granite work adorn the streets: one, a watering trough for horses, presented by Mr Maxwell of Munches, and situated at the junction of Maxwell and Craignair Streets; the other, a drinking fountain, erected at the Cross in commemoration of the Jubilee of Queen Victoria. Other two works of an outstanding kind were accomplished in Mr Shaw's time: the deepening of the reservoir at New Buittle, and the supersession

DALBEATTIE

of the private killing-places of the butchers by a public slaughter-house.

Perhaps the most notable event, however, in the provostship of Mr Shaw was the acquisition of a public park for recreative and other purposes. The ground was a free gift to the inhabitants of the burgh from Miss Copland of Colliston, one of the superiors, and consisted of ten acres of land, formerly pertaining to the farm of Islecroft, and lying at the side of the Dalbeattie Burn, to the south of the Dumfries road. The presentation of it was suggested by the inauguration of a movement, about eleven years ago, which has since been carried zealously forward by a voluntary committee, for the improvement of the general appearance of the town, by special attention to its streets and approaches, and the planting of trees and the placing of seats in appropriate places. Miss Copland's generous interest in their projects gave great encouragement to the Improvements Committee, who have since shown their appreciation of her gift by the efforts they have put forth to transform what was originally a piece of rough, uneven, stony ground into a park worthy of the town. By means of a concert, a bazaar, and a number of open-air gala entertainments, they succeeded in raising sufficient funds for their purposes, without requiring to apply for assistance from the burgh rates. Besides making general improvements throughout the town, they completely changed the aspect of the piece of ground presented to them, and were able to hand it over to the Town Council as an exceedingly attractive, well-equipped, and well-arranged park. Throughout the operations, Mr Josiah Ferguson acted as convener of the General Improvements Committee, Mr J. M. Austin was its honorary secretary and treasurer, and Mr Robert Wilson, the burgh surveyor, superintended the various works undertaken. To them the principal credit is due for the excellent results attained; but they were loyally and effectively supported in their disinterested efforts by the individual members of the committee.

Following upon Mr Shaw, the present provost, William Davie, draper in the town, was appointed in November, 1902. Mr Davie was born in Stirling, and settled in Dalbeattie over forty years ago. He had already been a Councillor for eleven years, when his genial disposition, conciliatory manners, and marked business ability induced his colleagues of the Town Council to raise him to the dignity of the provost's chair. Deeply attached to the town of his adoption, he has spared no pains in the supervision of its affairs; and it is largely the result of the regularity of his attendance at municipal meetings, and the wisdom and tact with which he carries through the business brought before them, that he has been retained in office till the present day. The work of the Councils over which he has presided has mostly lain in the direction of maintaining the general efficiency of the municipal organisation, and safeguarding the results of the schemes initiated by their predecessors. At the same time, however, advantage has been taken of every opportunity that offered to advance the interests of the town, and much activity has been shown in still further improving its amenities. Three years ago, by the kindness of Mr W. J. H. Maxwell of Munches, who had not only succeeded to the family estates but had served himself heir to the public-spiritedness of his father and his warm, personal interest in Dalbeattie, an important addition was made to the public park, by the annexation of an adjacent piece of ground, formerly known as " Daniel," and occupied as a cricketing field by the Dalbeattie Club. In honour of the donor, the land originally gifted by Miss Copland had been denominated the Colliston Park: similarly that presented by Mr Maxwell received the name of the Munches Park: the Dalbeattie Burn divided them, but a footbridge has been thrown across it, so that the two parks now form a complete and effective whole.

In the first twenty years of the burgh's existence, seven town-clerks held office for various short periods: James Grieve,

DR. M'KNIGHT. THOMAS HELME.

JOSEPH HEUGHAN. DAVID M'NISH.
PROVOSTS OF DALBEATTIE.

agent in the Union Bank, till 7th June, 1861; Robert McLachlan, accountant in the Union Bank, till 14th September, 1863; Charles Caven, till October of the same year; C. P. Richardson, solicitor, Castle-Douglas, till 12th February, 1864; R. W. Thomson, till 20th June, 1864; William Thomson, teacher in the Free Church school, till 18th June, 1874; and Francis Armstrong, the present burgh surveyor of Dumfries, till 12th May, 1879. On 11th June, 1879, James Little, solicitor, succeeded to the office, the duties of which he has now fulfilled for over thirty years, with increasing acceptance to the burgh and its commissioners. During that time he has been closely associated with the public life of the town, as well as with its municipal business, and has rendered valuable service in many confidential capacities by his wise counsel on legal and other matters. In conjunction with his business as solicitor, he conducts a branch of the Commercial Bank of Scotland, which was opened on 14th May, 1889, and put under his charge.

Contrary to what has happened in many small ports throughout the kingdom, there has been no appreciable falling off in the shipping trade of Dalbeattie in recent years. The conveniences afforded by the railway have no doubt served to divert traffic that would otherwise have been carried by sea; but enough has been left to the steamers and sailing vessels that visit the Urr to maintain the sea trade of the town at something like its former consequence. Originally known as the " Dub o' Hass," with its quays and quay walls dating from the end of the eighteenth or the beginning of the nineteenth century, the Port of Dalbeattie is still a factor of some importance in the life and business of the district. The trade done is principally with Liverpool and other north of England ports, and consists mostly in the export of granite and wood, and the import of manures and feeding stuffs for cattle. As a rule there discharge at Dalbeattie annually from 120 to 130 vessels, of which about a fourth are steamers, and the average carrying capacity of which is about 150 tons. Vessels up to 280 tons, however, are frequently loaded at Oldland and Steadstone quays, two miles further down the river; while cargoes of 300 to 350 tons for local merchants from Continental ports are landed at Palnackie. The exact figures for Dalbeattie port in 1907 were 106 sailing vessels and 23 steamers, while the imports amounted to 8,985 tons, and the exports to 12,674. Until 1891, the control of the harbour, and all authority in matters relating to it, were vested in the Road Trustees of the Stewartry; but in that year the Road Trustees were superseded by the newly-formed County Council, and, as the latter body had no powers given them to take over harbours and manage them, the port of Dalbeattie was left without any authoritative control. In these circumstances, the shipowners and merchants using the port took the management of it into their own hands, and appointed a committee of themselves to exact dues mutually agreed upon, and expend them on the upkeep of the river and harbour. In 1901, this informal committee applied to the Board of Trade for official sanction, and obtained the issue of the Urr Navigation Order, under which the management of the river from Almorness Point upwards, together with that of the harbours and quays at Palnackie and Dalbeattie, is vested in a body called the Urr Navigation Trustees. This body is elected triennially, and comprises six members from the Stewartry County Council, two from Dalbeattie Town Council, and four from the shipowners and traders paying dues at the port. The present chairman of the Urr Navigation Trustees is Mr Wellwood Maxwell of Kirkennan.

The first attempt to publish a newspaper in Dalbeattie was made by the late Robert Grieve, printer in the town. In August 1885, he began the publication of "The Dalbeattie and Colvend Visitors' Guide and Time Table" which, after running into fifteen numbers, ceased in October of the following year. In his library at Maxwellknowe, Mr Thomas Fraser has a complete collection of the various numbers, which comprise 260 pages in all. Though largely composed of advertisements, they also contain much interesting matter, including a serial story, "The Wife of Powbraid: A Tale of Colvend," by James Matthewson, Dalbeattie, and various lucubrations of local poets. For the last twenty years Dalbeattie has had a regular newspaper, the first number of the "Stewartry Observer and Wigtownshire News" having been issued by Mr J. D. McClymont from his printing office in High Street on 19th January, 1889. After being carried on by Mr McClymont for a short time, it was transferred to Messrs A. and I. A. Callan. Mr A. Callan withdrew from the business in 1892, since which time it has been solely conducted by Mr Ivie A. Callan. The Observer used to be a half-penny weekly, published on Friday mornings: it has lately been enlarged, and is now issued at a penny on Thursdays. For somewhat the same length of time, a book-publishing business has been carried on in Dalbeattie by Mr Thomas Fraser, formerly of High Street, now of Maxwellknowe. Among the works which he has given to the public may be mentioned "The Bards of Galloway," "Yarrow: Its Poets and Poetry," "Robert Kerr's Poetical Works," "Ingleside Musings," "Poetical Works of William Nicholson," Borland's "Border Raids and Reivers," Harper's "Rambles in Galloway," "The Galloway Herds," with an introduction and notes by the publisher, and Will Ogilvie's "Whaup o' the Rede." These books have had an extensive circulation among the inhabitants of Galloway and the Border country, and have helped to beget and encourage interest in their literature and history.

Among the industries of Dalbeattie not already mentioned is a saw mill, in the vicinity of the paper mill, owned and worked by Mr James Bell. Close beside it is a creamery, in the building where formerly was the Wilmington Flour Mill, which belonged to Mr Erskine, and was run for many years by the late Thomas Glendinning, until it was burned down about 25 years ago.

144 HISTORY OF THE PARISH OF URR

Besides Dr. Gillespie, who succeeded Dr. Lewis as medical officer of the parish, two other medical practitioners have been settled in the town for considerable periods: Dr. McKerchar, who at one time took an active part in public affairs, and Dr. Anderson, who has been closely associated with the Volunteer movement and the Territorial Army scheme. Both of them practise extensively in the country districts of Urr and other neighbouring parishes, as well as in Dalbeattie. The Volunteer movement, to which reference has just been made, was well supported in the town from its commencement, the Laird of Munches rising to the rank of Lieutenant-Colonel, while Mr Wellwood Maxwell of Kirkennan commanded a local company of the Galloway Rifles, some of the members of which volunteered for service in the late South African War. Under the new Territorial system, Dalbeattie is retained as the headquarters of a company, a contingent of which is now supplied by the Haugh-of-Urr.

The story of Dalbeattie may be fittingly concluded by a short account of the celebrations of the fiftieth anniversary of its formation into a burgh, which took place on Saturday, 18th July, 1908. The events of that day are still fresh in the public mind, and will not be soon forgotten in the town; but a reference to them will serve to indicate the present condition of the local industries, and the spirit of pride in their native place which continues to animate the inhabitants. The idea of a Jubilee demonstration originated with the General Improvements Committee, and was heartily taken up by the provost and Town Council, as well as the different sections of the community. A programme was arranged, embracing a grand procession through the town, a formal ceremony in the public park, and a series of athletic and other entertainments. Each department of the day's proceedings was under the superintendence of a special committee, and the general executive committee was composed of the conveners of the various separate committees, namely, Provost Davie, convener;

Bailie McClymont, Bailie Newall, Robert Wilson, John Simpson, John Jack, and Mrs Mundell. The weather was all that could have been desired, and everything passed off with complete success.

The procession started from John Street at half-past one o'clock, and perambulated the town by way of Maxwell Street, Craignair Street, Port Road, Port Street, and High Street, all of which were profusely and gaily decorated. The town band led the way, and was followed by a series of carriages containing, amongst others, the superiors of the burgh, Miss Copland of Colliston and Mr Maxwell of Munches, and the following representatives of public bodies: Provost Davie, Bailies Newall and McClymont, ex-Provost Shaw, ex-Bailie John Craik, Councillors J. J. Clark, Dornan, John Jack, David Mundell, Rae and Shennan, past and present members of the Town Council, with Mr James Little, town-clerk, Mr J. R. Saunders, burgh prosecutor, and Mr Robert Wilson, burgh surveyor; Mr Wellwood Maxwell of Kirkennan, chairman of Urr Navigation Trustees; Rev. David Frew and Mr James Austin, chairman and clerk of Urr Parish Council; Mr Thomas Fraser, representing Urr School Board; and Mr Ivie A. Callan, representing the Improvements Committee. Behind them came vehicles of various kinds, adorned with flags and bunting, and carrying spectacular representations of the different handicrafts and industries of the town. Among those who took part in this division of the procession were the employées of Messrs. D. H. and J. Newall, the Dalbeattie Granite workers, the Dalbeattie Creamery Company, the printers of Mr I. A. Callan, the men from Mr D. Cameron's shoeing forge, a party of Dalbeattie carters, the bobbin makers of Messrs Jackson and Messrs Lawson and Henderson, workers from the smithy of Mr William Morrison, the wheelwrights of Mr D. Cameron, Mr William Kennedy, joiner, and the carters and vanmen of Mr Alexander Wilson and Mr Andrew Wright, coal merchants, Mr J. J. Clark, ironmonger, Mr A. Caven, butcher, and Mr

Aitchison, fish merchant. Interspersed with the operatives were members of the Boys' Brigade, and the societies of Oddfellows, Rechabites, Foresters, and Shepherds, all of which, as well as the Freemasons, have branches in the town; and following them came a long parade of children from the public school and the school of St. Peter's Roman Catholic Church. The rear of the procession was composed of cyclists, male and female, in every variety of fancy costume. The strength of the last-named feature served to remind the onlookers that athletics are not neglected in Dalbeattie; indeed, at present, there are five flourishing recreation clubs in the town — the Cricket, Football, Golf, Bowling, and Quoiting Clubs. The whole formed an effective show, as it wended its way through the densely thronged streets; and its significance could scarcely be missed, as a representation of the social and industrial life of the town, and a demonstration of its progress during the fifty years of its existence as a burgh.

On the dispersal of the procession, the centre of interest was transferred to the band-stand of the public park, round which a large crowd gathered, to witness the ceremony of opening the Colliston and Munches Parks, which so far had not been formally inaugurated. Provost Davie presided, and introduced Mr Maxwell of Munches who, on behalf of Miss Copland of Colliston as well as himself, declared the parks gifted by them to the people of Dalbeattie open for the uses for which they were intended. In the course of an eloquent and interesting speech, Mr Maxwell congratulated the inhabitants of the burgh on the attainment of their municipal Jubilee, recounted the progress of the past, and impressed upon his hearers, especially of the rising generation, the duty of continuing the good work of improving and developing the town. At the same time he referred to the interesting fact that one of the householders present at the meeting of the 17th April, 1858, at which it was resolved to form Dalbeattie into a burgh— Mr William Wilson of 12 Craignair Street — still survived,

DALBEATTIE

though unable to take part in the Jubilee celebrations. Thereafter the provost presented Miss Copland and Mr Maxwell with gold keys, suitably inscribed, in recognition of their generosity to the town, and as souvenirs of the day's proceedings, for which they both returned thanks.

The day was brought to a close with a programme of sports and other entertainments, the most novel item of which was the flight of a balloon and the descent from it of a lady parachutist. It was estimated that five thousand people had been present at the various events associated with the celebration, many of them coming from a considerable distance. The result was highly satisfactory to the promoters, who could not but feel that their main object had been fulfilled, in the deepening of the pride of the citizens in the honourable traditions of their burgh, and the incitement of them to further endeavours for the advancement of its interests and well-being.

CHAPTER IX

Parish Boards and Associations

IN former days there was practically no corporate life in the parish, except such as gathered round the church, and found expression in the doings and deliberations of the Kirk Session and heritors. As general executive authorities, these bodies not only concerned themselves with the moral and religious welfare of the parishioners, but supervised the education of the young and the relief of the poor, and attended to other public matters as necessity arose. During the nineteenth century, a development in this respect took place: the management of public affairs was gradually devolved upon special boards or councils more directly representative of the people, and various associations were formed for the promotion of matters of general interest. Some account of the changes, so far as they have not already been noticed, remains to be given.

Education.

For the greater part of the century, the old parochial system of education, which had excited the animadversions of Dr. Muirhead, continued in existence; but, as time went on, an increasing attention was given to its working, and such improvements and extensions were effected upon it, as rendered it more adequate to the requirements of the parish. The heritors retained their former liabilities for the upkeep of the schoolhouses and the stipends of the teachers. Additional remuneration, however, had been secured to the latter, by the provision of some small endowments, and the exaction of fees from the children. A careful inspection of the schools was made every year by the parish minister, who was generally assisted in this duty by his brethren from the neighbouring parishes, or in later years by his colleagues of the dissenting churches. At the same time, he and his Kirk Session consulted with the heritors on the conduct of the schools and the appointment of the masters, and drew their attention to any weaknesses that might arise in the educational system. Alongside the recognised parochial establishments, too, a number of private places of learning, or " adventure schools " as they were called, sprang up in the different villages, the teachers of which were sometimes men of superior parts and college education, whose style of instruction was noway inferior to the general standard of the time.

The opening of the century found two schools established in the parish, for which the heritors were responsible: the original parochial school at Hardgate, and a branch school at Milton, which had been started some years before, for the convenience of the children in the higher-lying lands. The stipend available for the support of both teachers was 200 merks Scotch, or £11 2s. 4d. Sterling: of this £3 was paid to the schoolmaster at Milton, and the remainder was reserved for his superior at Hardgate. In 1818, new premises were provided for the latter by the purchase of a house in Hardgate —the original of the present teacher's residence—which was repaired and fitted up as a combined schoolroom and dwelling-house for the teacher. The total cost was £92 18s. 0d., and this was apportioned according to the size of their respective properties among the eight heritors in the immediate neighbourhood. Here Mr William Allan, who is still gratefully remembered in the district, laboured in the instruction of the young for forty years, during which time he enjoyed the respect and confidence of the community, and earned for himself the affectionate esteem of successive generations of pupils. A man of genial and obliging disposition, upright character, and marked individuality, Mr Allan filled a large and useful place in the life of his day, not only devoting himself punctiliously to the duties of his profession, but evincing a lively interest in the affairs of the parish, and giving ungrudging service in the promotion of its welfare. Appointed an elder and treasurer of the parish church in 1821, he succeeded to the session clerkship in 1839, and continued to fill these offices till his death in 1869, some ten years after he had retired from active work as a teacher. To the older natives of the parish, the name of Mr Allan still recalls all that was most notable and commendable in the "old parochial master." He was followed in Hardgate by a teacher of the name of Leishman, who only remained till 1863, when John Menzies, previously a teacher in Dumfries, was appointed. Mr Menzies was in office in 1873, when the old parochial system was superseded by the modern School Board, and he continued to work under the new conditions till the beginning of the present century, when he retired to Dalkeith, where he still resides, with a well-earned pension. He was a man of a similar type to Mr Allan, though somewhat more reserved in his disposition; and he occupied the same position in the parish church, as well as in the general life of the community. A strict disciplinarian, he was at the same time a capable and painstaking teacher, whose scholars reflected the greatest credit on him in their after lives; while his upright character, strong sense of duty, and courteous, dignified manners, combined to render him trusted and esteemed among all classes of the parishioners. Three years after he came to Hardgate, the heritors resolved to erect new and more commodious premises for the children, and throw the whole of the old schoolhouse into the private dwelling of the master. A separate school was accordingly built on the present site, which, with additions and alterations made upon it by the School Board, continues to serve the needs of the neighbourhood. In 1900, Mr Menzies was succeeded by the present teacher, Mr Quintin Aird, who had come to the district a few years previously to take charge of Crocketford School.

In Mr Allan's time, some old-world customs of country

WILLIAM ALLAN, HARDGATE.

JOHN LOWDEN, HAUGH-OF-URR.

school life, which have now disappeared, were in full vogue. At first, the children in rotation brought a peat for the fire on the winter mornings, but this was afterwards commuted to a payment of sixpence for coal-money. The "Candlemas Bleeze" was another recognised institution, the object of which was to supplement the salary of the teacher by a voluntary addition to the usual fees. At Candlemas term, each boy and girl in the school brought a present of money for the master, and the highest contributors of each sex were denominated "king" and "queen" respectively for the day. It is not surprising to learn that the healthy rivalry excited by the prospective rewards occasionally exceeded reasonable bounds, and had to be restrained by the good sense of the teacher. As a complimentary return for their donations, the children received a holiday, and were treated by the master to some slight refreshment, which at one time consisted of toddy (presumably in weak solution), but in later years was of more solid and less dangerous description. These usages were dropped in the time of Mr Menzies, when better provision was made for the upkeep of the school fire, and the salary of the teacher was put upon a less precarious footing.

The first notice of the parochial school at Milton in the nineteenth century occurs in the Kirk Session minute of 18th October, 1818, the year in which the new schoolhouse for Hardgate was acquired. There it is recorded that a vacancy had occurred, and that a meeting of heritors was to be convened on the 5th November following, for the purpose of filling it up. The person appointed seems to have been Thomas McEnallie, who, in the minute of 8th September, 1822, is described as the parochial teacher at Milton, and appears with James Paterson, shoemaker, to answer to a charge of disturbance of the peace in that village. Paterson had used insulting language to McEnallie, and the latter in a moment of irritation had resorted to personal violence. Both delinquents expressed their regret, were rebuked by the Kirk Session, and were ordered to make public appearance for their offence on the following Sabbath day. Later in the century, the Milton school was in charge of James Beck, who had started life as the teacher of an " adventure " school in Haugh-of-Urr. After his retiral from Milton, he lived for a time at Blackford, and acted as compulsory officer for the upper division of the parish under the first School Board. He was succeeded by Robert Harkness, who continued in office under the School Board till 1876, when John Smart was appointed. Mr Smart was schoolmaster of Milton for nearly twenty-five years, and an elder in the parish church for most of that time. A man of strong religious principles, he was sincerely interested in the welfare of his friends and neighbours as well as of the young, and was held in high esteem in the district. After his resignation of his office at Milton, he took up residence in Haugh-of-Urr, and was appointed registrar and session-clerk of the parish church, but he only survived for a short time. The vacancy at Milton was filled by the appointment of a female teacher, in the person of Mrs Fisher, who has been followed by Miss Robson, Miss Wilson, and the present school-mistress, Miss Liddle.

For many years the school was carried on in the one-story cottage, which now stands uninhabited on the north side of the bridge over the Milton Burn, and which served at the same time as the teacher's dwelling. Shortly before the School Board came into existence, a new school was erected by the heritors, which is still in good condition; and immediately afterwards a commodious dwelling-house was built for the teacher, on the opposite side of the road, at a cost of £300.

Though Springholm had no regular parochial school, its educational wants were almost as well attended to as those of the other villages in the parish. Besides "adventure" schools, which existed in it from an early date, and which at one time are said to have numbered half a dozen, it had a recognised public school fully three quarters of a century ago, which had been erected by voluntary effort, and was

PARISH BOARDS AND ASSOCIATIONS 153

vested in several neighbouring proprietors as trustees. This school stood in the playground behind the present Board buildings, and was presided over by William Stephen Dickson till his death in 1856. Mr Dickson's salary was chiefly derived from the fees of his scholars, which seldom exceeded thirty pounds per annum, but it was occasionally supplemented by voluntary contributions from proprietors and residenters in the neighbourhood. He was succeeded (after the short interregnum of a teacher called Riddell) by Adam Muir, who was in office when the school was transferred to the School Board, but retired in the following year; since which time Donald McGregor, William McAlister, and the present teacher, Miss Minnie McDougall, have been in charge. On the transference of Springholm public school to the School Board in 1873, it was at once resolved to remove the old buildings, and erect new and more suitable premises. The present school and teacher's house were accordingly built on the same site, but nearer the road line, at a cost of £700.

Crocketford School, which was also the result of local benevolence, and was built in the second quarter of the nineteenth century, is situated in the parish of Kirkpatrick-Durham. In 1873, it was handed over by the trustees in whom it was vested to the two School Boards of Urr and Kirkpatrick-Durham, for the joint use of the children of both parishes, under a formal agreement, by which the management devolves on a committee of three members from each School Board, and the right is reserved to the inhabitants of the village of using it after school hours, and on Sundays, for religious and other meetings. The teachers since the transference have been Messrs Bell, Menzies, McDonald, Quintin Aird, and Thomas Smith, M.A.

Few statistics of school attendance in the parish are available, until the days of School Board discipline and organisation. From the Statistical Account of 1845, however, we learn that in that year there was an average attendance of

154 HISTORY OF THE PARISH OF URR

80 scholars at Hardgate, and of 50 at Milton. Of the public school at Springholm no statistics are given; but the probability is that it had quite as many scholars as Milton. In the "adventure" schools, the attendance varied very considerably, according to the time of year, and the popularity of the teacher. In none of the schools was there anything like the regularity now made possible by the compulsory clauses of the Education Act. This is corroborated by a tradition which still lingers in the village of Milton, to the effect that one of the old parochial masters was saluted on one occasion by his last remaining pupil with the remark that there would be no school on the morrow, as *he* was not coming. The "adventure" teachers, as their designation implies, depended entirely for their subsistence on the fees and offerings of their scholars, which at no time afforded them a very substantial livelihood, and occasionally, it is to be feared, dropped almost to vanishing point. One of the earliest and most notable teachers of the "adventure" type was William McNaught, who carried on a school in Kells Cottage, Hardgate, from the beginning of the century till his death in 1839. During all that time, he was session-clerk of the parish church; and occasionally, to eke out his living, pauper children were committed to him by the Kirk Session for board and education, at a rate of £4 per annum. The free and easy method of the schoolroom in his time may be illustrated by the following story which is told on good authority. It was a habit of Mr McNaught to take a nap in the afternoons, during the hearing of school lessons; and, on awakening, he would try to cover his delinquency, by calling out to the boy whom he had left reading, and who was now supposed to be gravelled by some big word: "spell't, man, spell't." One Sunday in church, when a young stranger was preaching, whose pronunciation was somewhat hesitating and inaccurate, the dominie fell sound asleep. Everything went well enough, until the preacher, coming to a more than usually difficult word, made a sudden pause, when Mr

McNaught, abruptly wakened up by the arrest of the preacher's voice, and forgetting for the moment where he was, called out in his most professional tones: "spell't, man, spell't." Among other "adventure" teachers in the Haugh-of-Urr during the century were: Jean Thomson, who kept her school in the old house, now removed, which stood at the church gate; Robert Brown and Thomas McEnallie, whose place of instruction was the second house from the cross on the right-hand side of the road to Hardgate; James Beck, already mentioned, who occupied the second house to the west of the new hall; and two Smiths, father and son; while Robert Welsh, James Donaldson, and others, are still remembered in Springholm.

In the early years of the century, the only scholastic establishment in Dalbeattie was the school of William Sloan. It was carried on in a low, thatched cottage that stood on a knoll about the middle of High Street, and was long known in the town as the "Noggie." The attendance was small for the size of the town, usually ranging between 20 and 30 scholars; still, it was a beginning, from which in the process of time large results were to follow. The century was not far advanced when Mr Sloan was succeeded in the "Noggie" by James Copland, who for many years thereafter maintained his place in Dalbeattie as a popular and successful teacher. In 1814, he was ordained to the eldership in the parish church, the duties of which he discharged with great conscientiousness till 1837, when dissatisfaction with the appointment of the Rev. G. M. Burnside induced him to resign. In the interval some noteworthy changes occurred in the conditions under which his professional work was carried on. The roof of the "Noggie" having fallen in one day when the master and his pupils fortunately were at dinner, Mr Copland transferred his establishment to a house in High Street. Some time afterwards, the growth of the population in Dalbeattie suggested to the heritors the need for increased educational facilities in the town, and a more secure provision for the master; in 1828, accordingly, they proceeded to erect a regular parochial school —the building which still stands in Glenshalloch Place, but which was enlarged in 1854—and appointed Mr Copland to it as the first master. Here he laboured till his death, and was followed by a succession of worthy parish schoolmasters, Farish, Stewart, McAndrew, Beveridge, and Alexander Davidson, whose names are still cherished by some of the older inhabitants.

The transformation of Mr Copland's school into a regular parochial establishment gave occasion for a rearrangement of the salaries of the parish teachers, which was carried through at a meeting of heritors on 2nd April, 1829. At this meeting, the Rev. John McWhir produced a certified copy of a decision of the Barons of Exchequer, finding that the average price of a chalder of oat meal for the preceding twenty-five years was £17 2s. 2d.; and the heritors, having taken into consideration the extent and population of the parish, resolved that the school salary payable to the three schoolmasters in the parish for the next twenty-five years should be £51 6s. 6d., or the value of three chalders. This sum was allocated among the three schoolmasters in the following proportions, to be paid respectively by the heritors whose properties adjoined their schools: Haugh-of-Urr, £22 9s. 9d.; Milton, £10 16s. 9d.; and Dalbeattie £18. It was further determined that the school wages payable should remain as formerly; and the schoolmasters of the different schools were authorised and recommended to insist upon payment of these wages in advance. At the same time, the heritors begged earnestly to suggest to the schoolmasters the propriety of doing all in their power to shorten as much as possible the period of vacation, and to introduce the monitor system into their schools, with the view of instructing a greater number of scholars in the most effectual manner.

In 1845, there were 90 children in attendance at the Dal-

PARISH BOARDS AND ASSOCIATIONS

beattie parochial school; but by this time the Disruption had taken place, and a school had been opened in connection with the Free Church in the town. The latter was at first accommodated in the basement of a building in High Street, but was afterwards removed to the Commercial Hall, where it was carried on till suitable premises were erected for it in the vicinity of the church. During its short career of thirty years, the Free Church school was successively in charge of Messrs McGregor and Thomson. Besides these two schools there were in Dalbeattie, as elsewhere in the period before the advent of the School Board, the usual representatives of the voluntary or "adventure" system, with teachers of varying degrees of qualification. Thomas Maxwell, the first occupant of the chief commissioner's chair, began life as a teacher in the town. Thomas McEnallie, already mentioned as a teacher in Haugh-of-Urr, conducted a school in his earlier days in the building now known as the Commercial Hall, and is said to have been a good scholar and expert penman. At various times, schools were carried on by the following: Andrew Webster, originally intended for the ministry, in one end of the house of William Houston, nailer, at the Cross; John Johnstone in Copland Street; David Craik in Port Street; and Roland Aitken in William Street. In addition to these dominies, there was also a succession of lady teachers, whose work was confined to the instruction of girls and very small boys: Miss Kelly, whose school occupied the house in High Street which had formerly served as the Plough Inn; Mrs Craik, who had an establishment in Port Street; Mrs Riddick, who gave instruction in her own house at the burn-side; and, in the female school in Southwick Road, Miss Griffith, Mrs Alexander Lindsay, and, last of all, Miss Johnston, whose reputation drew many scholars from the surrounding district, as well as from the town, till she gave up work about a dozen years ago, and went to reside with her brother, the minister of Sheuchan. Humble as many of these seminaries were, they did a necessary and valuable work in their time, as a supplement to the old parochial system, which was no longer adequate to the wants of the age; and many good scholars were produced by them.

At its advent in 1873, the School Board found five schools in existence in the town, besides the school in connection with St. Peter's Roman Catholic church: the parochial school in High Street, presided over by Mr Davidson; the Free Church school in Mill Street, of which Mr Thomson was master; Miss Johnston's female school in Southwick Road; and the private schools of Roland Aitken and Mrs Riddick in William Street and Burn Street respectively. The parochial school became at once the property of the School Board, and the Free Church and female schools were transferred to it shortly afterwards. The voluntary schools were carried on for a few years by Roland Aitken and Mrs Riddick, and, after the former, by Samuel Maxwell; but they were unable to meet the requirements of the Education Act, and were consequently dropped. The schools taken over by the School Board were not only in an overcrowded condition, but were also unsuited to the modern necessities of education; prompt measures had accordingly to be taken to provide more ample and appropriate accommodation. The female school was repaired and extended, and an order issued for the exclusion of boys, even of the tenderest years; while plans were set on foot for the erection of a large public school in Southwick Road, to accommodate the children attending the other two schools. The new school was opened on 5th May, 1876, and cost about £2500, including £300 paid for the site. Some difficulty was experienced in arranging the headmastership, in view of the conflicting claims of Mr Davidson and Mr Thomson; but ultimately it was decided that both of them should be appointed to the new school, with equal salaries, separate rooms, and independent staffs, though Mr Davidson was to be recognised as the principal teacher. The arrangement was a makeshift, which led to considerable

PARISH BOARDS AND ASSOCIATIONS

bickerings, especially among the clerical members of the Board; but it was perhaps the best that could be made under the circumstances. Mr Davidson only held office for two years, resigning on 13th May, 1878; while Mr Thomson continued for other four years, giving up his situation on 8th June, 1882, in consequence of the Board's adoption of a resolution by which his salary was affected. On the withdrawal of Mr Davidson from the headmastership, Andrew Dunn received the appointment, which he retained till January, 1881, when he was succeeded by William Smith. Mr Smith was not only a capable, energetic, and highly successful teacher, but an effective public speaker, and an ever-ready helper in every movement which had for its object the improvement of the social and intellectual tone of the town. His sudden and comparatively early death in 1898 was deeply regretted in the town, especially among his fellow-members of the parish church, the interests of which he had worked earnestly to promote, as elder, session-clerk, and master of the choir. He was succeeded in the headmastership of the school by Mr Alexander Baxter, the present holder of the office.

The progress of Dalbeattie public school, since its institution in 1876, is one of the most notable features in the life of the town. The average attendance has increased from 326 to 645; the staff from 7 to 20, with a drill instructor; and the grants earned from £272 7s. to £1641 7s. 10d. Extensive improvements and enlargements have been made upon it in recent years, including the addition of a Higher Grade department, with the result that it is now one of the largest and best equipped schools in the south of Scotland. No similar expansion, of course, has been possible in the other schools of the parish, owing to the different conditions under which their work has been carried on; instead, the average attendance in all of them shows a greater or less decrease, having fallen in Hardgate from 102 to 82, in Milton from 38 to 20, in Springholm from 53 to 43, and in Crocketford from 63 to 58. The female school had an average attendance of 52 scholars in 1876, and this was well maintained till its close; and St. Peter's R.C. school at the present time has nearly 90 children under regular instruction.

The early School Boards had an onerous task put before them, and some difficult and delicate problems given them to solve; and great credit is due to them for the zeal and energy with which they applied themselves to the ordering of the educational affairs of the parish. To meet the expenditure incurred by them in connection with new buildings and repairs, various sums had to be borrowed from the Public Works Loan Commissioners: £835 in 1874, £2500 in 1875, and £500 in 1887; but these have now all been paid off. In the days of the old parochial system, three small legacies had been left to the parish for educational purposes: £30 by George Sofflay, who was proprietor of Fell in 1799, for behoof of the public school in Dalbeattie; £25 by William Muirhead, merchant in Carlisle, for the same school; and £87 by Mrs Milligan, Haugh Head, for Hardgate and Dalbeattie schools. Only the last-mentioned of these endowments remained, when the School Board came into office; and it was handed over to them by the Rev. J. M. Sandilands on 11th November, 1876, along with £10 of accrued interest. The total was made up to £100 and lent to the Parochial Board, as a bond upon the cemetery; but was paid back to the School Board about ten years ago by the Parish Council.

The extension which has taken place in the operations of the School Board since its institution may be inferred from the fact that in 1873, the first year of its existence, the amount required to make up the deficiency in the School Fund was £400, involving a rate of 4d. per £, while in recent years it has been over £1000, and has required a rate of 1s. per £; these rates, of course, as in other cases, being divided between owners and occupiers of property.

The first chairman of Urr School Board was Mr W. H.

Maxwell of Munches. He was unwearied in his attention to its affairs, and by his natural tact, practical wisdom, and liberal views of education, not only assisted materially in smoothing over the difficulties of its earlier days, but was largely instrumental in shaping its future policy, and giving it the enlightened tone which continues to characterise it. He was succeeded, at his death in 1900, by his son, Mr W. J. H. Maxwell. So far, also, the Board has only had two clerks, Mr John Lowden till 1895, and since that time, Mr James Little.

Relief of the Poor

For the first forty years of the nineteenth century, no change was made in the method of administering poor relief, which was still regarded as the business of the Church, and was attended to officially by the minister and Kirk Session. During the ministries of Dr. Muirhead and Mr Alexander Murray, relief continued to be given in the old casual way, as occasion demanded; but in 1815, when Mr John McWhir had succeeded to the incumbency of the parish church, a more regular, methodical system was adopted. The necessitous persons in the parish were put upon two lists, according as they were entitled to temporary or permanent relief, and these were revised quarterly, at stated meetings of the Kirk Session held for the purpose on the first Sundays of January, April, July, and October. The church collections, which had been considerably increased from former days and now amounted to over £60 per annum, were the principal source of the poor funds, the only other available revenue at first being the interest of a sum of £100, left for the poor of the parish by Mr Michael Herries of Spottes, and still held by the Kirk Session for that purpose. As time went on, however, and the number of poor increased to such an extent that the income derived from these sources proved quite insufficient to meet current demands, the heritors periodically imposed a voluntary assessment on themselves, and some of the more prominent of them, such as Mr

Stothart of Blaiket, Mr Copland of Kingsgrange, Mr Herries of Spottes, and Mr Maxwell of Munches, gave occasional private donations. The funds thus put at their disposal were administered by the Kirk Session with great care, the accounts of their treasurer being audited at each quarterly meeting, and disbursements authorised according to the balances found to be on hand.

The first roll of Mr McWhir's time, dated 28th November, 1814, contains the names of 13 poor persons, to whom quarterly allowances of eight and ten shillings are granted; and the total expenditure upon the poor in that year seems to have amounted to about £52. In the following year the number on the roll was 19, and by 1833 it had risen to nearly 40, entailing an expenditure of £120 a year. Thereafter the pauperism of the parish increased with great rapidity, owing to the rising population of the villages, and the depressed condition of agriculture; with the result that the Kirk Session were involved in many anxious discussions of ways and means, and the heritors were required with increasing frequency to pass self-denying ordinances for voluntary assessment.

In 1842, it had become quite evident that the system of poor relief hitherto in vogue was no longer adequate to the growing necessities of the time, and that something further would require to be done. The expenditure for the previous year had been £300, which had been met by £64 out of the church collections and a voluntary assessment of £236 upon the heritors; and it was plain that these sources of revenue could bear no further strain upon them. A meeting of heritors and Kirk Session was called for the second day of August, to put in force certain powers that had been conferred by Act of Parliament a few years before. At this meeting, which was held in the parish church and was presided over by Mr John Herries Maxwell of Munches, it was resolved to raise a sum of £350 for the support of the poor in the succeeding year, by a legal assessment upon all heritors and householders in the parish,

PARISH BOARDS AND ASSOCIATIONS 163

with the exception of those occupying houses under £3 of rent, and to appoint a committee of heritors and householders to manage the affairs of the poor under the assessment, and to meet and confer with the Kirk Session on all matters connected therewith. The committee was called the Poor's Board for the parish, and was at first presided over by Mr John Sinclair of Redcastle, who at this time took a considerable interest in parochial affairs. Mr Allan, session clerk, was appointed clerk and treasurer to the Poor's Board, and Dr. James Currie, Dalbeattie, acted as its medical officer; the former receiving a salary of £15, and the latter being paid by account, according to what he did. Another doctor, it may be mentioned, took an active part in the business of the Board, Mr James McKenzie, surgeon, Springholm. The following assessors were appointed to value the lands and houses in the parish for the purpose of levying the new poor rate: Thomas Crosbie, Little Kirkland; Samuel Thomson, Markfast; Anthony Rigg, Torcatrine; and William Dickson, Crofthead. It was, perhaps, not so much any just reason for dissatisfaction with their decisions as resentment against the tax itself that led 35 of the farmers and householders to appeal against the assessments put upon them. Few of them, however, received any relief from the Board, which was compelled to be just rather than generous, since it now had upon its roll 77 adult paupers, and 7 orphan children. In the second year of its existence, it had to raise a sum of £400 by assessment, involving a rate of 9d. per £; and, in the following year, the situation became so accentuated that the Board unanimously resolved to demit office, as "they could no longer act with safety to themselves, and usefulness to the public." A meeting of heritors was convened to deal with the crisis, and the members of the Poor's Board were persuaded to resume their function, with Mr John McMorine of Glenarm as their chairman, and on the understanding that, besides funds to meet the allowances already granted, there should be placed at their disposal a sum not exceeding £40 for cases of emergency, while the minister and Kirk Session should have the entire control of the collection at the church doors, subject to the salaries of the kirk officers. The state of the poor at this time is described in the minutes of the heritors as " deplorable " and " starving "; and soup-kitchens had been opened at Dalbeattie, Springholm, and Haugh-of-Urr, to provide for the most necessitous cases. Under these circumstances, the Poor's Board took up their task again, and continued to grapple with its difficulties till November, 1845, when the Parochial Board, a regular body for the administration of poor relief constituted by the Poor Law Act of that year, came into existence. In their last year of office, their expenditure had increased to £528, necessitating a poor rate of 1s. per £, which at that time realised £544.

The Parochial Board was constituted of representatives of the ratepayers, the heritors, and the Kirk Session, and was empowered to deal with all matters connected with the relief of the poor, including the levying of the necessary assessments. It was maintained in office for exactly fifty years, during which time it performed a necessary, important, and often arduous public work, no less to the benefit of the poor of the parish than to the satisfaction of the ratepayers. The circumstances of the parish, with a number of declining villages in it and a rising industrial town, compelled the members of the Board at times to impose a burden of no mean weight upon themselves and their constituents; but it was recognised to be an inevitable burden, which they did their best to reduce to the lowest possible dimensions. Their work, being necessarily of a routine character, does not present many outstanding points of interest; but a few facts may be noted regarding their officials, and the general trend of their operations.

During the fifty years of its existence the Parochial Board had remarkably few changes of officials. The first chairman was Mr John McMorine of East Glenarm, who had served his

WELLWOOD HERRIES MAXWELL OF MUNCHES.
FROM ENGRAVING BY JAMES FAED, AFTER PAINTING BY
SIR GEORGE REID.

PARISH BOARDS AND ASSOCIATIONS

apprenticeship to the administration of poor relief in the old Poor Board. He remained in office till 1856, when he was succeeded by Mr Wellwood H. Maxwell of Munches, who had interested himself in the work of the Board from its commencement, and had also been associated with the previous administrative body. He retained the chair till the Parochial Board was superseded by the Parish Council in 1895. The first and only clerk, collector of rates, and inspector of poor, was Mr John Lowden, Haugh-of-Urr. Dr. James Currie, who had been medical officer to the Poor's Board, continued his services in that capacity to the Parochial Board till his death in 1856. Thereafter Dr. Thomas McKnight was appointed; but, at the close of a year's service, a resolution was carried in the Board, on the motion of Rev. Mr Sandilands, that the medical officer should henceforth reside in the middle of the parish, and Dr. McKnight retired rather than leave Dalbeattie. As no suitable man, however, could be got to reside in Haugh-of-Urr on the terms offered by the Board, this resolution had to be rescinded, and Dr. Lewis, Dalbeattie, received the appointment on 7th July, 1857, retaining it during the remaining period of the Board's existence. For registration purposes, the parish was divided into two districts, coinciding with the ecclesiastical divisions already assigned to the church of Dalbeattie and the old parish church respectively. The first registrar of the Dalbeattie district was Mr William Stewart: he held office from the passing of the Registration Act of 1854 till August, 1886, when he was succeeded by the present registrar, Mr Robert Maxwell, who had already acted for several years as his assistant. In the upper or landward division likewise, there were only two registrars during the term of the Board's existence: Mr William Allan, and after his death in 1869, Mr John Menzies. The latter continued in office under the Parish Council till 1900, and was followed by Mr John Smart. On the death of Mr Smart, a few months later, the present registrar, Mr Quintin Aird, received the appointment.

In the first half of its career, the labours of the Board were particularly heavy, as the amount of poverty prevailing in the parish was greater than it has ever been since. Until 1870, the number of poor upon the roll seldom fell below 120, and not infrequently rose above 130, necessitating an average poor rate of 1s. 4d. per £. The highest year seems to have been 1857, when the number of poor relieved was 138, and the assessment imposed 1s. 7d. The amount produced by the annual assessment rose gradually with the valuation of the parish, and in 1870 reached the sum of £1309, as the result of a rate of 1s. 2d. The expenditure in the same year was £1467, and the difference was so far from being made up by the medical relief grant and the receipts from other parishes, which were the only other sources of income, that there was a loss upon the year's working of fully £50. After 1870, the condition of things in the parish, so far as the administration of poor relief is concerned, became more favourable, with the result that the number of poor on the roll gradually fell below 100, and the rate levied below 1s. per £. The number of poor has varied considerably since, but has scarcely ever touched 100. In recent years the rate has not appeared to show a proportionate decrease, but this has been largely owing to changes introduced in the method of assessment, and more liberal allowances granted to the poor. The figures for the year ending in May, 1908, were as follow: number of poor on the roll, 75; poor rate falling on owners, 6½d., on occupiers, 7d., total 1s. 1½d.; income, including assessments, government grants, and receipts from relatives and other parishes, £1390 10s. 7d.; total disbursements, £1289 18s. 10½d.

On 8th April, 1856, a petition was presented to the Parochial Board from the ratepayers of Dalbeattie, requesting them to arrange for a separate burial-ground for the lower division of the parish, the old burial-ground at the parish church having become insufficient for their requirements. The Board at once took action in the matter; and, after obtaining the sanction of the sheriff, purchased from Mr Maxwell of Munches a piece of ground extending to about an acre, and by 1858 had it fenced and laid off for the required purpose, at a total cost of £180. At the same time, a scale of charges was drawn up, and a committee appointed to manage the new burial-ground, which was to be called the Dalbeattie Cemetery, with Mr Thomas Maxwell, who had taken an active part in its acquisition, as convener. In 1870, when Mr Thomas Maxwell still acted as convener of the cemetery committee, an additional acre was added to the burial-ground, and suitably enclosed at a cost of about £100; and in 1876, when Mr Dugald McLaurin had succeeded to the office of Mr Maxwell, a dwelling-house was erected for the caretaker, on which £180 was spent. It was in connection with the latter undertaking that the sum of £100, as already mentioned, was borrowed from the School Board. After the Parish Council had succeeded to the duties of the Parochial Board, the demand again arose for increased burying space; and about seven years ago the existing accommodation was almost doubled by a further addition, at an expenditure of £400. The most active members of the cemetery committee in the prosecution of this work were the brothers John and Andrew Craik.

The Parish Council took the place of the Parochial Board in 1895, and has since fulfilled the office of administering poor relief in the parish with discrimination and care. Its first chairman was Mr Thomas Fraser: he held office for three years, and was succeeded by Mr John Craik, who fulfilled a similar term; after which, in 1901, the present chairman, Rev. David Frew, was appointed. Dr. S. A. D. Gillespie has acted as medical officer to the Council, and Mr James Austin as clerk, inspector, and collector of rates, during the whole term of its existence. The Landward Committee consists of five members, and has been presided over by Major W. D. Herries, younger of Spottes, since its commencement. For the same length of time, Mr James Austin has officiated as its clerk.

HORTICULTURE

In 1896, an association was formed for the promotion of an interest in horticulture in the parish, under the name of Urr Parish and Dalbeattie Horticultural Society. During the thirteen years of its existence it has held, alternately at Haugh-of-Urr and Dalbeattie, an annual exhibition of flowers, plants, vegetables, and dairy produce, with honey, baking, jellies, and other subsidiary articles. In recent years a poultry and pigeon section has been added, which has met with a large measure of support; and on each occasion when the show has taken place at Haugh-of-Urr a programme of sports has been submitted. Financially and otherwise, the society has enlisted the encouragement and support of a large body of parishioners and others, so that its operations have been attended by a gratifying success, and the number and quality of the exhibits at its annual shows have been regarded as highly creditable to the district. Its first president was the Rev. David Frew, who has continued since to act in that capacity, except for a year, when Mr James Little, Dalbeattie, was in office. The succession of secretaries and treasurers has been: Messrs James Kennedy, James A. Catto, Robert Slater, and Quintin Aird, for the landward division of the parish, and Messrs Frank J. Johnston, W. Fergusson, John Turner, and J. Martin in Dalbeattie. Mr Aird has done the principal work of the office during the last nine years, and it is largely to his efforts on its behalf that the past success and present healthy condition of the society are due. The annual income averages about £65.

CURLING

The Urr Parish Curling Club is an old institution, dating from the 21st February, 1838. On that date a meeting of the curlers of Urr was held at the Haugh, when it was decided to form themselves into a society for the parish, and rules and regulations for the game were adopted. Dr. Alexander

PARISH BOARDS AND ASSOCIATIONS

McNeillie of West Glenarm was appointed president; Anthony Rigg, Torcatrine, vice-president; and James Lowden, Haugh-of-Urr, secretary and treasurer. The following were the members of the first committee: Messrs Hyslop and James Kerr, and Dr. Currie, Dalbeattie; Messrs Gibson, Cocklick; Thomson, Chapelton; Thomson, Markfast; Crosbie, Haugh-of-Urr; John Garmory, Haugh-of-Urr; John Smith, Milton; and Hope, Cronie. At a further meeting on 30th November, 1838, additional rules and regulations were adopted, and representatives from Springholm seem to have been present. In the seventy-one years of its existence the club has had twelve presidents: Dr. Alexander McNeillie of West Glenarm, 1838-1845; Thomas McGeorge, Glen of Spottes, 1845-1851; Alexander Thompson, Chapelton, 1851-1853; John Thomson, Blaiket Mains, 1853-1860; Alexander Young-Herries of Spottes, 1860-1875; William Thompson, Barr of Spottes, 1875-1878; John Carter, Haugh-of-Urr, 1878-1884; James Dinwoodie, Auchenreoch, 1884; John Halliday, Springholm, 1885; Alexander McNeillie Kissock, West Glenarm, 1886; Thomas Henderson, Newark, 1887; and Fergusson Wood, Springholm, who has now filled the office for twenty-two years. The number of secretaries has been five: James Lowden, Haugh-of-Urr, 1838-1845; his son, John Lowden, 1845-1885; William McAlister, teacher, Springholm, 1885-1892; Andrew Kirkpatrick, Auchengibbert, 1892-1895; and John Burgess, Springholm, the present secretary, who has acted since 1895.

Dalbeattie has now a curling club of its own, but the parish club continues to give a good account of itself, and in the season capital games may be witnessed at its different centres, Auchenreoch and Milton Lochs, and Spottes Pond. At one time there seems to have been another sheet of water at Blackford, on which curling could be indulged in; for, according to a minute of the Curling Club in 1842, it was decided to hold the competition for the rink medal in the following winter on Blackford Loch. The rink medal, it may be mentioned, was presented to the club by the first president, Dr. McNeillie, and has not only been the occasion of many an exciting tussle in the past, but is still an object of keen competition among the parish curlers.

CHAPTER X

THE ANTIQUITIES OF THE PARISH

THOUGH not very numerous, the antiquities of Urr are of varied interest, and sufficiently important to warrant special notice. Some of them belong to the remote and unrecorded past: others recall the social and ecclesiastical life of the middle ages. They are distributed with tolerable evenness over the parish.

THE MOTE OF URR

This well-known earthwork, to which the name of "The King's Mount" has also been given, is regarded by competent authorities as one of the finest extant specimens of the ancient mote. It is situated on the western bank of the river Urr, within a mile of the parish church, and about $2\frac{1}{2}$ miles above Dalbeattie. A branch of the Haugh-of-Urr and Dalbeattie road crosses the water by a ford at its south-eastern extremity, and passes thence into Buittle. About fifty years ago, when the railway to Castle-Douglas was opened, an effort was made to have a stone bridge for vehicular traffic erected at this point, and plans were actually prepared which may still be seen in a house in the neighbourhood; but the scheme failed to meet with adequate support, and had to be abandoned. A strong wooden foot-bridge, however, resting upon stone piers, was built by voluntary subscription a few hundred yards down the river. It proved so great a convenience that in 1904, when it began to show signs of wearing out, it was renewed and strengthened by a joint committee of Urr and Buittle Parish Councils at the expense of the rates.

The Mote stands in a broad, alluvial meadow, which is surrounded by hills of a considerable height, except on the northern side, where the valley opens out upon the uplands beyond. At any distance from it, these hills have the effect of dwarfing its appearance, so that an actual inspection of it is necessary in order to realise its imposing dimensions. Compared with structures of a similar kind, it is no less exceptional in its size than remarkable for its fine state of preservation. Viewed, as it usually is for the first time, from the opposite bank of the river, its outlines seem as clearly marked, its various features as regular and well-proportioned, as if it were of comparatively recent construction. In form it appears to be an elongated, oval hillock, rising abruptly from the level of the river bank, the southern side a long but fairly easy slope, the other sides steep almost to the extent of being precipitous, and divided into three parallel sections or stories of diminishing size, the lowest being by far the largest, and the uppermost very much narrower though somewhat higher than that which intervenes. Approached from the southern side by way of the foot-bridge, the ascent of the basal section or story reveals the fact that it is encircled on the top by a trench of the depth and width of a small canal. The inner slope of this trench is considerably higher than the outer, and leads to a broad and spacious platform, from which again, across another trench, rises the steep, conical mound which forms the summit of the whole. This platform and mound, with their encircling trenches or fosses, constitute the Mote proper, and in antiquarian language are termed respectively the base-court and citadel. It is convenient to use these terms in considering details of structure and dimensions.

Accurate measurements of the Mote have been taken by Mr F. R. Coles, and are given in the Proceedings of the Society of Antiquarians of Scotland (vol. xxvi. pp. 137ff). According to Mr Coles, the superficial dimensions of the base-court are 460 by 220 feet in all, or 228 by 220 feet in the part lying north and clear of the citadel: its perpendicular height above the level of the river bank is about 60 feet: the trench which en-

MOTE OF URR.—Plate 2.

FROM ENGRAVING IN GROSE'S "ANTIQUITIES," 1797.

closes it has a slope of 18 feet on the outer side and one of 33 feet on the inner, and measures from 6 to 9 feet in width at the bottom. The citadel rises fully 25 feet above the level of the base-court, or quite 85 feet above the river bank: it stands at the south end of the base-court, and nearer to the western than the eastern side: unlike the base-court, which is an irregular oblong, it is nearly circular in shape: the two diameters of the summit are 100 feet and 92 feet: the trench which surrounds its base is 537 feet in length, 10 to 12 feet in width, and has an average depth of 14 feet. Though the base-court has been frequently ploughed, traces of ramparts may still be discerned, especially along the southern and western sides. At present there are two entrances to it — places where the sides of the trench have been levelled down to facilitate access —one at the north-western, the other at the south-eastern corner, but only the former appears to have been an original approach. The latter bears all the signs of having been made in recent times, probably in connection with tilling operations, to admit the passage of the plough and other agricultural implements. Near the original entrance at the north-western corner is a heap of small stones; but these are not supposed to have any particular significance, having simply been gathered in the course of working the soil. The dampness of the ground at a spot near the south end of the base-court trench betokens the presence of a spring, which may have been of service in former days. There is no approach to the summit of the citadel, except an irregular line of footprints evidently of modern formation. Here, at one time, lay a large, round, granite boulder, a little to the north of the centre, but it disappeared some thirty or forty years ago.

The Water of Urr at present is confined in its course to a single channel on the east side of the Mote. It seems, however, in former days, to have divided itself into two streams, some two or three hundred yards to the north, one of which passed round the west side of the Mote, and through the adjoining meadow, to reunite with the other at a little distance below the present foot-bridge. The line of this old channel may still be traced in the markings of the soil, as well as in the configuration of the river bank at the points at which it left and rejoined the main stream. Besides these visible proofs of its existence, indirect witness to it is borne by the fact that it remains the boundary between the parishes of Urr and Buittle, and is given as such in the Ordnance Survey maps. The loop thus formed by the river would add a feature of some practical significance to the Mote in ancient times, by turning the ground on which it stood into an island.

In the Old Statistical Account of 1794, Dr. Muirhead states that about thirty years before, some outworks remained upon the southern slope of the Mote, seemingly erected by the Romans, and having some resemblance to their mode of fortifying. At the time of writing, however, these outworks had been obliterated by the plough; and, as Dr. Muirhead does not condescend upon a description of them, it is now quite impossible to determine what the nature of them may have been. That they were really Roman is open to serious doubt, especially as the only authority for the statement ventures upon the further opinion that there would be upon the Mote of Urr "sufficient space for accommodating a legion, with auxiliaries." During the time the Romans were in Britain the legion consisted of not less than 6000 foot-soldiers, several hundreds of cavalry, and a large body of auxiliaries. Manifestly such a force could not be accommodated with any degree of comfort within a space of 12,000 square feet.

Erections of various kinds have probably been raised from time to time upon the Mote, only to pass away again through the tear and wear of the elements, and the direct action of man. In illustration of the rapidity with which time and agricultural operations together result in changing the aspect of things, Mr Coles draws attention to some shapeless, grass-grown mounds and ridges that appear upon the southern slope of the Mote, at the corner where it touches upon the bank of the river, and mentions that they are the remains of a house, called Stepend or the house at the ford, which was still in occupation about seventy years ago, when the Ordnance Survey map was made. That it was inhabited much more recently than that is attested by some of the older people in the district, who can recall occasions on which the occupants were put to considerable discomfort, if not brought into actual danger, by one of those sudden rises of the river to which it is still liable. The ruins of another house, with an enclosure of a Scotch acre of land, are to be seen on the south-western side of the slope, in the direction of Milton farm-house. It was occupied within the last thirty years, and with the land attached to it formed a separate property called The Mote, which had been of much greater extent at one time, and had been for generations in the possession of the Walker family. Recently it was acquired by the neighbouring proprietor of Milton.

The discussion of the origin and history of the Mote of Urr labours under the obvious disadvantage of having no written records to depend upon. So far the silence of early historical documents upon it has not been broken. Even the keen and indefatigable antiquarian Dr. Christison has been unable to find any mention of it before the middle of the fifteenth century. In the Exchequer Rolls, or early accounts of revenues and rents in Scotland, it is frequently mentioned between the years 1456 and 1503, along with the Mote of Earlston, as a farm from which an annual rent is drawn. In the Registrum Magni Sigilli, or Register of the Great Seal, an early record of royal grants and licences in Scotland, two references occur to the Mote of Urr in connection with grants of land by King James V.; "1535 Moite de Wr," and "1541 Moit de Ur." Beyond these official entries of a comparatively late date, nothing relating to it has so far come to hand among the historical remains of the past. In the absence of formal, direct testimony, its date and early uses can only be inferred from a consideration of the structure itself, and the results so far reached by the study of motes in general. These old earthworks, of which there are many less imposing examples scattered over the Stewartry, and several within the parish of Urr, have only recently begun to receive the attention they deserve, and opinion is still somewhat undecided regarding them. Broadly speaking, however, the old ideas of their pre-Roman origin and use in Phallic or nature worship have mostly been given up, and a theory increasingly holds the field, which refers them to Saxon influence in the period succeeding the Roman domination, and ascribes a military, defensive character to them. According to this theory, they were built and used as fortresses, to which resort might be had in times of danger, or which might be permanently occupied by the chiefs and their retainers, in the rude, unsettled days between the departure of the Romans and the building of stone and lime fortifications. Other purposes may also have been served by them, such as those of a general meeting-place, or place of justice and judgment: indeed, as the strongholds of the chiefs, and the most suitable places for the promulgation and administration of such laws as existed, it is exceedingly likely that these purposes were served by them: but in most cases it is tolerably certain that the military character was predominant. The form of the motes was designed with a view to defence, and this object was still further carried out by enclosing the base-court and citadel with lines of ramparts and wooden palisades, the former of which can generally be traced, though the latter has naturally disappeared. In the Bayeux Tapestry, a panorama of sewed work depicting the invasion of England by William the Conqueror, and preserved in the public library of Bayeux, a representation is given of the fortified mote of Dinan. From this, as well as from some old documents relating to motes on the continent, it is inferred that wooden houses were generally

THE ANTIQUITIES OF THE PARISH

erected within the palisades, and that a sloping bridge or gangway connected the top of the citadel with the exterior of the fortress. As to the time when these earthworks, with their wooden erections, ceased in Scotland to be occupied as places of strength, it is safe to assert that the process began with the introduction of Norman influences into the country, and was completed by the beginning of the fifteenth century. The Norman conquest of England took place in 1066, and a century or two would suffice to admit of its effects penetrating into the northern kingdom; so that the beginning of the decline of the old Scottish motes may be dated about the end of the twelfth century. About that time, castles or keeps of stone and lime, after the Norman style, began to supplant and render obsolete the native fortifications of earth and wood. Even, however, when deserted by the chiefs for grander and more secure habitations, the motes might continue to be occupied by the lesser nobles and gentry, or might be used at times for other of their ancient purposes. Accordingly they cannot be held to have been entirely discarded before the beginning of the fifteenth century, after which the mention of them in old Scottish charters purely as land-names shows that they had finally been diverted from their original uses.

The application of these general considerations to the Mote of Urr, conjoined with an examination of its structure, suggests the most probable solution of its Sphinx-like enigma. So far as can be determined from surface abrasions and protrusions, the original body of the Mote was a natural, stony hillock, or mass of rock, earth, and gravel, which was found ready to hand in the island formed by the two channels of the river. At first, perhaps, it was regarded as a sufficient security in itself from human and animal foes; but afterwards, when the Romans had left the country, and Saxon influences were predominant, the notion was conceived of strengthening it by giving it the form of a mote. On some sides at least of the original hillock, the slopes were made steeper and more inaccessible by cutting and packing: the outer trench was dug, and the debris from it thrown upward and levelled to form the main platform or base-court: within this, again, the second trench was cut, and the citadel reared out of the materials which it afforded: while more cutting and packing were done along the edges of the trenches to shape them into ramparts, and a third trench was made which has left some traces on the southern slope. Possibly, to complete the design, supplementary materials had to be obtained from the bed of the river or the surrounding plain. The Mote being thus constructed, the next step was to raise those wooden erections which we have reason to believe existed upon it: the palisade round the base-court and the citadel, the shelters or houses, and the sloping gangway which gave access to the summit. With these works upon it, and a sufficient force to maintain it, the Mote of Urr would be almost impregnable to contemporary assaults, and would probably rank as the foremost stronghold of its time. A reminiscence of its consequence may be embodied in the name Firthhead, which occurs in the immediate neighbourhood, and is supposed to refer to the "head fort" of the district, though other derivations are given of it.

With regard to the date of the Mote and the length of time during which it was occupied, nothing more specific can be positively advanced than that, like other structures of the kind, it was built and used in the period before the introduction of the Norman keeps. As it is, however, a typical example of a Saxon mote, and exceptionally large and well-preserved, there is nothing improbable in the conjecture that it belongs to the later years of the Saxon dominancy in Galloway, which extended over the seventh and eighth centuries. On the other hand, it may be assumed that its glory as a place of defence began to fade about the beginning of the thirteenth century, after the strong stone castle of Buittle arose in its vicinity. Whatever use may have been made of it afterwards, the notices of it in the Exchequer Rolls and charters of the fif-

THE ANTIQUITIES OF THE PARISH

teenth century are decisive of the fact that, by that time at least, it had ceased to be a fortress, and had become merely a sub-division of land.

The Mote of Urr has been claimed by Mr Skene and other antiquarians as the site of Caer-bantorigum, a native town existing in the time of the Roman dominion, and mentioned by Ptolemy, a geographer of the second century, as one of the principal places of the Selgovae. A good deal may be said for this identification, but it is by no means certain, and must still be left open to question, especially as there are three other motes or forts in Galloway, which have the same claim made for them. It may be pointed out, however, that the discussion is in no way affected by the view now taken of the probable date and purpose of the Mote of Urr. A native village, such as Ptolemy mentions, may have existed at the advent of the Romans on the island and hillock enclosed by the waters of Urr, though the Mote was only formed some centuries later. It is highly probable that the advantages of the spot, in the way of defence, were recognised from the earliest times; so that, if the argument points that way, there is no reason why in its pristine condition it may not have been the site of Caer-bantorigum.

It only remains to mention an interesting tradition of the Mote, from which it is popularly supposed to have received the name of "The King's Mount." As the residence of an early chief or king, the historic structure may have otherwise acquired this name; but the legend has clung so persistently to it as to suggest a foundation in fact. It pleases the imagination to have it so; for in that case one glimpse at least is given into the forgotten past, one memory survives of the many, varied scenes of human life and activity witnessed by the Mote in the course of its long and chequered existence, which have passed away without leaving the vestige of a record behind. King Robert the Bruce, it is said, in the course of the wanderings imposed upon him by his enemies in the early part of his career, found himself towards morning in the vicinity of the Mote, and there, though weary and footsore, was encountered by an English knight, Sir Walter Selby, and compelled to give him fight. At the moment, the wife of one Mark Sprotte, who lived upon the Mote, was busy preparing a bowl of porridge for her husband's breakfast. Seeing the king in danger, she rushed from her cottage, and coming up behind the Englishman caught him by a lock of hair, or as some say by the knees, and brought him ignominiously to the ground. Too magnanimous to take advantage of his humiliating fall, his opponent sheathed his sword, and allowed him to rise. Thereafter the two knights washed their bloody hands in the Water of Urr, and adjourned to the cottage of Dame Sprotte for rest and refreshment. The only entertainment available was the brose or porridge intended for breakfast; and this Dame Sprotte set down to Bruce with a single spoon, as she would not have bite or sup given to an Englishman in her house. Partly to defeat her vigilance, and partly to reward her loyalty and attention to himself, Bruce told her to go out and run, and promised to give her, when he came into his kingdom, the land she encompassed while he was supping the brose. Setting out upon the business with a good will, she made what use she could of her opportunity; while, relieved of her presence, Bruce and his enemy shared the frugal meal, taking sup about from the spoon. In due time the grant of the land, amounting to twenty Scotch acres, was formally confirmed to the Sprottes, who became the Sprottes of the Mount, and retained it in their family for five hundred years. The only condition attached to its tenure was that, when a king of Scotland happened to pass through the valley of the Urr, a refection of brose was to be presented to him in "King Robert's Bowl." It is to be hoped that the possibility of being subjected to this ordeal has had nothing to do with the scarcity of royal visits to Galloway in later times.

THE ANTIQUITIES OF THE PARISH

Nothing particular being known of the remaining motes in the parish, it will be sufficient to give a brief description of them. They are very much smaller than the Mote of Urr, and simpler in design; but they probably belonged to the same general period, and were intended to serve a similar purpose.

EDINGHAM MOTE

Only four small hillocks of stones remain, in the vicinity of Edingham Castle, to attest the existence of this mote, and afford an indication of its form and dimensions. It seems to have been irregularly oblong in shape, and to have measured about 45 feet from east to west, and about 42 feet from north to south. It stood upon an elevation of 150 feet above sea-level, but was not within sight of any other motes. Seventy years ago its remains must have been more extensive and distinct, as they received notice upon the Ordnance Survey map.

LITTLE RICHORN MOTE

This is a large and evenly shaped mound, upon the eastern bank of the Urr, about a mile below Dalbeattie. It occupies a square corner formed by the junction of the Little Richorn Burn with the Urr, and measures 15 feet high at its greatest elevation, 175 feet from east to west, and 150 feet from north to south. The west side, adjoining the river, is practically straight, and slopes down to the water's edge: the north and south sides are straight, but converge slightly, and are rounded at the corners where they join the east side, which is curved and somewhat smaller than the others: a trench about 15 feet wide surrounds the whole, except upon the side that abuts upon the water. In the spring of 1891 some excavations were carried out upon this mote, and the results were given in the Transactions of the Dumfries and Galloway Natural History and Antiquarian Society for the following year. The only thing of note discovered was a sloping line of stonework, composed of roughly hewn granite blocks, and averaging about 6 feet in width, which extended from the south-western corner to the middle of the curve on the east, about 158 feet, then ceased for a space, but reappeared for a length of 44 feet towards the north-western corner. Nowhere else was such stonework found; neither along the edge of the river, nor in the outside rampart. The discovery gave rise to a difference of opinion; some authorities taking the view that the stonework was part of the foundation of an upright wall, and that consequently the mound had originally been a fort; others, with Mr Coles, whose account of the matter is here followed, inclining to another conclusion. In the absence of further evidence, the proper character of the Little Richorn mound must be left an open question.

Fort, Milton Loch

The forts, as a class, are to be distinguished from the Saxon motes, being earlier in time, and of native origin. There is said to be some evidence of their existence at the very dawn of Scottish history, in the period immediately succeeding the departure of the Romans. Their purpose would be much the same as that of the Saxon motes, which partly superseded them in the Lowland districts, but partly also coexisted with them, as the main fortresses of the country, until the introduction of the stone and lime castles.

The fort of Milton Loch is a particularly striking example, alike on account of its length, and the peculiarity of its situation. It stands on a narrow neck of land which juts out into the Loch from the western shore, and which, if there is anything in its name—Green Island—may at one time have been disconnected from the mainland. This so-called island seems to be of rocky formation on the south, but softer and more peaty on the north, and is so far taken up by the fort, that only a border of 20 to 50 yards in width runs between it and the waters of the Loch. The lines of the fort have apparently

MILTON LOCH.

PHOTO. BY J. AND J. BROWN, CASTLE-DOUGLAS.

THE ANTIQUITIES OF THE PARISH

been determined by the configuration of the ground on which it is constructed; at any rate it presents a distinctive appearance, being considerably longer and narrower than most structures of a similar kind. It consists of an irregularly oval rampart and external trench, enclosing an area of 221 feet by 84, with an entrance about 20 feet broad on the west side, and a sharp, narrow cutting through it, fully half-way round on the north side, which looks like an opening made for draining off the water. The rampart, which is bold and strong near the entrance, diminishes both in height and breadth as it curves away from it, and its slope throughout exhibits two very different gradients or degrees of steepness, the upper half running at a much sharper angle to the perpendicular than the lower. Inside the rampart three small mounds may be observed, apparently composed of stones, one on each side of the entrance at irregular distances from it, and one near the focus of the oval at the east side. There is also a square-cut, oblong hole in the ground, exactly opposite the entrance, which seems, from the dampness which gathers about it, to have been a well or spring. The trench on either side of the entrance widens out to a right-angle, so as to present a straight front to the mainland. The whole remains of Milton fort, taken in connection with its isolated position, suggest that in its day it must have been a stronghold of considerable consequence.

WATERSIDE FORT

This is an earthwork similar in character to the fort on Milton Loch, but in a much worse state of preservation. So little indeed remains of it, that it has escaped the notice of the Ordnance Surveyors, and is not marked upon their map. It stands in a clearing of the wood that crowns the high bank of the Urr at the bend behind Waterside Farm. The Mote of Urr lies only about a mile below it, on the opposite side of the river, but is not visible from it. Communication between them is supposed to have been maintained by means of the earthwork on Milton Park Farm, called the Camp or Castle Hill, which stands about midway, and is in full view of both. The valley of the Urr appears to have been dotted with motes and forts in this zigzag fashion, with the result that a chain of connection would be established throughout its course. The original form of Waterside Fort can only be conjectured now from the traces left, though these afford a tolerably clear idea of its dimensions. They simply amount to a hollow, uneven depression, in the centre of a ploughed field, which is carried round in the figure of a horseshoe, the extremities of which are 210 feet apart, and the curve circumference measures 510 feet. In the construction of the fort, advantage seems to have been taken of a slightly elevated piece of ground, with a bank or ridge running round it, and a small stream flowing along one side. What remains is evidently the trench, which probably was completed by a rampart, and may have had a second trench and rampart in close conjunction with it. So much at present may be reasonably inferred, but the fort is so clearly in process of disappearing, that its existence may soon become a memory of the past.

Standing Stone on Redcastle Hill

On the rising ground above the farm-house of Redcastle, about half a mile to the east of the Mote of Urr, there is a large, unhewn block of granite, standing upright in a field, with no other object near it. Its height above the ground is about 10 feet, and it is so deeply embedded in the earth, that hitherto no onslaught of the elements nor effort of man has sufficed to shake it. To all appearances it has been conveyed to its present situation in some remote age, and erected for a specific purpose. There is nothing, however, to throw light either upon the date or the object of its erection. Similar stones are found elsewhere, and have given rise to considerable discussion, one opinion being that they marked a place of sacrifice or religious assembly in prehistoric times, and another that they commemorated some notable achievement or event. The latter is regarded as the more probable explanation, at least in the present instance; though what it was that the stone was intended to mark, whether the scene of a singlehanded combat, the site of a battle, or the burial-place of a chief, cannot now be ascertained. As Dr. Muirhead puts it, in his reference to it in the Old Statistical Account: "what person or what event this monument of antiquity was meant to commemorate, no mortal pretends to say, tradition itself being silent on the subject."

In the centre of another field on the same farm, at the side of the Dalbeattie road, and looking towards the Mote, there is another standing stone of much smaller size, which is apt to engender curiosity; but it is of no historic significance, as it was erected within the memory of an old man recently dead, for the comfort and convenience of the cattle.

Edingham Castle

This is an old ruin, of a single story in height, standing a little to the south-east of Edingham farm-house. It is built of granite, with a mixture of whinstone, and measures about 30 feet in length and 21 in breadth. Its walls are 3 feet thick, and show signs of having been arched over to support another story or two above, a portion of the staircase to which may still be seen on the left-hand side of the doorway. A thick cover of ivy helps to preserve the stones and hold them together, while a few surrounding trees give shelter and distinction to the spot on which they stand. The remains are evidently those of a small tower or keep, such as was used as a residence by the gentry of three or four hundred years ago, and is exemplified in various other ruins in the neighbourhood. Timothy Pont's map, drawn up early in the seventeenth century, shows a house of some consequence on the site of the present ruins; and, in the Sibbald Manuscripts of a century later, "Edinghaim" is mentioned as one of the considerable houses of the time, along with "Kilwhonaty, Fairgirth, Carguinnan, Drumcayran, Achinskioch, Castel of Wraiths, Drummillen, ye Castel of Terreglis." In the sixteenth century, the lands of Edingham were in the possession of the Livingstones and the McGhies: from 1612 onwards, for over a hundred years, they were held by the Morrisons: and Edingham Castle, probably built before their time, would be successively the habitation of these families. When the proprietor became non-resident, it would continue to be occupied by the tenant, and would only fall into disuse, like so many similar places, when the demand arose for the modern style of farm-house.

Chapel and Graveyard Sites

Of the chapels and graveyards which existed in the parish in Roman Catholic times so few vestiges remain that no description of them is possible. Two of them, the chapels of Blaiket and Edingham, have so completely passed out of existence, that even their exact situation cannot now be determined. The sites of others, as traditionally known, are marked upon the Ordnance Survey map. The principal is the chapel of St. Constantine, with its associated graveyard, on the farm of Meikle Kirkland. Besides this, there are chapel sites on Chapelton and Aucheninnes farms, and in the Spottes glen, and a supposed graveyard site on Greenhead Hill.

CHAPTER XI

OLD CUSTOMS AND MANNERS

AMONG the customs of former days that have gradually been given up, the celebration of Old Hogmanay may claim first notice. It took place on the 12th of January, as according to the old style of reckoning the year began twelve days later than in modern times. Old Hogmanay is almost a forgotten festival now; even the children have abandoned the last semblance of its observance; yet, so recently as fifty years ago, in one village at least, within a few miles of Urr, the celebration of it still lingered as a great social event. The chief feature of the occasion was the performance of a quaint and somewhat mysterious ceremony. The village, like many other old Scottish villages, lay round a public green, with a common well in the centre of it. Towards nightfall the inhabitants turned out in their strength; and, scattering in different directions, ransacked the neighbourhood for articles of a portable and cumbersome kind. Everything that promised to be useful was laid under contribution—carts, barrows, ploughs, rollers, hencoops, feeding troughs, and field gates—irrespective of the wishes and convenience of the owners. These having been transported to the green, a wide and fairly effective barricade was soon formed round the well. For the following night and day, the space enclosed was held to be forbidden ground. No one was permitted to enter it or draw water from the well. The forgetful villager, who had omitted to provide himself with a sufficient supply for the interval, had to pay the penalty of his want of forethought, and go without, if he could not borrow, the necessary element. The attempt to surmount the barricade was regarded as offensive to the community, and likely to ensure ill-luck to the offender. It brought upon him the immediate wrath of his neighbours, and the prospect of many untoward happenings during the coming year.

The atmosphere of the nineteenth century was unfavourable to the survival of a custom of this kind, and slowly but surely killed it. With the rise of the modern spirit, the older members of the community began to discourage a practice, the origin and meaning of which had long been forgotten, and which was attended not only with inconvenience, but sometimes even with loss. The younger folks were not so much concerned with its formal observance as with the practical joking and horseplay for which it served as excuse and occasion. In their hands it was transformed into a kind of saturnalia of petty tricks upon the more sedate and eccentric inhabitants. Their humour was vented, their ingenuity expended, in such mild methods of torture as the overturning of water-barrels, the stopping of chimneys with divots, the blocking of doors and windows, and the tying up of "snecks." With a primitive mechanism of pins and strings, too, they could produce strange rappings upon the window panes, and cause considerable annoyance and alarm. The resentment begotten of these practices gradually induced the more law-abiding of the young folks to desist from them. The others were eventually frightened into giving them up. The last traces of a venerable old custom thus passed ignominiously away, leaving no shadow of regret behind them, but a general sense of relief.

The meaning of this barricading of the village well is shrouded in the mists of antiquity. An expert in primitive customs and folk-lore, when consulted on the subject some years ago, refrained from speaking with confidence about it, and left the villagers to plume themselves on providing a nut too hard for scholars to crack. The humorous suggestion, of course, has been made that it originated in an anti-teetotal demonstration, and was intended to concuss the locality into the use of spirituous liquors for at least one day in the year. Teetotalism, however, was not so general or aggressive in former times as to incite so violent and effective a protest. Some, accordingly, would find the roots of the ceremony in some outstanding event of old tribal days, such as the sudden seizure of the well by a neighbouring enemy, or the surreptitious poisoning of it, upon a far-off Hogmanay night. The most probable account of it, however, is that which refers it to an ancient sacrificial custom or ceremony of propitiation. In heathen times, as is well known, each well and river was supposed to have its presiding deity or tutelary spirit; and the Old Hogmanay custom may have originated in a religious rite directed to the spirit of the village well. It may have been the habit of the rude forefathers of the hamlet to placate the local spirit at the beginning of the year in order to secure the favour of pure and plentiful water during the following twelve months.

Until recent years another very old custom continued to be observed in connection with the marriage ceremony. When everything was ready at the house of the bride, and the appointed hour had come, her friends and neighbours assembled to await the arrival of her prospective spouse. On the news of his approach, a select body of young men sallied merrily forth, and met and arrested his carriage about half a mile away. Dividing themselves into two teams, one representative of the bride, the other of the bridegroom, and denominated respectively the bride's and bridegroom's "parties," they got into position for a race back to the house. A fair start was given them, and off they set at full speed. The struggle was keen and exciting, every muscle being strained, and a great variety of alertness being exhibited, to the infinite amusement of the onlookers old and young. The winning post was the bride's father, stationed at the door of the house, amid the assembled guests, and holding a napkin aloft. This was snatched from his hand by the foremost of the racers, to whose "party" accordingly the victory was awarded with acclamation, and to whom some liquid refreshment was given to regale himself and his fellow-competitors.

This custom, which was known as "racing for the napkin," seems to have been a survival or variation of a practice once fairly general in Scotland, called "the riding of the bruise or broose." Indeed, some of the older inhabitants of Urr remember to have seen and even participated in it in this more exalted form. "The riding of the bruise," as the name implies, was a horse race upon a more elaborate and prolonged scale than the simple pedestrian contest that took its place. Assembling at the house of the bridegroom, which might be miles away from their ultimate objective, the horsemen disposed themselves into two groups, according to their relationship with the bridegroom or the bride, and pitted their steeds against each other in a race to the bride's house. Usually they did not start till the bridegroom was so far on his way that they could only hope by furious riding to reach the house before him. Then they clattered away on their various mounts, over hill and hollow, through thorp and town, with a great show of zeal, making the echoes ring, and rousing as much excitement and pleasantry as possible on their way. The winner was rewarded, not only with the napkin, the symbol of victory for himself and his party, but also with a bottle of the wine of the country, which he could dispense at his discretion.

Considered in either of its forms—as a simple foot race or a lengthy equestrian competition—the symbolism of this ancient usage is tolerably clear. The napkin represents the bride, for whose possession the opposing groups of runners are supposed to contend. On the one hand, the party of the bridegroom aims at securing her and carrying her off to his home: on the other hand, the party of the bride is enlisted in her defence, and strives to anticipate the other party and baulk its designs. This piece of by-play, had it been confined to a limited area and comparatively recent years, might possibly have been regarded as merely reminiscent of exploits connected with the runaway marriages of Gretna Green. Doubtless, in the romantic days of the blacksmith-priest, it would occasionally be enacted with a realism denied to it in later times. The persistence, however, and extent of its observance seem to render this an inadequate explanation.

For its real origin we have probably to go back to a much earlier time—to the old tribal days, indeed, when capture was the recognised method of obtaining a wife. Forbidden by the law of exogamy to intermarry with their own kindred, and surrounded by tribes of an unfriendly disposition, men who did not care to remain wifeless had no resource but to seize and carry off the women of their neighbours. Many a hot race and keen tussle would be the result. These would necessarily pass unrecorded, but would not fail to leave their impression upon the savage mind, and would ultimately give rise to a fairly well-defined body of tradition. We only need further to allow for the power and play of tradition in shaping the customs of a people to see how the old barbarian usage of espousal by capture would pass gradually, through a mimic makebelieve, into the friendly game or contest associated with the marriages of a more peaceful age. So closely are we knit together in the same bundle of life with our remotest ancestors. The forms of their savage wooing, however altered, may still be traced in the refined ceremonials of our enlightened age; for where the "racing for the napkin" and the "riding of the bruise" have been entirely given up, if not indeed forgotten, the groomsman still remains, and he is admittedly the lineal descendant of the best man or helper of the primeval bridegroom in the capture of his wife.

Another custom that has gone from country life is the old institution of ministerial catechising. As a recognised branch of clerical routine, this old Scottish usage is defunct. Long ago it was relegated to the region of the lost arts. Older people remember a time when the visitation of the minister was still a "visitation" indeed, especially to the younger members of the family, as disconcerting questions were apt to be asked, and lengthy devotional exercises were engaged in; but even these have been generally given up, and the call of the parson now resolves itself into a genial talk upon sublunary affairs, only occasionally concluded by the offering of a short prayer. Other shadows of the old-time practice linger upon the stage in the catechetical course to which young communicants are subjected, and the annual Bible knowledge examination conducted by the minister in country schools. But the substance of it is long since fled; the thing itself is gone, never again in all probability to tax the energy and erudition of the minister, or the patience or endurance of his flock. In its day it served a useful purpose and met a clamant need; but, with the growth of knowledge and the passing of the interest in dogma, it was bound to fall into desuetude.

And yet there is a pleasure in recalling that rigorous intellectual discipline to which our forefathers submitted in the interests of religion. What a scene must often have been witnessed in the old country school, the high-roofed barn, or capacious kitchen! The whole population of the immediate neighbourhood gathered together in the presence of their minister to give an account, as well as a reason, of the faith that was in them! Deep and varied must have been the emotions that swept over the assembly, as the highest and holiest doctrines of religion were elaborately dissected and explained. Many a good story is told of the blundering answers of the catechumens, so that we may well believe the gravity of the ordeal was not infrequently relieved by a touch of humour or farce. Still, the prevailing spirit must have been profoundly serious; more so, perhaps, than we can appreciate, in those days of religious instability and impatience of dogmatic instruction.

There is an old-world pamphlet by the minister of a parish adjoining Urr, which serves to throw light upon the method pursued in catechising. It is entitled, "A Specimen of Plain and Practical Catechising by John McNaight, A.M., Minister of Buittle," and bears to have been composed by him, and published in 1783, with a view to the edification of his people when he himself was no longer able to instruct them. The pamphlet is cast in the form of a verbatim report of a catechising diet, and may be taken as representative of the procedure at one of these functions. After prayer, and calling of names, the pastor takes the boys and girls at school in hand, "and all other such like little young ones present." He puts them through the Shorter Catechism, so far as they can go; and, while complimenting some of them on saying it from beginning to end, expresses the hope that next time he examines them they will also give him a part of the Larger Catechism. The Ten Commandments, the Lord's Prayer, and the Creed are next repeated and explained. Then follows a series of extempore questions and answers, in which the pastor sometimes appears as the respondent, and the children evince a desire for information and religious precociousness, which might be the envy of the modern juvenile. An appropriate exhortation brings this part of the programme to a close. In the two succeeding portions, the same process is repeated, first with the unmarried lads and lasses, then with the husbands and wives, the sexes being taken up separately, and the range of topics widened and deepened with the advancing maturity of the catechumens. There are many digressions, often suggested by requests for fuller light on the part of the audience, and the net result is the presentation of a tolerably complete system of eighteenth century theology. The whole is intensely interesting as a revelation of the theological atmosphere in which our forefathers lived and moved and had their being, as well as the unbounded confidence they reposed in the Church, as the channel of eternal truth.

With the passing of ministerial catechising, and other ecclesiastical changes, may be noted the gradual disappearance of the old-fashioned type of minister's man. As an important parish functionary, the familiar of the minister, he is fast becoming a rara avis, and will soon be numbered with other specimens of the extinct. His time-honoured office threatens to collapse, to succumb to the spirit of the time, like that of the Poet Laureate, or the King's Historigrapher or Limner.

If the minister's man must go, it is well that he should go in such good company; for what a man he was, or rather, what an epitome of all that is faithful and serviceable in man! He was "the man" par excellence: the pivot of domestic comfort in the manse, of religious efficiency in the parish: replete with manly virtue, sound wisdom, and handy accomplishment: indispensable to the daily routine, the weekly rest, the Sabbath sermon. No mere servant, but a whole retinue of servants rolled into one, he did not so much perform duties, or occupy an office, as administer a system. In his day— not his day of life merely, but his ordinary working day—he played many parts: ploughman, coachman, gardener, gravedigger, and valet. On Sunday the whole care of the flock devolved upon him, the whole charge of the ordinances, with the exception of the conduct of divine worship. Always the stand-by of the minister, he was frequently the medium of communication, sometimes even the buffer, between him and his parishioners. Tall and spare as a rule, with a face of considerable refinement, a gravity of deportment that clerics might envy but could not surpass, and a beard that would have adorned the highest office in the Russian Church, he magnified his own position, and lent enhancement to that of the minister. With his man at his back, the minister could speak bravely with his enemy in the gate. He could keep himself in touch, too, with the circumstances and doings of his parishioners, without condescending to gossip, or submitting to familiarity; for the man was discreet withal, and knew his place, as well as the things that were better left unsaid, the things it was not necessary or good for the minister to know. What quaint and worthy specimens of the class may still be recalled! Not so long ago the aged minister of a Lowland parish, who had passed his professional jubilee, could still be seen going about his work, accompanied by a man who had been with him during all the years of his pastorate. Looking upon the two old men, one could not help thinking of the world of memories they must have had in common, happy, sad, and indifferent; and how much each in his own way must have been to the other.

The minister's man of the olden time was the only real rival of the minister in popularity with the story-teller. Many a good story has been told, illustrative of his pawky humour, shrewd sense, and keen observation. His loyalty to his clerical superior could always be taken for granted, yet no one could hit off his weaknesses, foibles, or peculiarities better than he. He had his own opinion, too, of the men and events that came within his purview, his own idea of the course and management of parochial affairs, and could express himself with clearness and pith. Not infrequently he exhibited an illuminating wit and clever sarcasm. To strangers he was a perfect storehouse of information regarding the customs and people of former days. The returning native will miss him, as he revisits the homes and haunts he has known, and most of all as he stands in the old God's acre of the parish, to refresh his memory, and have his heart quickened, with thoughts of the dead.

A matter of wider social interest than the passing of old customs and institutions is the general change proceeding in the life and manners of the country. Neither the minds of the people nor their ways of living and behaving run in the same grooves as formerly. The developments of the nineteenth century have tended to obliterate the old distinction between town and country, so that it is almost a slander now to ascribe bucolic ignorance, or even idyllic simplicity, to any considerable section of the inhabitants of rural districts. It is neither a deception of the memory, nor a mere flight of fancy, that leads the older folks to remark so often upon the different condition of things at the present time from that which existed in their younger days. Great and important changes have certainly been in process, and it still remains to be seen whether these are for better or for worse.

For one thing, there is a change in the attitude to religion, which no longer holds the place it did in the lives of many country people. The old-fashioned piety, that found the Church a necessity, that regarded family worship as a duty, and found pleasure as well as profit in the reading of devotional books, seems to be passing away; at least it is not so conspicuous as it used to be; and there is no longer the keen interest in dogma of the catechising days, nor the ready submission to the authority of the Church, which made possible the system of public discipline and rebuke. To a great extent, of course, the explanation of the change is to be sought in the spirit of the age, which is more assertive and independent than that of former times, and less amenable to considerations of fear in the province of religion. Subsidiary causes, however, have also been in operation, such as the popular election of ministers, the multiplication of churches in country places, the spread of cheap literature, the provision of public games and amusements, and the greatly increased interest in politics, consequent upon the lowering of the franchise.

The manners and ways of life of the people also reflect the changed conditions of modern times, being less marked by individual characteristics, and more uniform with those of the towns. The result may be ascribed in large measure to the change in the educational system which was instituted a generation ago, and is now exhibiting its fruits. The instruction given in the Board schools tends to develop a uniform type of mind and character which must have its effect upon the tendencies of the day. An illustration of the change may be taken from the form of mutual salutation in popular use. It is fast becoming stereotyped: a simple, friendly inquiry in set phrase on the one side, and a formal expression of thanks on the other. It was not so in the time of the fathers: there was more individuality, more current significance, and consequently more variety, thrown into their greetings in the markets and elsewhere. Survivals of the ancient usage in this respect are still encountered in these prosaic days, which are not unworthy of attention. Some of them, of course, may be dismissed without consideration as unmeaning; but others betray a waggish inventiveness in the individual, and many, like place-names, have a background of social and historical significance. In some measure they reflect the past and present conditions of life in the district, and reveal the temper in which the inhabitants have habituated themselves to deal with them. A few examples of these individually characteristic salutations, overheard in a south country town on a recent hiring day, may be given as an indication of the change that is passing.

"Hoo's your health?" inquired one farmer of another, with a decided emphasis upon the final word, which could not be mistaken for the usual provincial inflection of the voice. Evidently he meant to restrict the scope of his inquiry, and to have the answer confined accordingly to the one matter of health. There was a deliberate avoidance of a more general expression of interest. Apparently he did not wish to know of his friend's affairs, so far as they related to his mind, family, or estate. His anxiety was explicitly limited to his bodily condition. This self-imposed restraint opens up a wide field for conjecture. The true Galwegian, it may be said, is a reticent man, and likes reticence in others. He has also a horror of gossip and inquisitiveness, and shuns the very appearance of either. These are characteristics bred in the race by long experiences of turmoil and persecution. But, besides that, a general disinclination may be noticed among Galloway farmers to discuss the trials and difficulties of their occupation. If not originated, it has at least been confirmed, by recent years of agricultural depression and wet seasons. It is felt that what affects one affects all, and is therefore to be patiently borne, not made the theme of casual conversation.

"Hoo are ye wearin'?" This was the salutation of a middle-aged cotman to an elderly friend, whom he evidently had not seen for a considerable time. It was a triumph of satire. He addressed his acquaintance as a piece of machinery, whose iron constitution might be taken for granted, but the collapse or wearing out of which, through the excessive grind of the daily routine, was only a question of time. This superficial exaggeration, however, only served to hide the real pathos of the meeting, which doubtless appealed to both, though neither was disposed to own it. In the days gone by, they had "neeboured" each other, in wind and rain, in cold and heat, toiling together in the harvest field, struggling with the plough, or herding or turnipping the sheep. There was no need for inquiry on either side as to how things had gone in the interval. The cotman's life does not vary much with change of scene or master, and each of them knew very well how the other had been spending the time. The same arduous labours, the same exposure to the elements, the same hard fare, would be their common lot. All curiosity on these points could be suppressed, and attention directed to the one salient feature of the effects which they had left. "Hoo are ye wearin'?" touched at once upon the only variable factor in the progress of the years, and the answer that came with the promptness of conventional usage showed how deeply the iron of the cotman's lot has entered into his soul: "O, jist haudin' thegither."

"Dod, man, are ye aye leevin' yet?" exclaimed a big-boned, happy-faced ploughman to a little, sharp, determined-looking fellow, who had first accosted him. It was no doubt meant as a friendly greeting; yet the tone of the query, like the words, expressed nothing but profound surprise. Under the circumstances the effect was exceedingly ludicrous. The little fellow was left to discover for himself the reason of the wonderment that he had lived so long. It could not be the uncertainty of his health in former days, for that would have implied an unfeeling joke at his expense of which no ordinary Galwegian is capable. There might, however, be a facetious reference to an unusual spirit of independence in him, an adventurous disposition, or a combative and opinionative temperament, which might reasonably be supposed to have brought him into trouble, if not actually to have accomplished his decease. On the other hand, the affectation of surprise may have been an indirect expression of sympathy with him in the hardness of his lot, or an implied compliment to the strenuousness with which he sustained it. In any case, it carried one's mind back to the old covenanting days in Galloway—the "killing times" as they are still called—when it was a real wonder to meet a friend, after the lapse of years, or even months, and find that he was "aye leevin' yet."

SPOTTES HALL.

ECCLESIASTICAL HISTORY

CHAPTER XII

BEFORE THE REFORMATION

DEFINITE facts relating to religious matters in the parish only begin to emerge in the twelfth century. It was only then, indeed, that parochial divisions were created in Scotland, and that Urr, as a parish, came into existence. Previous to that, there is no separate information regarding either its social or religious history, and we are dependent entirely upon inference from the few ancient remains that are left, and what is known of the state of things generally in Galloway. A detailed account of the religious customs and beliefs of the ancient Galwegians hardly seems necessary; but a brief sketch may not be out of place.

The earliest type of religion throughout the province would be a crude kind of animism: that is to say, a vague belief in the existence of good and evil spirits, moving and working in the phenomena of nature, and present not only in human beings and animals, but also in plants and lifeless things. Such a belief is apt to arise within the savage mind, as the interpretation of its own experience in waking action and the dreams of the night. It naturally inspires dread, and the desire to propitiate those mysterious powers, which are as capable of working harm as good. Hence there would be associated with it magical arts and incantations, and a rude kind of worship—mostly in the form of sacrificial offerings to the dead. The soul was supposed to have a shadowy existence of its own, and, at death, to transmigrate into another body, or animal, or natural object; it was well, therefore, to placate it, and do it reverence, lest it should avenge its wrongs, real or fancied, by bringing trouble or disease upon the offender. How far these old superstitions continued to persist, after new faiths were introduced, it is impossible to say; perhaps they spring up naturally in the ignorant mind; at any rate, it was well into the eighteenth century before the belief in ghosts and witchcraft was discredited.

At the beginning of the Christian era, this primitive animism had developed into Druidism—a highly-organised nature-worship, which prevailed among the Celts, not only in Britain but in Gaul. Historians of the present day hardly profess to know so much about the Druid religion, as those who wrote a generation ago; still some facts may be taken as established. It was presided over by a class of priests called Druids, the chief of whom was the Arch-Druid, to whom great authority and reverence were given. Generally speaking, these priests administered what we call public affairs. They attended to the education of the young, such as it was; disputes were referred to them for settlement; they sat as judges in cases of misdemeanour, and determined the punishment. It is doubtful whether they had any idea of One Supreme God, or a future state of the soul under other conditions than the present; they seem rather to have worshipped a number of gods, derived from reflection upon the powers of nature, and to have believed in the transmigration of souls, that is, their passing from one form of embodiment to another. Their chief divinity was the sun, to whom they paid high honour and frequently sacrificed human victims. Their moral teaching seems to have been purer than that of most heathen religions; they taught their people " to reverence the Gods, to do nothing evil, and to practise manly virtue." They held the oak tree sacred, and regarded with even greater veneration the mistletoe that grew upon it. They had their festivals, too, of which the chief were Beltane and Samhain; these continued to have recognition of a kind, long after the religion that originated them passed away. In Urr, at the end of the sixteenth century, and later in some places, Beltane was still a common term of reckoning: Mr John Brown's salary as reader was fixed at " XX lib. ijs. ijd., and ten mair sen beltym 1572." Beltane fell on the first day of May. Samhain, which was observed on 1st November, was advanced a day, and changed into Hallowe'en, or the Eve of All Hallows or Saints, which still drags on a lingering existence.

It was this religion—modified to some extent by contact with the Romans—that confronted the Christian faith on its first appearance in Galloway. The earliest evangelist of Christianity, whose name and work are known to us, was St. Ninian—a native of the Solway shore, either upon the Cumberland or the Galloway side, who had made a pilgrimage to Rome, and been indoctrinated in the faith. Landing on the Isle of Whithorn about 396, he built a church there, called the Candida Casa or White House, and established a monastic retreat or school of Christian learning, from which he carried forward the work of evangelisation over a wide tract of country. His influence is said to have reached as far north as the Grampians; in any case, he and his emissaries met with great success throughout the Scottish Lowlands, which generally abandoned their old religion, and embraced the Christian faith. One of the earliest regions to receive the new light would be the Vale of Urr. We can imagine the herald of the Cross—Ninian or another—making his way down the winding banks of the river, and sowing the seed of the Word as he went. The people would be rude and ignorant, but not without a point of contact in their natures for the blessed truths and elevating influences which he dispensed. It is hardly likely that a church was built, or a regular system of worship established. The people, on assenting to the Gospel, would simply be baptised in companies, or even crowds, and thereafter enjoined to observe the more outstanding principles of the new life. A preacher might be left among them to continue the work, or their instruction might be renewed from time to time, as occasion served, by passing evangelists. The process of converting and confirming the Celts of Galloway would have points of similarity with the earlier expansion of the Christian religion over the Roman Empire.

St. Ninian died in 432; and, in the years that followed, the traces of his work were almost entirely swept away. Events in Galloway were unfavourable to the continuance of the Christian faith. After the withdrawal of the Roman power, the old life of war and plundering was resumed, and the great bulk of the people, instigated by the heathen bards that still survived, renounced the religion they had been so easily persuaded to accept. For centuries considerable obscurity hangs over the history of Galloway, and what is known points to constant internal strife, and fierce struggles with intruders from without. It would seem that the light kindled by St. Ninian was never entirely quenched: in the sanctuary at Whithorn, if nowhere else, it continued to shine with flickering strength: now and again it was reinforced from other quarters, and shed its rays more widely: but, for the most part, paganism was in the ascendant, and maintained its ancient grip upon the people. Early in the ninth century, a fresh heathen influence was brought to bear upon the province; the Norsemen descended upon the shores of the Solway Firth, and established a footing in Galloway which they maintained for over two hundred years. These warlike wanderers from the north brought with them a whole scheme of mythology, with elaborate and picturesque tales of the doings of their gods and goddesses, and ideas of a heathen Paradise and place of punishment for the wicked, which must have strongly infected the imagination of the inhabitants; the more so, that they did not resent their presence, but lived on terms of amity with them. Traces of the Norse occupation are still to be found among the place-names of Galloway; perhaps, also, in the physical characteristics and habits of the people. The drinking of healths, for instance, though not confined to Galloway, is said to have been derived from their custom of pledging their gods in their cups. Their favourite deities were Odin, Thor, and Freya; and these have given their names to three of the days of our week. Their great festival of Jul, observed about the 25th of December, accounts for the name of Yule and the element of feasting and merriment still associated with Christmas.

The eleventh century witnessed the beginning of a great improvement, both in the social and political affairs of the province, and in its religious condition. The authority of the Norsemen waned and disappeared; and Galloway, which for centuries, under a variety of rulers, had been more or less independent, became definitely merged in the dominions of the Scottish king. Through the influence of Queen Margaret, the Consort of Malcolm Canmore, and afterwards through the exertions of her son David I., the "sore saint to the crown," a revival and reconstruction of the Church took place throughout Scotland. By the twelfth century bishoprics had been created, many magnificent religious houses built, parishes erected, a parochial clergy organised, and, besides rich endowments of land given to the Church, tithes instituted for its support. The process of delimiting and equipping parishes is comparatively clear. In some cases, the lord of the barony or manor would find an old religious house already on his ground, with a district attached to it; but, in most cases, he would have to build a new church, and appoint a priest for his vassals, with an adequate endowment of tithes from his soil. In the case of Urr, there was probably a combination of arrangements. It is known to have been a barony from a very early date, and the limits of the barony would determine the boundaries of the parish. At the same time, there may have been a church already existing; for there is documentary evidence to show that, soon after the erection of the parish, or about the middle of the twelfth century, there were two churches in Urr—one at Meikle Kirkland, and another at Blaiket. The reasons for this double provision, and the comparative contiguity of the churches, which would only be separated by a mile or at most two, can only be guessed now. In those days the churches, though built of good hewn stone and lime, and thus greatly superior to the rude buildings that preceded them, were yet mostly of very small size, measuring no more than twenty or thirty feet long, and fifteen or sixteen feet wide. The extent and population of the parish might necessitate two such churches—the one to accommodate the inhabitants of the lower end, and the other those of the upper; while the clergy of the period might have good cause for desiring to be as near each other as possible. The site of the Kirkland church, with graveyard attached, is still ascertainable, and continues to be marked upon the Ordnance Survey map. It stood a short distance behind the present cot-house, on the right-hand side of the road that leads up to Auchengibbert. All traces of the Blaiket church have long since disappeared; nor is any mention made of it in the Statistical Account of the parish, written in 1627 by the minister of the time, though he refers clearly enough to its ancient neighbour.

The church at Kirkland, which was usually regarded as the parish church, was dedicated to St. Constantine, the patron saint of various other churches in Scotland. There is considerable dubiety about the identity of St. Constantine. Three persons of the name have been brought forward as claimants to the dedication of Urr Church. Two of them were old kings of Scotland—Constantine II. and Constantine III. The former is said to have founded the church of Dunkeld between 810 and 820. If so, he must have lived to a good old age, for he was defeated and slain in battle by a band of Danes from Ireland in 876, at Inverdovat in Fifeshire. He was buried in Iona, and was supposed to have had his sainthood attested by the occurrence of miracles at his tomb. Constantine III. belonged to the following century. Resigning his crown, he entered the abbey of Kilrymont; and, after

BEFORE THE REFORMATION

spending five years as its abbot, died in 943. These two royal saints had the same festival day in the Church's Calendar— 11th March; but it is doubtful if either of them became the patron saint of Urr. That honour probably belongs to an earlier Constantine, who lived and laboured as a missionary in the days of St. Columba. He is said to have founded a monastery at Govan; and, after winning most of the inhabitants of Cantire to the Gospel, to have suffered a martyr's death at the hands of unbelievers about the end of the sixth century. Various accounts of his origin are given—that he was a British king, who gave up his estate on the death of his wife, a king of Scotland, a monk from Ireland—but the question is now incapable of decision. In any case, he must have been a man of great religious energy and devotion, to have had so many churches dedicated to his honour.

Regarding the dedication of the Blaiket church, we have more certain and satisfactory information. Known generally as Kirkbride of Blacket, that is to say, the church of St. Bride or St. Bridget, it was evidently dedicated to the well-known saint of that name, who was held almost in equal veneration in Ireland with St. Patrick and St. Columba. The allusion in St. Patrick's Confession to "a blessed maiden, very fair, of noble birth, and of adult age," whom he baptised, and to whom he afterwards gave the veil, is supposed to be to her. As usual with these old saints, the true story of St. Bridget's life has been distorted and obscured by the inventions of later years; but it seems certain that she was a woman of exceptional beauty and goodness, who founded a nunnery at Kildare, and devoted her life to the education and religious training of girls. The veneration accorded to her in Ireland gradually extended to Scotland, and numerous churches were dedicated to her, especially in the south and west.

The two churches of Urr were within the bishopric of Glasgow. Then, as now, the Urr Water was an ecclesiastical boundary, and divided the see of Glasgow from that of Galloway. At first the Urr churches had the status of parsonages; that is to say, they were churches, independent of an abbey or other religious house, whose priests were appointed by the lord of the manor, and drew the whole tithes and land-rents pertaining to their cure. It was not long, however, till a change occurred. In the twelfth century, monastic establishments began to multiply in the land, and acquire an ascendancy which seriously affected the independence and usefulness of the old parish churches. It became a fashion with the king and his gentry, not only to endow them with liberal gifts of land, but to attach parish churches to them, with their tithes and other appurtenances. In this way, three-fourths of the churches of Scotland became directly connected with monasteries, and were managed by them, to the detriment of the position of the parish clergy. The church-rents and tithes of the parishes went to swell the wealth of the monasteries, which appointed what were called vicars—poor and badly-paid priests, working under them—to serve the cures. Fergus, lord of Galloway, having been implicated, about the year 1130, in a rebellion against the Scottish Crown, was forced to take refuge in the abbey of Holyrood. Afterwards restored to the king's favour, he again mixed himself up with political disturbances, and had to retire a second time to the abbey, where he became a monk, and died in 1161. He and his son Uchtred, who succeeded him, conveyed to Holyrood abbey many of the churches of the south, of which they had the patronage. Among these were the two churches of Urr, which thus became vicarages, and continued as such to the Reformation. Of the priests who officiated in them, the name of one alone has been preserved, that of Johan Vicaire de Urres, which appears in the Ragman Roll.

The charter by which the Blaiket church was conveyed to Holyrood is held by the McDowalls of Logan, in the parish of Kirkmaiden. The text of it is given in full by McKerlie in his *Lands and their Owners in Galloway*. It is in

BEFORE THE REFORMATION

monkish Latin, and somewhat to the following effect: " Uchtred, son of Fergus, would have all men know that he has granted and made over in perpetual gift, for the safety of the souls of king David and his son Henry, king Malcolm, and his own father Fergus and ancestors, to the church of the Holy Rood in Edinburgh and the clergy there serving God, the church of St. Brigide of Blacket, with all its appurtenances [which are detailed], to be held free of every exaction for all time." No doubt the abbey left the vicar with only a miserable pittance to struggle along as best he could. The grant of this church, as well as that of St. Constantine at Kirkland, was confirmed to Holyrood in 1240, by William, Bishop of Glasgow. There was also a confirmation by Eustace Baliol, one of the witnesses to which was Hugh Sprot, burgess of Urr. At the Reformation, the patronage of the church of Urr was transferred to the king, under the Annexation Act of 1587. For a time (1633-1688), during the attempt to revive Episcopacy in Scotland, it was vested in the bishopric of Edinburgh; but on the re-establishment of Presbyterian government at the Revolution of 1688, it reverted to the king. The right of presentation to Urr remained with the Crown, except for the short period 1690-1711, until the abolition of patronage in 1873, when full liberty was granted to the people of electing their own ministers.

It is strange how old names survive; not only are there two farms in the parish—Meikle and Little Kirkland—whose names still proclaim them to have been old possessions of the Church, but the stipend of the minister, in the latest modification by the Court of Session (1903), is regarded as composed partly of parsonage and partly of vicarage teinds. The same reflection is suggested by the name of Chapelton farm. It was no uncommon thing, in olden times, for a wealthy and pious proprietor to erect a private chapel on his land, and pay a priest to minister in it to himself and his servants. In all probability, a place of worship of this kind stood in the vicinity of Chapelton; indeed, there is a thorn bush on the farm, which is supposed to mark its site. Near Spottes Glen, again, there is a field called the Chapel Yard, where some remains of ancient masonry may still be seen, and from which a stone lintel, evidently belonging to a place of worship, was taken some time ago, and built in, for preservation, over a doorway in the Glen Farm. Chapels are also known to have existed at Edingham and Aucheninnes. Besides these genuine witnesses from antiquity, there is a farm called Hermitage in the parish, which might suggest the location of one of those old anchorite's cells, which were common in Scotland so late as the eleventh and twelfth centuries, and in which the solitary devotee inflicted austerities on his body for the good of his soul. The name Hermitage, however, does not appear in the Statistical Account of 1627; and, as the local pronunciation till recently was Heritage, which would give quite a different signification, it is probably of modern derivation.

The facts so far ascertained enable us to form a fairly clear idea of the ecclesiastical situation in Urr, in Roman Catholic times. The churches of St. Bridget and St. Constantine would be available for the parishioners generally, and would be served by vicars of Holyrood, who would receive for their support a small moiety of the parochial endowments, the rest going into the coffers of the abbey. At Chapelton, Glen of Spottes, Edingham, Aucheninnes, and probably other places as well, there would be chapels maintained by individual landowners. In the early days of zealous devotion and unquestioning faith, the system would work well enough; but, as time went on, Urr would most likely share in the general degeneration of Church life which took place throughout the land, and would be ready for the great Protestant Reformation of 1560, which swept the old order away, and brought in the new.

URR CHURCH AND MANSE.

PHOTO. BY J. AND J. BROWN, CASTLE-DOUGLAS.

CHAPTER XIII

MINISTERS BETWEEN THE REFORMATION AND THE REVOLUTION.
1560-1688.

FROM the Reformation to the present day, the ministerial succession in Urr has been practically continuous. During that time there have been fifteen individuals in office—some tolerably distinguished in the literary or ecclesiastical world—none, so far as our authorities go, altogether unworthy of their sacred calling. Of course, there is considerable variety in the amount and value of the information available regarding their different lives. Generally speaking, it grows in detail with the advance of years; but in one conspicuous instance at least, that of Rev. John Hepburn, it is provided with exceptional liberality. Occasionally, though fragmentary, it is more than ordinarily suggestive, and enables us, from a few scattered notices, to reconstruct in our imagination a life of great industry and usefulness, which otherwise might have been buried in the forgotten past. On the whole, it affords a record of service, continued for three and a half centuries, of such an able and strenuous kind as deserves pious remembrance.

REV. JOHN BROWN. 1567-1608.

The first name to emerge from the strife and turmoil of the Reformation period is that of Mr John Brown. This common Scotch name must have covered a character of uncommon energy and ability, if we may judge from the apparent avidity for work of the gentleman who bore it. To understand his situation, it is necessary to recall the general condition of ecclesiastical affairs at the time. The Church was in a state of ferment and transition. One great difficulty with which she was confronted was that of finding an adequate supply of ministers, to take the places vacated by the Roman Catholic clergy. As yet, no provision had been made for the training of a Protestant ministry; and so, for some time, there was a scarcity of men of sufficient qualifications for the pastoral oversight of the parishes. In many cases, several parishes were conjoined under the care of one individual: in others, they were left vacant altogether for a while: and in still others, they were supplied with lay readers—men of inferior attainments to the ordinary clergy, whose duty was to read the Scriptures and the Common Prayers to the people, but not to perform marriage or administer the Sacraments. The readers, however, were permitted to give an occasional exhortation; and, as their office was admittedly a temporary expedient to meet a practical difficulty, those of them who exhibited outstanding gifts in public discourse, and were men of acknowledged piety, were ultimately raised to the full position of ministers. This is what happened in the case of Mr John Brown. Appointed reader in Urr in 1567, he was ordained minister of the parish in 1572; and, within two years thereafter, had the parishes of Irongray, Kirkpatrick-Durham, and Kirkgunzeon added to his charge. This arrangement would doubtless suit the gentry of the time; who, here as elsewhere, would be ready enough to lay greedy hands upon the unappropriated teinds and other property of the Church. How it worked in practice we cannot tell now; but, when we consider the extent of the respective parishes, the state of the roads, and the means of locomotion in those days, we may conclude that the most moderate allowance of church ordinances and pastoral attention must have entailed extraordinary exertions and sacrifices, not only on the minister, but on the people as well. It hardly increases our wonder to learn that Mr Brown also preached sometimes at Kirkbean; or that, as a local tradition has it, he delighted in such lengthy discourses as almost brought him under the censure of the Presbytery.

His salary does not seem to have been proportionate to his exacting and multifarious labours; yet, in those days of simple living and scarce money, it probably sufficed for his needs. As reader in Urr, he received twenty-one pounds eleven shillings and eleven pence Scots, or a little over a pound Sterling. After his ordination in 1572, other ten pounds Scots were added to his stipend, and on his removal to Irongray in 1574, it was finally fixed at sixty pounds. The manse of Irongray, then as now, would stand not very far from the hill now popularly known as Johnny Turner's, from which a wide view is obtained of the surrounding country. Full of cares and labours, Mr Brown may sometimes have retired to this coign of vantage, and looked with despair rather than pride, upon his far-spreading diocese. He died in 1608, and was buried in Irongray churchyard, where an ancient stone, restored in 1885 by a reputed descendant, commemorates his ministry.

Mr Alexander McCarmonth. 1585-1602.

In his later years, Mr Brown seems to have been accorded some assistance in his onerous duties, by the appointment of readers in the different parishes under his charge. Alexander McCarmonth was his reader in Urr, and he took office in 1585; but beyond these facts nothing more is known of him. No doubt he would receive the usual small salary of a pound or two a year, and do his best to maintain the flickering flame of devotion, in the absence of other ministrations.

Rev. John Thomson, M.A. 1602-1615.

After Mr McCarmonth, a fully qualified minister was appointed, in the person of Rev. John Thomson, M.A., whose father, William Thomson, had been vicar at Terregles in Roman Catholic times, and throwing in his lot with the Reformed Church, had remained as reader there. He was presented to Urr by King James VI. on 12th March, 1602. Probably at first he was more or less subordinate to Mr Brown, who was still alive, and occupied a position resembling that of a modern assistant and successor. Four years later he seems to have succeeded to the full charge, as we learn that then he was "continued" or confirmed in the pastorate of Urr. To mark that event, or, as is more likely, to signalise the building of a new church under his direction, his initials were inscribed on the back of the wooden pulpit, with the date 1606 underneath. Amid all the changes of structure that have taken place since, the panel that contains this inscription has been faithfully preserved; and, twelve years ago, when the introduction of an organ necessitated its removal from its original position, it was carefully taken down, and re-inserted in the right-hand side of the pulpit. There it may still be seen—a silent witness to the noteworthy qualities of head or heart that prompted so honourable a memorial. "Being dead, he yet speaketh."

Rev. Alexander Robertson, M.A. 1615-1639.

Mr Thomson was succeeded in 1615 by Rev. Alexander Robertson, M.A. To his hand we owe the first Statistical Account of the parish, to which reference has already been made.* From the light it casts upon the state of affairs during his incumbency, we can infer a considerable advance in ecclesiastical matters, from the early Reformation days. No longer merely a station supplied by a reader, or part only of a badly paid cure, the Church of Urr now numbers on its roll the respectable total of six hundred communicants, and provides its minister with a stipend of six hundred merks, or, in sterling money, nearly forty-five pounds, which for those days was by no means a contemptible living. The old church also has been taken down, and removed from Meikle Kirkland to the present-day site, where it had been re-erected on a larger scale, probably during the incumbency of Mr Thomson. All this suggests considerable activity on the part of successive

* Page 24.

ministers, as well as a growing religious life among the people. Other information is given by Mr Robertson, relating to the general affairs of the parish, and may be found in connection with the previous mention of his manuscript. We may read his character, to some extent, between the lines of this document which he has bequeathed to us. On the whole, it leaves us with the impression of a man thoroughly alive to the practical questions of his time, and deeply interested in the welfare of his people and his church. That his sympathies sometimes took a wider range is evidenced by the fact that, in 1632, he contributed forty merks towards the building and library of Glasgow University, where he had graduated twenty-five years before. He died in June, 1639, aged about fifty-two. He was twice married, and had issue by both wives. Mr Alexander Robertson, preacher, who suffered death at Edinburgh on 14th December 1666 for his share in the Pentland rising, is said to have been a son by his first wife. His second wife, Grissell Gordoune, survived him, and seems, from the Minute Book of the War Committee of the Stewartry of Kirkcudbright (1640-1641), to have been a woman of some consequence. On 1st September 1640, she is ordained "to present her silver worke, viz.:—the twa piecess that was bought by the paroche of Urr for the use of the Kirk, and sex silver spoones pertaining to the aires of the said minister;" and on 13th November, "the Committie, for the ungodlie words and filthie speiches utterit be Johne Makartnay against the umqle. Minister of Urr his wife, efter tryall taken be the said Committie thairof, ordaines the said Johne, upon Sounday next, to ryse out of his seat efter sermone and confess his fault in declameing, by words, of the gude name and fame of the said relict and to crave first God's mercy for offending him, next the said relict's for the offence done to hir, and then the parochinares' for his evill example, and then his minister to resaive him and the said relict to tak him be the hand, and to pey to the Commissar Depute for his fyne fiftie merks monie." Such was the penalty of defamation in those days. It may be suggested, as a probable explanation of the dispute, that the minister's wife was the same Grissell Gordoune who, as daughter to John Gordoun, had sasine of the lands of Blaiket in November 1628. The Makartnays were connected with the Blaiket family, and succeeded to the property about the middle of the century.

Rev. George Gledstains, M.A. 1640-1666.

Mr Gledstains took his degree at St. Andrews in 1627, and in 1638 was admitted helper to Mr Halbert Gledstains, minister of Troqueer, of whom he was probably the son. Transferred to Urr in 1640, he received his presentation from King Charles I. in 1641. Soon after his settlement, the extant Presbytery records begin, and by their occasional references to him and his parish, afford sufficient testimony to the zeal and faithfulness with which he discharged the duties of his office. The representative of the Kirk Session in the Presbytery seems to have been regularly appointed, some of the elders mentioned in the minutes as hailing from Urr bearing such locally historical names as MacKairtnae, MacJore, and Muirhead. Delinquents were scrupulously brought to book: and Popish malignants were proceeded against with a rigour only to be justified by the circumstances of the time. So keen was the oversight exercised, that moral defaulters and adherents of the old faith, seeking refuge in Urr, were immediately put in process, till they provided themselves with a testimonial from their former parishes. An entry in the Presbytery minutes gives us a glimpse into the work Mr Gledstains was doing in Urr, his relations with his people, and repute among his brethren. In June 1650, Mr Gledstains was appointed to attend the forthcoming General Assembly at Edinburgh; and, before proceeding thither, he requested the Presbytery to arrange for a visitation of his parish. This was accordingly done; and on 6th August 1650, the brethren who had visited Urr reported that "they found all matters there in a very good frame and posture, especially upon the minister point, who both by his doctrine, life, and discipline, received a large and ample commendation of his people." Troubles, however, were in store for Mr Gledstains and his people, as well as for other faithful ministers and flocks throughout the land. Under Charles II. the attempt was renewed to re-establish Episcopacy in Scotland, and those who remained staunch upholders of the Presbyterian system were driven ruthlessly from their parishes. It is a significant fact that the minutes of Dumfries Presbytery break off abruptly in 1665, and do not resume again till 1687. There is nothing to show what share Mr Gledstains may have had in the more severe sufferings of the Covenanters; but in 1666 he was ejected from Urr, and, doubtless, it would be suffering enough for him to be parted from his attached people. Perhaps, also, like others of his brethren, he was compelled to endure bodily hardships, and skulk like a criminal "in dens and caves of the earth." In the troublous times that followed, Urr certainly received a fair share of attention from the king's troops. It is just possible, however, that his lot was milder, and that he had a safe, if not a comfortable place of refuge to which to retire; for, judging from the subsequent position of his family, he may have been a man of considerable means. In 1676, his eldest son acquired the lands of Crocketford and Little Merhorn in the parish of Kirkpatrick-Durham; and he, and his sister or daughter after him, retained possession of them for seventy years. In 1676, however, Mr Gledstains died; so that it still remains uncertain how he fared during the ten years that elapsed from the time of his "outing" from Urr. His wife, Agnes Currie, was still living in Crocketford in 1707; so, at least, says McKerlie; but Scott in his Fasti gives her name as Jane Porteous, and asserts that she died in Dumfries on 28th May 1703.

REV. JOHN LYON, M.A. 1666-1688.

On the " outing " of Mr Gledstains in 1666, Mr John Lyon, M.A., who had studied at St. Andrews, and been ordained by George, Bishop of Edinburgh, on 15th September, 1665, was intruded in his place. He belonged to the class of Episcopalian " curates," whose services were detested by the general body of the people, and whose memory, in subsequent generations, was held in popular execration. It was natural that it should be so. These " curates " were foisted upon the parishes in opposition to the will of the people: they were strangers to their parishioners, and out of sympathy with their habits of thought and feeling: they had usurped the places of their own beloved pastors, and were enjoying the stipends of which they had been unjustly deprived: they were in league with their oppressors, and, if not the cause, at least the occasion of the persecutions under which they groaned. This was enough, apart from their own personalities and the principles at stake, to make them popularly disliked. Throughout the " killing times," the tragedy being enacted in the country, especially in the west and south, had its epitome in Urr: fear, hatred, distress, on the one side: misunderstanding and repression, on the other. The incumbency of the parish was no bed of roses for Mr Lyon. The people, naturally of an obstinate, determined cast, were made sullen and revengeful, by the sufferings and injustices inflicted on them; as occasion served, they were always ready to heap petty annoyances upon the " curate "; few attended his services, unless under constraint, and, even then, it was to find fault with his utterances, rather than to profit by his ministrations. No man could have done them good under these circumstances. Once, at least, their hostility took a more pronounced form. Raiding his manse in his absence, they wreaked their animosity on his household goods, and carried off his wife a prisoner to the hills, whence, we presume, she was soon restored to her sorrowing husband. It is not clear whether they expected to find him at home; and, if so, what they would have done to him. Probably their intentions were not homicidal; indeed, we may be almost certain of that, from what happened afterwards at the Revolution. Then, when the change of Government gave them their opportunity, they contented themselves with simply "rabbling him out." That was bad enough, however, as many a poor "curate" was to learn. Storming his house, according to the fashion of the time, they turned the inmates to the door, threw their goods and chattels after them, and ordered them to be gone out of the parish, and never let themselves be seen in it again. The "curates" escaped scatheless, but were thrown homeless and penniless upon the world. According to a local tradition, Mr Lyon's sympathisers, who were not inconsiderable in number, accompanied him a short distance on his way. Gathering them together round the great stone that still stands on the farm of Redcastle, about a mile from the manse, he addressed to them some farewell words. The scene would no doubt be a touching one, and should not be altogether forgotten in casting up the accounts of the time. It was not long till Mr John Hepburn, a preacher more acceptable to the people, who had been skulking in the neighbourhood, waiting for such a turn of events, appeared in the pulpit, and inveighed in no measured terms against the Episcopal hirelings.

We have a curious glimpse of Mr Lyon in after years, which throws a strong backward light upon the character and circumstances of his ministry. On 22nd July 1699, fully ten years after the Revolution, a letter was received by the Presbytery of Dumfries from the Moderator of the Commission of the General Assembly, requesting information of him while he acted as Episcopal minister at Urr. Evidently, being in straits, he had applied to the Commission for employment. About this time, through the "rabbling out" of the "curates," just as after the Reformation, through the ousting of the Roman Catholic clergy, there was a dearth of ministers; and the Church had resolved to avail herself of the services of those Episcopalians, whose qualifications and past conduct were above reproach, and who were willing for the future to conform to Presbyterian principles. The fact that Mr Lyon applied for re-instatement suggests that he had not much to fear from ecclesiastical scrutiny. It is interesting to see how the Presbytery dealt with the matter: what a fine sense of justice they affected, yet how scantily they meted it out to the distressed "curate." To begin with, they appointed one of their number to make inquiries, and, solely on his report, drew up their answer to the letter of the Commission; in other words, they left it to a single individual to collect what tales he might of events that happened many years before, and, without the least pretence of sifting, remitted these to Edinburgh—knowing well the prejudice that existed against the person concerned, and the issues for his worldly prospects that depended on their judgment. No wonder Mr Lyon appeared in person at their next meeting, with a petition for a fairer and fuller inquiry. Their letter to the Commission had accused him of gross immoralities; and he was surely within his right in demanding that some kind of proof should be led, and a more thorough examination made into his life and doctrine while he was in Urr. The Presbytery could not resist this plea, and did what they should have done at first—agreed to visit Urr, and call for witnesses. It is symptomatic of their relations with the incumbent of the time, Mr Hepburn, that they were doubtful of his willingness to expedite their arrangements, and instructed the ministers of two adjoining parishes to make the necessary intimations from their pulpits.

The Presbytery met at Urr on 5th October, 1699. Mr Lyon compeared; and three of the leading men of the parish, George McKairtney of Blaiket, William McGeorge in Larg, and Thomas McGeorge in Glenarm, handed in an indictment against him. They could not, however, speak to any of the counts from personal knowledge (this was surely suspicious in men occupying their position in the parish, and taking the lead in the prosecution), but named witnesses who might be called to substantiate them. These were ordained to be summoned to appear before the Presbytery at Dumfries on that day week. Mr Lyon was served with a copy of the libel, and undertook not to proceed against the witnesses as slanderers, if they should fail to make out their case. We may read what significance we please into this precaution of the Presbytery.

The formal trial took place at Dumfries on 12th October. Mr Lyon again compeared, and gave in answers to the libel. He also lodged objections to the witnesses as ultroneous, but agreed to refer the whole matter to their oath. The charges were formulated under the following four heads, which were taken in turn, and duly considered. I. "Once or twice he taught publicly from the pulpit, that a man could not be a Christian, nor obtain salvation, without taking the test:" the test being the oath abjuring the Covenant, and acknowledging the reigning king, enforced during the persecutions. Three witnesses, John McGoun in Little Larg, John Hanna in Little Culmain, and Hugh McGeorge in Garmartin, were produced to speak to this charge, but Mr Lyon took exception to all of them. The first had never been his hearer: the second was addicted to Mr Hepburn's principles and party: the third (poor fellow) was hypochondriac for four or five years at the time alleged, and so not compos mentis. Evidently they all belonged to that class of recalcitrant hearer, who only attended church at the point of the bayonet. But what was there in the charge after all? Mr Lyon's language might be rather hyperbolical, but his meaning was plain, and perfectly consistent with his own ecclesiastical profession. He himself had taken the test, and doubtless considered it his duty to impress upon his parishioners the necessity of following his example. His motives may have been as humane as they were conscientious. II. "He used to have rash oaths in his common discourse." The first witness to this count was Samuel

Copeland in Little Kirkland, Mr Lyon's beadle; and he, though he must have been often with him, could not say that he ever heard him use an oath. The only other witness, James McMine in Howcroft, averred that he once "heard Mr Lyon swear by God his Maker, that Mr John McAdam, schoolmaster in Kirkland, shall not keep Galloway." The words had been uttered in the heat of a quarrel: sticks had been broken on the occasion. Who knows what provocation the sorely bested minister may have received? Besides, it was pointed out by Mr Lyon that the witness, still youthful, must have been a mere child at the time to which his evidence referred. Surely words, presumed to have been spoken in such circumstances, and reported by a single witness of so unreliable a character, would scarcely be considered now to justify a charge of habitual swearing. III. "He was sometimes drunk." The beadle was again called, but could only testify to seeing Mr Lyon once affected with liquor; and even then he was able to walk all right, though "not speaking in his usual voice." This simply raised the apparently insoluble question, as to where the line ought to be drawn between drunkenness and sobriety. Another witness, Edward Garmorie in Grange, "thought he was drunk one night when the dragoons came on him;" but, as he was unwary enough to add that this happened six or seven years before, whereas it was over ten years since Mr Lyon had left the parish, his memory was evidently not to be trusted. IV. "He had a great hand in causing the troopers harass and oppress many of the honest people of Urr." This charge had not even the appearance of support, and entirely broke down. Six witnesses were called, but none of them would swear that Mr Lyon really had a hand in the persecutions: all they would say was, that they suspected him.

It must be admitted that Mr Lyon came very well out of the trial, considering that both judges and witnesses were strongly prepossessed against him. Altogether it seems a case for a verdict of not proven, if not, indeed, of full acquittal;

but the Presbytery, either from nicety of conscience, or disinclination to allow an Episcopalian delinquent to escape, were at no pains to absolve him. Since they could not condemn, they refrained from passing judgment at all, and simply ordered the whole evidence to be transcribed and transmitted to the Commission in Edinburgh, Mr Lyon being graciously permitted to have an extract copy of it. This, of course, left him still in the position of an accused person. How he fared with the Commission, and what became of him afterwards, we do not know; but we take our leave of him with a feeling of kindness and commiseration. Whatever his faults may have been, they were mostly the faults of his time and class; he had a difficult position to fill, and probably received as much injustice as he inflicted. It says a good deal for him that, after a ministry of twenty-two years, maintained under the most discouraging conditions, in a time of great laxity, so little occasion of stumbling could be found in him. How many of the Presbytery that sat in judgment on him would have emerged blameless from a similar ordeal? Certainly some of them needed for themselves the charity they failed to extend to him; for, according to their own records, it was only a few years till several of their number (and there were only twelve at that time altogether) had to be dealt with, and ultimately deposed, for misdemeanours of a graver and grosser sort than any laid, even in suspicion, at his door.

CHAPTER XIV

Rev. John Hepburn, M.A. 1688-1723

IN Mr John Hepburn we encounter an exceptionally strenuous personality, one that seemed to find its habitat amid the storm and stress of ecclesiastical contention. For many years after the Revolution, his excessive zeal and irregular ministerial behaviour not only brought himself into notoriety, but caused serious dispeace in the Church. His personal character was so free from reproach, his motives were so manifestly sincere, his claim to be the legitimate representative of Covenanting principles was so plausible, and himself so pertinacious, that he gained a considerable following throughout the country, and wielded a wide-spread influence. A leading light and organiser of the "praying societies" that arose at this time, and afterwards gave impetus and volume to the dissent from the Establishment, he has been called "the Morning Star of the Secession." It was difficult for the church courts to know what to do with him. The attempt to discipline him taxed their ingenuity to the utmost. Throughout his time their records are largely occupied with proceedings against him. Leniency was tried, but found of no avail; coercion was resorted to, but was hardly more successful; even imprisonment served only as a temporary check upon his movements, and failed to break or bend his stubborn spirit.

The son of a Morayshire farmer, Mr Hepburn was educated at Aberdeen University, where he took his M.A. degree in 1669. Eight years afterwards he was ordained in London by an English Presbytery. This was sometimes questioned in after years, but he steadfastly affirmed it, and refused to accept further ordination. He seems to have received three separate calls to Urr, all more or less irregular, and the subjects afterwards of much acrimonious debate. In 1680, while Mr Lyon was still Episcopalian minister of the parish, a call was offered to Mr Hepburn, "subscribed by the plurality of the people, to preach the Gospel occasionally amongst them, as his conveniency and safety would allow;" in 1686, they gave him another call more generally subscribed; and again, as they asserted later, " in 1689, before there was any formal Presbytery of ministers at Dumfries, they legally and unanimously presented to him a call, to settle and abide with them, promising subjection and obedience in the Lord." Complying with the first of these invitations, Mr Hepburn appeared in the parish in the thick of the persecuting troubles, and began to do duty irregularly in it; but he soon brought upon himself such notice from the authorities as necessitated his going into concealment. What exactly it was that roused their resentment — whether his mere presence and unauthorised ministry, or some overt act of lawlessness—does not appear; but, in May 1684, he was declared fugitive. Keeping in touch with the people, however, he patiently waited his opportunity; and at the Revolution, when Mr Lyon was "rabbled out," he was ready to take his place. At once entering upon the pastorate, he began that restless career of controversy and agitation which lasted for over thirty years.

It is an open question whether he ever was regularly and officially inducted. Undoubtedly he was the choice of the people, and to him and them alike that was equivalent to "the called of the Lord:" their loyalty, their almost passionate devotion to him, never wavered, in spite of the strain put upon it by his frequent absences and eccentricities; he retained their confidence to the end. Throughout the proceedings against him, too, he was recognised by the courts of the Church as the minister of Urr, whatever may have been the basis and motive of such recognition. There is no notice, however, of his formal induction in the minutes of Presbytery;

on the contrary, many of the entries seem to indicate that such a ceremony never took place. On more than one occasion, Mr Hepburn, when brought to book for his vagrant tendencies, claims the liberty, which could only belong to an unattached minister, of preaching in vacant parishes. At the outset of his ministry in Urr, the Presbytery order him several times to be written and spoken to, for going about irregularly within their bounds; and, on his appearing at their meeting on 10th September, 1689, while welcoming him in brotherly fashion, they advise him to accept a call to some definite parish. A week later, a deputation from Irongray appears with a unanimous call to him, which the Presbytery press him to accept, but with which, after some delay, he declines to comply. For several years thereafter he is treated as a member of Presbytery, reproved for his absences from the meetings, and appointed to preach as their representative in various places, as well as to act as their correspondent with the Presbytery of Wigtown; yet on 20th July 1692, Mr George McKairtney of Blaiket and others from Urr come before the Presbytery, asking their help to get the Privy Council to give the stipend of Urr to Mr Hepburn, "whose preaching they allow;" and on 16th August Mr Hepburn presents himself with some of his parishioners, asking whether he is a member of Presbytery or not, and why the Presbytery do not grant their request regarding the stipend. To this demand the Presbytery return the significant reply that, as complying with the call from Urr, he is permitted to sit with them, but, as not definitely settled there, he is really not a member. In 1705, in the course of proceedings against him, the representatives of the Presbytery denied "Mr Hepburn either to have had or have legal right to the Parish of Orr;" and, later still, Mr Veitch of Dumfries greatly incensed the supporters of Mr Hepburn by questioning the validity of his ordination, which led them to retort that he had himself previously admitted its validity, when he expressed his willingness to receive him as his colleague. On the whole, the inference seems to be that Mr Hepburn never was really inducted into Urr; and that the Presbytery, while protesting, were driven by force of circumstances to adopt a policy of opportunism towards him. Considering his following in the country, and his hold upon the parish, and being unable to compel him to submit to a formal induction at their hands, they for the most part allowed his position to go unquestioned, and treated him generally as the minister of Urr. What they could not cure, they made shift to endure.

From the outset of his ministerial career Mr Hepburn identified himself with the malcontents in Church and State; and, intruding himself into other parishes, vigorously denounced what seemed to him the defections and corruptions of the time. The Revolution settlement was distasteful to him: it did not recognise sufficiently the authority of the Church, and was too lenient towards her former oppressors. He resented the oath of allegiance demanded of the clergy, and abused his brethren for the docility with which so many of them were ready to take it. The laxity of the Church aroused his indignation, as seen in her toleration of the "curates," her willingness to receive them back again into her service, and her anxiety to avoid controversial disputations, accommodate herself to the new state of affairs, and settle down to do what practical good she could. To his mind it was all a backsliding from Covenanting principles, a lowering of the banner of truth, and a carnal compliance with the world. There were many who agreed with him, especially in the south and west. Banded together, in a loose kind of organisation, under the name of Christian societies, they lifted up their testimony against the defilements of the Church and the sins of the State. Some of the society men held aloof from both, and refused all association with them: these afterwards found other leaders, such as Mr MacMillan of Balmaghie, and developed an existence that continued in separation from the Establishment, and became the Reformed Presbyterian Church. Mr Hepburn and his adherents, however, diverged from them at this point; as they expressed it, "they could not find freedom to disown totally the existing constitution of Church and State, and judged it most like to Scripture pattern to own what was good in both, and to protest and bear witness against the defections of both, by pleading in face of judicatories for redress of grievances." The "Hebronians," as they were called, did not, like the "MacMillanites," become a sect; but continued in the Church, and were gradually assimilated to the general body of constitutional Presbyterians. Mr Hepburn's course might be the wiser, but, in the circumstances, and with his temperament, it could not but be the more difficult. He had to steer between Scylla and Charybdis: the irreconcilable section of the society men repudiating him and venting themselves bitterly against him, he was exposed to a cross controversial fire—on the one hand, from them, and on the other hand, from the authorities of the Church.

There is no obscurity about the aim of Mr Hepburn, nor any question of the conscientiousness with which he pursued it. He desired the reform of the Church upon constitutional lines, and never could see that this either necessitated his voluntary detachment from her organisation, or warranted the infliction upon him of ecclesiastical censures and penalties. He always professed, as in duty bound, to be seeking the peace of the National Zion; and was candidly amazed at the storm he sometimes succeeded in raising. This may be partly accounted for by the vigour and piquancy of his language, which must have been very trying to his opponents. In the elaborate vindication which was issued by his followers, entitled "The humble pleading for the good old way," we have a fair example of his controversial methods; in his own numerous appeals and statements of grievances, he shews himself possessed of no mean literary style and power of thought; but it was in his public ministrations that the full force of his keen and active intellect made itself felt. His prayers are said to have been strangely fervent. His preaching frequently produced upon his audience the most wonderful visible effects, some of them being constrained to cry aloud, others falling upon the ground, struck into a swoon. It was all very well for Mr Veitch of Dumfries to remark sarcastically that "he had, indeed, a way of couping folk," but such manifestations undoubtedly witness to his strong personal force, stirring eloquence, and unimpeachable sincerity. A few of the more telling phrases, with which he adorned his discourses, and denounced the evils of his time, have been preserved to us, owing to the fact that they were reported to the Church courts, and inserted in the libels drawn up against him. On one occasion he prayed, with sublime egotism, "Lord, send forth labourers into Thy Church in this land; what can one man do?" Preaching at Balmaghie, after the deposition of Mr MacMillan, he quoted Matt. 24. 48-51 against the Presbytery of Kirkcudbright, and said "they had been doing the devil's errand"; also "that the Church had gone off its foundations, that ministers clapped people's heads, and profaned the Sacrament of the Lord's Supper, by giving it to drunkards and swearers, and that, if they got not another religion, they and their religion would go to the bottomless pit." Other choice quotations are: "The fasts kept by ministers since the Revolution do nothing but add fewel to the flames of God's wrath, and do nowise appease the same:" "The oath of allegiance to Queen Anne is the Black Oath:" "Ministers held formerly of Christ, but have changed their holding, and now hold of the Queen, and have put Christ's crown on her head:" "The stipend is their motive and temptation, and if people were worth their ears, they would give these ministers no stipend:" "They are neither curates nor Presbyterians, but lukewarm Laodiceans, that God would spue out of his mouth:" "The Black Curates killed Jesus Christ, and the Presbyterian ministers and professors of this nation have laid the stone on His head." No wonder his vilified brethren remonstrated with him; and, when he refused to listen to them, and continued to invade their parishes, not only preaching against them, but baptising and marrying in their despite, put in motion the machinery of ecclesiastical law against him.

The Presbytery displayed considerable patience in their dealings with Mr Hepburn: as the Assembly also did afterwards, when his case went to it. Besides their own grievances, they had complaints from other Presbyteries against him; but they were in no hurry to proceed to penal measures. Every opportunity was given him of desisting from his irregularities, and submitting to reasonable discipline. Letters were addressed to him, and private conferences were held, without result; a visitation of Urr was resolved upon, but had to be abandoned, owing to the departure of Mr Hepburn contumaciously for London. There was nothing for it but to refer his whole affair to the Commission of the General Assembly. This was done in due form, and on 30th April 1695, the decision of the Commission was received, "admonishing Mr Hepburn to desist from preaching, baptising, and marrying in other parishes, and confine himself to one parish, to which he hath or may have a call; otherwise Urr and Kirkgunzeon [which also seems to have been in Mr Hepburn's hands] will be declared vacant, and new ministers put in them." To most men this would have been a sufficient warning, but it had no effect upon the fiery ardour of Mr Hepburn. Within a week of its receipt, he had flagrantly contravened the Act of the Commission, by officiating and baptising in Torthorwald and Troqueer. It was impossible to pass over such a serious flaunting of authority; Mr Hepburn was duly cited three times to explain himself before the Presbytery, and, not appearing, was declared contumacious; thereafter the Assembly took the matter up, and, their triple summons likewise having been disregarded, on 4th January, 1696, they suspended him from the ministerial office. The Act of Suspension, as recorded in the minutes of Dumfries Presbytery, shews the leniency with which the Assembly treated Mr Hepburn. An offer is mentioned as made by them, to drop all procedure against him, on condition of his promising to walk orderly, take a settled charge, and submit himself to the judicatories of the Church. Power, also, is granted to the Presbytery of Dumfries, to remove his suspension, or, of course, as a necessary alternative, to depose him, according to his future behaviour. The widespread influence of Mr Hepburn, and the importance attached to his case, are shewn by the fact that intimation of the sentence is ordered to be made in the New Church of Edinburgh, and in all the churches of Dumfries, Ayr, and Glasgow Synods. They are further evidenced by the difficulty that appears to have been encountered in carrying out this order. Some of the brethren had to be seriously dealt with by their Presbyteries, before they dared to intimate the sentence to their congregations. One of the Dumfries Presbytery, Mr Andrew Reid, appointed to preach shortly afterwards in Urr, had a reception from the parishioners which sufficiently indicates the state of feeling there: "several persons, having presented a protestation against him and the Presbytery, barricaded the Church door, drove his horse through the corn-fields, robbed him of his bridle and one of his stirrups, and called him a soul-murderer and other abusive names." Evidently it required some degree of physical courage to enforce discipline at Urr in those days. It was only after a year had elapsed, that the Presbytery, as a body, ventured to visit the obstreperous parish, and then (a fact that considerably discounts their temerity) there were neither elders nor minister to meet them. On 24th October, 1697, they met with the people, and exhorted them to get themselves elders, so as to be in a better condition for calling a minister; at the same time they arranged that the vacant stipend should be applied, as was usual at that time, to the repair of the church and manse, and some useful bridges. It does not appear that any attempt was ever made to fill Mr Hepburn's place. Meantime what had become of him? Ignoring the authority of the Assembly, no less than that of the Presbytery, he had continued in his devious courses till the law laid hold upon him, and, after a prosecution before the Privy Council, shut him up in Edinburgh Castle. From Edinburgh he was transferred to Stirling; where, according to pamphlets of the period, he still exercised his gift, and delivered his soul of its burden, through the bars of his prison windows. Thither many of his followers resorted to him, "travelling," as Mr Hill Burton says, "from his own peculiar Western district, to drink of the pure fountain of Covenanting truth."

On 3rd February 1699, his suspension was removed by an Act of Assembly, and he was permitted to return to Urr, after his three years' absence, and resume his ministry. His incarceration seemed to have had no more effect upon him than the milder measures formerly taken against him. Far from moderating his excesses, he threw himself more strenuously than ever into the special work he had cut out for himself, associating more closely than before with Mr MacMillan, and adding to his former testimony against the ways and works of the Church, the new grievance of his recent suspension. The Presbytery wrote to him, inviting him to their meetings, but no reply was vouchsafed; "for peace and unity's sake" they sent a deputation to confer with him, but all the answer they received to their advances was that "he would do therein as the Lord would give clearness and call." To his former obstinacy, there was probably now added a feeling of embitterment begotten of the penalties he had endured. The old complaints were renewed: the old futile negotiations followed: the case passed again from the Presbytery to the General Assembly's Commission: and on 8th June 1704, another sentence of suspension was passed upon him. The Presbytery again had a lively time, during which Mr Andrew Reid had a fresh experience of the amenities of Urr. Appointed to read

AUCHENREOCH LOCH.

PHOTO. BY J. AND J. BROWN, CASTLE-DOUGLAS.

the sentence of suspension to the people of Urr, and to cite Mr Hepburn to the next meeting of the Commission, he proceeded to the church on a fine Sunday in July, accompanied by an officer and two witnesses, but found no congregation convened, or likely to be convened, and had to content himself with affixing a copy of the intimation to the church door. He himself seems to have escaped maltreatment on this occasion, but his companions were not so fortunate; they were violently assaulted by the parishioners, beaten to the effusion of blood, despoiled of their papers, and had their clothes so rent that the Presbytery had to order them new ones. So serious was the riot considered, that an express was sent off to Edinburgh, to acquaint the Moderator of the Commission and Her Majesty's advocate therewith. Something of the spirit that animated the people of Urr seems to have evinced itself in other parishes. Eight ministers were reported to the Presbytery, as having neglected to intimate Mr Hepburn's suspension, and were ordered to do so under pain of censure, "as their negligence might foster the division, and procure dislike to the ministers who had made the intimation." A month afterwards, the Presbytery were informed that "intimation had been made in most parishes, except where it was judged utterly inexpedient."

During the ensuing autumn, answers to charges, complaints, reasons for removal of suspension, and other papers, were poured in abundantly upon the Commission by Mr Hepburn and his followers. Ultimately it was arranged that a meeting should be held at Sanquhar on the first Wednesday of February 1705, between a committee of ministers and elders and representatives of the factionaries. Nothing came of the meeting, however, except a civil pretence of clearer understanding on both sides; and on 9th April 1705, Mr Hepburn, being still averse to working in conjunction with his brother ministers, and in subjection to the judicatories of the Church, was solemnly deposed from the office of the Holy Ministry. "He had not given nor taken Communion for sixteen years: he had treated his former suspension and warnings and tender dealings as if they had not been: he had been guilty of a continued tract of erroneous seditions, and divisive doctrines, and schismatic courses, wherein [saith the Assembly] he is obstinat, refusing to be reclaimed."

Protests were immediately forthcoming from himself and his parishioners. The latter, in a paper subscribed by many hands, and acutely reviewing the whole history and arguments of the case, declared their firm and faithful adherence to him as their minister, notwithstanding the Assembly's sentence. His supporters in other parishes, too, prepared papers, and had them read before their respective congregations, and afterwards affixed to the church doors, expressing their indignation at the treatment accorded to him. No wonder the ministers of these congregations temporised, and refrained from intimating Mr Hepburn's deposition to their people. To himself it seemed to make little practical difference: he returned to Urr, and preached, and performed the other parts of his ministerial work, as freely and assiduously as before. He was nothing, however, if not consistent, and the state of alienation from the Church, being contrary to his expressed convictions, weighed heavily on his soul; consequently he never ceased to ply the Assembly with petitions for his reinstatement. These were nearly successful in 1706, and a year afterwards were completely so, much to the annoyance and dissatisfaction of the Presbytery of Dumfries. Probably the Assembly were puzzled to know what to do with a man on whom the terrors of the law made no impression, and were glad of any pretexts, such as his more orderly behaviour since his deposition, and his promise to endeavour to promote the unity and peace of the Church, to get him off their hands. At any rate, on 12th August 1707, it was carried by a great plurality of votes, that he should be reponed to his ministry at Urr. To many at the time this decision of the Assembly seemed mistaken leniency: it still appears a wonderful stretch of tolerance.

Nothing daunted or abashed by this experience, Mr Hepburn betook himself to his old ways, and behaved as arbitrarily and eccentrically as before. With his accustomed vehemence and virulence he opposed the union of the Parliaments in 1707; and, five years later, his wrath flamed forth anew on the restoration of patronage in the Church. On the outbreak of the Jacobite Rebellion in 1715, there was naturally some anxiety and speculation as to the course which he would take. His want of affection for the established order of things was so well known, that it was not unreasonable to suspect him of some inclination for a change. True, he was getting old, but the fiery spirit survived, and it was quite within the range of possibility that a man of his temper and manifold grievances might join the insurgent force that Lord Kenmure was raising in Galloway. These suspicions were communicated to Mr Hepburn by a friend, and his reply is extant; in it he repudiates them most warmly for himself and his adherents, disowns the name of Jacobite, and declares his resolution to withstand the Pretender so far as his station and influence would allow. One thing his enemies had omitted from their calculations—his hatred of Popery, and of the principles generally with which the House of Stewart had been identified. This, after all, was a stronger feeling in his mind than dissatisfaction with the existing Government; it asserted itself in the hour of trial, and kept him loyal to the reigning house. The tradition still lingers in the parish of his antipathy to the Roman Catholics, and the rigour with which he treated them. It is even averred that he denied them liberty of burial in the churchyard, and actually exhumed and removed to the confines of the parish, the bodies of such as were surreptitiously interred in his absence. A story is told of an interment that took place while he was from home, which illustrates this point: it is said to have been that of a Roman Catholic, but more probably was that of an Episcopalian. His son, a young lad, was looking on indignantly during the hurried proceedings, and at the words, " a blessed resurrection" in the Burial Service, he could control himself no longer, but burst forth with the angry ejaculation, "I doubt his blessed resurrection, but I am sure he will have a speedy one, if my father were back." Whether this be true or not, it is a fact that he collected among his parishioners all the books that savoured of Popery, and made a bonfire of them on the Corse Hill. Tradition adds the embellishment that he caused the most bigoted Papist in the parish to blow the fire. Evidently to one of his thinking, the return of the Stewarts could be no welcome prospect; on the contrary, the bare possibility of it was enough to stir his Covenanting blood, and rouse him to take the field to prevent it. Things might be bad under the established system, but they were infinitely worse under the old régime which it was proposed to restore; and so he buckled on his sword, and called his parishioners to arms, for the defence of Church and State. Marshalling them, 320 strong, on the hill behind the church, he put them through their drill; then, unfurling his flag, set out with them, a drummer at their head, for Dumfries.

Alarm and excitement prevailed in the town, owing to the persistent rumours afloat of an impending attack on the part of Kenmure and his followers. The burghers, hearing of Hepburn's approach, were not inclined to place too much reliance on his late-born zeal for the existing constitution. While yet a few miles off with his men, they sent to him on 31st October Bailie Gilchrist and the Laird of Bargaly, to ascertain his intentions, and if possible, secure his help in the defence of the town; but the redoubtable Hepburn, true to his crotchets even in this moment of danger, would give them no satisfaction. Probably, though decided enough on the main issue, he was disposed to be a little masterful, now that the tables were turned, and those in authority stood in need of his assistance. At any rate his reply to the deputation was, that he and his people "had no freedom in their conscience to fight in defence of the constitution of Church and State as established since the sinful union." Thereafter he posted his men on Corberry Hill, a strong position on the Galloway side of the old bridge of Dumfries; but, though the Provost himself came out to solicit him, and offered him his choice of posts among the defending forces, he would not come to terms, and steadfastly refused to set foot within the town. There were some, of course, who charged him with deliberately sitting upon the fence, and waiting to see what way the game would go; but the simplest, most probable explanation of his conduct is to be found in his life-long prejudices and cantankerous scruples. The bulk of the inhabitants believed in him, and supplied him amply with provisions; and no doubt, if the occasion had arisen, he would have justified their confidence, and given full proof of his loyalty. The expected attack, however, did not come off; Kenmure avoided Dumfries, and passed hurriedly southward to join the Jacobites in the north of England, his departure, as is well known, inspiring the old song—

"Kenmure's on and awa', Willie!
Kenmure's on and awa';
And Kenmure is the bravest lord
That ever Galloway saw."

There was nothing left for Hepburn but to march his men home again; his flag was furled, and along with the drum laid past in the manse; the drum has disappeared, but the flag still remains, the memorial of his warlike zeal and enterprise.

He lived for eight years after this, but eschewed public affairs, and devoted himself to the duties of his sacred calling. Changing somewhat in his closing days, he became a warm advocate of union and peace. In March, 1723, he passed quietly to his rest. Though almost certainly buried in Urr, no record of his interment is to be found in the churchyard. There may have been a reason for this in the strong antipathy he had aroused amongst the Roman Catholics and Episcopalians. To the south of the church a broken stone commemorates his sister-in-law, Mrs Jean Leslie, who died on 27th January 1700, and his widow, Mrs Emilia Nisbet, who seems to have lived on in the parish, and died on 11th September 1740. She was the daughter of Alexander Nisbet of Craigentinny, and left a son, Mr John Hepburn, who became one of the ministers of Edinburgh, and the grandfather of a Scottish nobleman, through the marriage of his daughter Emilia in 1742 with Daniel Carmichael of Mauldsley, the father of Andrew, sixth Earl of Hyndford. Immediately behind the church, again, there is a stone erected to the memory of his daughter Jean, who married John MacJore, the laird of Cocklick, in 1726, and had a son John, who succeeded his father, and remained in possession of the farm till 1799. There is no mention, however, of Mr Hepburn himself All the other ministers of Urr, from the Revolution downwards, have their appropriate memorial: he, alone, by no means the least worthy, fills a nameless, unremembered grave.

CHAPTER XV

Ministers from 1723 to 1806.

Rev. Christopher Wright 1723-1735

IT was no easy task Mr Christopher Wright essayed, when he ventured upon the pastoral charge of Urr, in succession to Mr Hepburn. The spirit of the late minister lived on in many of the parishioners, and hopelessly divided them from others, who were anxious for a better understanding with the general body and courts of the Church. So far as appears, Mr Wright was painstaking and judicious; but he did not quite succeed in reconciling the contending elements, and the division in the parish eventuated in the formation of a separate congregation, which exists to the present day.

On the occurrence of the vacancy, the Presbytery took what precautions they could to ensure a harmonious settlement. Mr Wright had come into their bounds the year before, as a licensed preacher of the Gospel, with satisfactory testimonials, and in the interval had been teaching the school at Kirkpatrick-Durham. A few Sundays after Mr Hepburn's death, he was appointed to supply the vacant pulpit. The right of pr·sentation, as in other cases where it had formerly vested in the bishops, now belonged to the king; and, on 13th June 1723, the Presbytery instructed their clerk to write to His Majesty's Advocate, asking him to intervene with the king to delay any proposed presentation, till the will of the people should be ascertained. At the same time, two of their number, Mr Hill and Mr Watson, were appointed to repair to Urr, and, after service, to convene and consult the people. The result was that a petition from Urr was laid before the Presbytery, in favour of a call to Mr Christopher Wright, signed by many of the heritors and heads of families. It was noticed, however, that the names of the men who had officiated as elders in Mr Hepburn's time were significantly absent. These afterwards appeared at the Presbytery with a written protest against the call, and a demand for the removal of grievances; but "the paper of objections was found of no import, and intended merely to obstruct the planting of the church." Owing to the long divided state of the parish, the Presbytery had no knowledge whether the objectors were elders or not; and so, disallowing their protest, they approved and concurred in the call. Mr Wright passed his trials satisfactorily; and, though another attempt was made to obstruct procedure after the serving of the edict on the congregation, he was duly ordained and inducted on 24th October. The minister who presided on the occasion took as his text, Acts 20. 24: "None of these things move me, neither count I my life dear unto myself, so that I may finish my course with joy," &c. Mr Wright, however, was in no immediate danger, as he received the hand of fellowship (which was more than a mere form in those days) not only from the Presbytery, but from heritors and heads of families, "as many as could draw near."

It is indicative of the circumstances in which he afterwards found himself, that it was nearly three years before he was able to supply the places of the recusant Kirk Session. On 7th January 1724, he reported to the Presbytery that he had no one to assist him in exercising discipline in the parish, or administering charity to the poor. The Presbytery appointed a committee to help him in obtaining elders, and after prolonged negotiations, six suitable persons were ultimately found willing, and admitted to office. Another matter that involved delicate handling had then to be taken up: the re-allocation of the church seats. This was successfully carried through by the end of 1727. On two occasions Mr Wright was chosen a commissioner from the Presbytery to the General Assembly. In those days, this entailed a long and toilsome journey, and a considerable absence from the parish. Occasionally we have glimpses of him in the Presbytery minutes—now prosecuting a Papist, now complaining of a man guilty of forgery and cheating over a horse. On the whole, he seems to have been an energetic and efficient minister; though his attitude to the new Library House, built and furnished by the Presbytery at Dumfries, requires some explanation. On the face of it, it seems to imply that he was not given to reading; at any rate, on 14th October 1731, the following curious enactment was passed: " Messrs Hill, Miller, Mack, and Wright, who refuse to contribute their proportions for building the said Library House, or supporting the Library, shall in all time coming be excluded from all power in managing the said Library, from all use of books belonging to the same, or benefit otherwise; and all members or others concerned, are hereby discharged to give them in loan any of the Library books, under the pain of half a crown for the first fault, a crown for the second, and the loss of their own privileges for the third fault; and the Library keeper shall be strictly enjoined not to give any of the books out of the Library to any of the recusant brethren, under the penalty of a crown toties quoties." In those days, when there were not so many specifically religious objects to collect for, money was often raised for useful public works, by a general collection throughout the Church, as well as by the appropriation of vacant stipend. Urr seems to have been ready to give its mite on such occasions. On 6th March 1734, Mr Wright reported to the Presbytery that he had collected 6s. 8d. in his parish for the building of a bridge over the Stinchar. It was customary to open the meetings of Presbytery by what were called an exercise and addition: at the November meeting Mr Wright performed this duty, his subject being Hebr. 1. 8: not long afterwards, his brief ministry came to a close. He died on 12th January 1735; no doubt having done what in him lay to assuage the bitterness of feeling in the parish, though without having been able altogether to eradicate it.

How much he suffered from it, and whether it had any effect in shortening his days, we cannot now tell. That it still existed in considerable force, is evident from the fact, that the brethren present at his burial advised the Presbytery again to send a letter to His Majesty's Solicitor in London, asking that no presentation be issued "till the inclinations of the people be known, in respect of the peculiar circumstances of the parish." In the same letter, the Presbytery solicited his interest with the king, to secure for Mrs Wright and her family of five children an additional half-year's stipend. As yet there was no fund in the Church to meet such a case, and something had to be done to assist them in their necessitous situation. Mrs Wright, whose maiden name was Sarah Patoun, afterwards removed to Dumfries, where her father was minister, and taught sewing till her death in October 1747.

Rev. Thomas McKinnell. 1736-1769

Though not so well remembered as other ministers of Urr, Mr Thomas McKinnell was recognised in his day as a man of outstanding energy and ability. Minister of Dunscore before he became minister of Urr, he exerted himself very effectively in improving the parochial equipment in both these charges. For many years he took a large and active interest in the business of the Church courts, officiating as Clerk both to the Presbytery and the Synod. Judging from these facts, and the number of calls he received from parishes within the bounds, he must have been held in high esteem throughout the Presbytery.

Beginning life as an under-teacher in Dumfries, Mr McKinnell afterwards gave himself to the study of divinity, and on 4th April 1721 received a testimonial from the Presbytery, bearing that he had behaved himself becomingly within their bounds, "in which," it is mentioned, "he had been born and bred." Licensed by the Presbytery of Lochmaben in 1722, he received his first call to Dunscore on 11th April

1723. As usual in those days, some opposition was offered from the vacant parish; but, after due consideration, the call was sustained; and, on 27th August 1723, Mr McKinnell was ordained and inducted. The further appointments of Presbytery and Synod Clerk were conferred on him in 1727. Soon after his settlement in Dunscore, he set about extensive repairs upon the church and manse, and had the glebe and stipend properly defined and allocated. As early as 5th September 1727, representatives from Lochrutton appeared before the Presbytery, with a call to him from that parish; it had to be departed from, however, owing to the strong opposition offered, and the attachment evinced for him, by his own parishioners. To keep him amongst them, they voluntarily undertook to increase his stipend from 730 to 800 merks; and, as it was paid in small sums by many hands, the laird of Craigenputtock agreed to save him the trouble of lifting it for seven years. The whole transaction was creditable alike to minister and people. Again, on 20th March 1733, Robert Fferguson, Fourmerkland, Holywood, who claimed to be the patron of Holywood Kirk, appeared before the Presbytery with a presentation in favour of Mr McKinnell; who, however, asked to be excused from an immediate answer to it, on the grounds that " he considered patronage a heavy grievance to the Church, and that the people ought to be consulted." Thereafter a regular call was got up and put into his hands; but the people of Dunscore showed such anxiety to retain him, and entered such strong reasons against his transference, that the matter had to be referred to the Synod, and ultimately fell through. Two years later, the vacancy occurred in Urr, upon the death of Mr Christopher Wright. A delay of six months having taken place, the right of appointment devolved upon the Presbytery. They, however, being satisfied with the orderly procedure so far observed in Urr, agreed to a petition, signed by most of the heritors, all the Kirk Session, and a great many heads of families, asking them to allow a hearing of one or two young men, and meantime themselves to supply the pulpit fortnightly as formerly. Two young men from Penpont—John Dickie and John McNaught—were invited to preach before the congregation; but apparently they did not give satisfaction, for, on 2nd September 1735, another large and influential petition was presented to the Presbytery, desiring them to moderate in a call to Mr Thomas McKinnell. This was duly done, and the call approved, sustained, and put into Mr McKinnell's hands. Again there was serious opposition from the people of Dunscore, and the matter had to be referred once more to the Synod. This time, however, the prosecutors of the call were successful; and by 5th May, 1736, they were in a position to ask the Presbytery "to have Mr McKinnell put into Orr, as arranged by the Synod, as speedily as possible after 15th May, both on his own account, and on account of the long vacancy." His admission accordingly took place on 20th May, Mr Hamilton of Holywood preaching on the occasion from the text, Acts 20. 28.

It was not long till Mr McKinnell began to busy himself in characteristic fashion with the church property of his new parish. Early in 1738, he reported to the Presbytery that the manse and offices of Urr were in a ruinous condition, and asked them to make a visitation and inspection of them. After considerable delay, and many negotiations, in which he seems generally to have had the sympathy and support of the heritors, a new manse was built and occupied in 1743. Seven years afterwards, he took action in regard to the church, and, with the hearty co-operation of the heritors, soon had a new one erected. About the same time, as a matter of necessity no less than right, he called upon the Presbytery to allocate him a peat moss for fuel, which was accordingly done; the piece of ground selected, as most contiguous to the manse, being on the farm of Tarscrechan, now Torcatrine. Apart from these ecclesiastical concerns, he seems to have been plentiful in labours for the moral and spiritual welfare of the people, and indefatigable in discharging his duties as a member of Presbytery. The frequent references to him in the Presbytery minutes attest the interest he took in the general business of the Church, and the zeal with which he watched over the backslidings and defections of his flock. In 1756, he was a commissioner to the General Assembly. In the same year, an alarm of invasion by the French was raised throughout the country, and the Presbytery arranged to meet in parties for prayer, and exhorted the people to do the same. In accordance with this arrangement, the ministers of Kirkpatrick-Durham and Kirkgunzeon met with Mr McKinnell in the manse of Urr. As time went on, his pastoral cares seem to have grown upon him, and absorbed, if they did not exceed, his failing energies. He resigned the dual clerkship in the Church courts, "on account of his distance from the Presbytery and Synod seats, and the exacting demands of his large and populous parish." A custom of the time was to hold what were called privy censures at some of the meetings of the Presbytery: that is to say, the brethren convened in private, before entering upon the ordinary business, and examined each other as to the zeal and faithfulness with which they were discharging their duties. On two occasions Mr McKinnell had to report that he had omitted the annual dispensation of the Lord's Supper: once, "because of his uneasiness of body;" and, at another time, "because of his lateness in coming home from the General Assembly, and an engagement to assist a neighbour." Of course, in those days, the celebration of the ordinance was a vastly different matter from what it is now; it involved elaborate preparations, and was attended by a large concourse of people from surrounding districts. We are reminded of this, when Mr McKinnell adds, by way of further excusing himself, that "it having been dispensed in several neighbouring congregations, such of his people as desired it had opportunity to partake; and that he is determined to have it observed at home with the first convenience." His later years were darkened by domestic afflictions, which he is said to have borne with exemplary patience. He continued in the faithful discharge of his duties almost to the very end, preaching to his people only a few days before he entered into his rest. He died on New Year's Day 1769, aged over seventy years. He was twice married; first, on 11th March 1724, to Euphan, daughter of Andrew Broun of Boghead, who bore him two sons and two daughters, Andrew, Robert, Margaret, and Janet, and who died on 17th September 1739; and, again, on 9th June 1748, to Janet Gordon, by whom he had one son, Alexander. There is a stone in the churchyard to the memory of the former; but the latter, who survived him, and died on 14th September 1784, was probably buried elsewhere.

Rev. James Muirhead, D.D. 1770-1806

The next incumbent of Urr was essentially "the scholar and the gentleman." He belonged to one of the leading families of the neighbourhood—the Muirheads of Crochmore in Irongray, who were closely related to the Irvings of Logan in Buittle, and claimed descent from the Muirheads of Muirhead and Lachope in Clydesdale, one of whom, Andrew de Muirhead, at an early period, had been Bishop of Glasgow. It is probable that James Muirhead, merchant in Dumfries, who presented to the church of Urr in 1735 the two silver communion cups, still in use though recast, was a connection of the same family.

Born in 1741, Dr. James Muirhead had every advantage in the way of upbringing. His early days were spent in the vicinity of the parish to which he was afterwards called to minister; his later education was received in Edinburgh, where he studied at the University, and associated with some of the leading men of that remarkable time. Edinburgh, in the latter half of the eighteenth century, was in great renown, not only as a place of fashionable resort, but as a centre of literary and scientific activity; and young Muirhead seems to

THE REV. JAMES MUIRHEAD, D.D.
FROM A PAINTING IN THE POSSESSION OF HIS GREAT-GRANDSON, COLONEL FINDLAY.

have felt all the charm and fascination of its life, and thrown himself with zest into its cultured society. Among the men whom he had the privilege of knowing were David Hume, Principal Robertson, Dr. Drysdale, Dr. John Brown, and Dr. Blair; and, as he himself afterwards told Dr. Murray, his successor in Urr, "he was the bosom companion of Gilbert Stuart, Mr Naysmith, Mr Smellie, and the club which wrote in the Edinburgh Magazine and Review." He did some literary work himself, beginning with articles in the Review and in some of the London periodicals that course of occasional writing, which he continued throughout his life.

For a while he seems to have hesitated in his choice of a profession. Of strong physique and active habits, he thought at first of entering the army; but soon abandoning that idea, he took to the study of the law, to which probably the bent of his mind inclined him. Ultimately, however, he decided to enter the Church; and, as Urr became vacant soon after the completion of his course of training, he received in 1770 the presentation to that parish. The appointment was not altogether acceptable to the parishioners; but his strong personality, sound learning, and quaint humour, soon reconciled them to it. As Dr. Murray expressed it in his funeral sermon to the people of Urr: "His entrance among you was made under particular disadvantages. The assertion of experience—the assertion of our Saviour Himself—that a prophet is of no honour in his own country, he found to be true. Brought up amongst themselves almost from his childhood, in the neighbourhood of a parish so divided in religious sentiments and opinions, he had to struggle with a variety of prejudices, which he at last so thoroughly overcame, that I have only to appeal to yourselves—to the esteem in which you held him—to the place which he obtained in your affections—for the truth of the assertion." There is no doubt of the sound qualifications he possessed for the ministry, and the faithfulness with which he discharged the duties of his office. Endowed with much native ability, he had received an education, and enjoyed an experience, superior to the generality of those who at that time embraced the sacred profession. He had seen a good deal of the world; he had associated with all sorts and conditions of men; consequently, he had a keen insight into human nature, and a sound judgment in practical affairs. He was deeply versed in the Classics, and in other branches of learning; and during his incumbency of Urr he not only continued to cultivate his gifts, and extend his acquirements, but studied to make them both subservient to the purposes of his sacred calling. His preaching was plain and practical; he discharged his other duties, "with cool, calm, unassuming, and regular steadiness." His early skill in the laws of his country enabled him to be of great service to his parishioners, in the way of composing their differences, in an age when legal advice was difficult to obtain, and legal redress uncertain. The minute book of his time testifies to the scrupulous regularity with which he disbursed the poor funds at his disposal. As there was no poor rate, these consisted almost entirely of church collections, which on ordinary Sundays ranged from two to ten shillings, though at Communion time, when the services extended over several days, there might be a total drawing of two or three pounds. The number of poor persons requiring relief seems to have averaged about nine or ten; so that the sum awarded to each of them rarely exceeded a guinea per annum. This, however, would go further in those days than it does now; it seems also to have been considerably augmented by private charity. More might, perhaps, have been done for the poor, but for the amount of bad money which in Urr, as elsewhere throughout Scotland at this time, found its way into the collections. On 3rd July 1786, there is an entry in the Session book to the effect that £1 10s. had been received for bad brass in the Kirk box. The rule being that marriages and baptisms should be performed in presence of the congregation, and a small fine levied on those who had them done elsewhere, as well as a fee of eight pence charged for registration in the Session book, there resulted a slight addition to the income, which was still further increased by fines imposed in certain cases of discipline.

While engaged in the work of his parish, Dr. Muirhead pursued his scholarly studies to such purpose as to gain for himself a considerable reputation, as well as the degree of Doctor of Divinity, in 1796, from his old University. Most of his literary productions, however, have either disappeared in the pages of defunct magazines, or, having been written merely for private perusal and amusement, exist only in manuscript form. His best known piece is a poem called "Bess the Gawkie," which has been reprinted in the "Bards of Galloway." There is also extant a clever translation by him from Martial's ode "Ad Vacerram." The statistical account of the parish, too, contained in Sinclair's great work of 1794, is by his hand. In it he makes many interesting observations on the life of his time, while he also exhibits the shrewdness of his judgment on passing events, by his reflections, for instance, on the effects of the political and religious disturbances of the past on the development of the country, and his arguments for a more liberal educational policy, and the removal of an oppressive coal tax. That he possessed a keen sense of humour is apparent from many of his compositions; but, still more, from the numerous stories which tradition has gathered around his name. Some of them may be open to doubt, but the fact that they are attributed to him argues at least a known compatibility with his character. An intimate friend of Dr. Muirhead was George Cairns, the laird of Kipp, of whom many humorous stories are told, and who is described on his tombstone in Urr churchyard, as "one of the most original and eccentric characters of the eighteenth century." It is said that, on one occasion, he was spending the day at the manse of Urr, and Dr. Muirhead took him down the glebe, and challenged him to catch his pony. The timid beast, however, would not allow Cairns to approach it; so the minister scoffingly remarked that he would require the assistance of his boy. "See, how it comes to him," said the Doctor, "while it flees from the laird of Kipp." "That's easily explained," said his friend, "ae beast, of coorse, kens anither." One of the best stories about Dr. Muirhead concerns his relations with the inevitable minister's man. For some time the person who fulfilled that function in his establishment had severely tried his patience by his frequent omissions and delinquencies; so one day he informed him he would require to dispense with his services. "I'm na gaw'n withoot a testimonial," said the recalcitrant beadle; "ye're bund tae gi'e me a testimonial." "Maybe," said the minister; "but you had better not insist on it." He did insist on it, however; so they both retired to the study, and the minister proceeded to draw up the document required. He wrote on for such a length of time, that at last the beadle interrupted him with the remark; "I'm sure there's na need for a' that writin'." "Wait a bit," was the reply; "I must tell all you've done, since you came to me, and I have not got yet to the story about the geese you stole from Halmyre." Another anecdote may be given, as illustrative of his method of dealing out justice to his litigious parishioners. Two men came to him with a dispute about a gun. The one had sold it to the other, under a guarantee of its capabilities; but the purchaser asserted that, after many trials, he could not get it to shoot. "Let me see it," said the minister; and he took it in his hand, and began leisurely to prime it. "Now," said he to the complainer, when he had finished, "stand you against that tree, and I'll fire the gun at you, and we'll see if it will go off." "O no," said the other, "I would not care to risk that." "Indeed," said Dr. Muirhead, "then you think after all that the gun may shoot; I am afraid you have not the courage of your convictions; you had better pay the man his money and be gone."

The Doctor's humour was not always of the most agreeable type; occasionally it took the form, especially in his writings, of clever, caustic irony, that spared neither friend nor foe. During the heat of an election, he had a sharp passage of arms with the poet Burns, in which the latter had rather the worse of the encounter. The poet began it by lampooning the minister in an election ballad—

> " Here's armorial bearings
> Frae the manse of Orr,
> The crest, an auld crab apple,
> Rotten at the core."

Dr. Muirhead replied in a severe and biting epigram, which cut Burns to the quick, and wrung from him an angry retort. Only once before, perhaps, in the poetical epistle from a tailor, had the bard been subjected to such satirical treatment. Even a practical joke was not beneath the consideration and enjoyment of Dr. Muirhead. On one occasion, it is said, to embarrass his neighbour, Dr. Lamond of Kirkpatrick-Durham, he invited himself and a number of his friends to pay a surprise visit, at dinner time, to that worthy's manse. The available supplies consisted almost entirely of a fowl, which the housekeeper, Babby, had prepared for Dr. Lamond's own meal. The company sitting down to make the most of it, Dr. Muirhead was called upon to say grace, when he delivered himself somewhat to the following effect: " Lord, grant Thy blessing upon this humble and solitary fowl. Make it even as the five loaves and two fishes—enough for us all—with a few fragments left over for Babby."

The stipend of Urr, in Dr. Muirhead's day, was £83 6s. 8d., with an allowance of £5 for communion elements. However it may have been with him in the earlier part of his career, towards its close he came into the enjoyment of considerable affluence. In 1800, he succeeded, through his relationship with the Irvings, to the property of East Logan; and about the same time, by deed of entail of Mr Michael Herries, the estate of Spottes came into the possession of his eldest son, who assumed the name of his benefactor, and was known thereafter as William Muirhead Herries. Shortly afterwards, Dr. Muirhead removed with his family to Spottes Hall; continuing, however, in the performance of his ministerial duties till 1806, when he obtained the services of an assistant and successor. He died on 16th May 1808. He was succeeded in the Logan property by his second son, Charles Herries Muirhead. This gentleman and his brother, the laird of Spottes, died within a few days of each other, the one on the 6th, and the other on the 15th March, 1823. Their mother, who had been Jean Loudon before her marriage to Dr. Muirhead in 1777, survived till 2nd December 1825. A daughter married Robert Skirving of Croys, and became the mother of the late Adam Skirving, whose daughter, the present proprietrix of Croys, is thus the great-granddaughter of Dr. Muirhead.

CHAPTER XVI

Rev Alexander Murray, D.D. 1806-1813

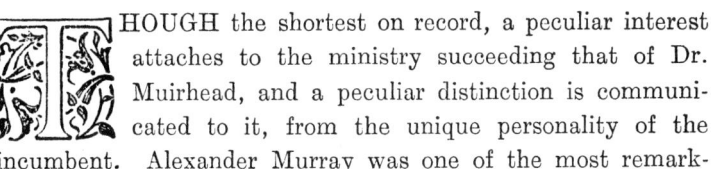

THOUGH the shortest on record, a peculiar interest attaches to the ministry succeeding that of Dr. Muirhead, and a peculiar distinction is communicated to it, from the unique personality of the incumbent. Alexander Murray was one of the most remarkable men of his time. Born in the humblest circumstances, without other advantages than the genius and power of work with which nature had endowed him, he made his way during his short-lived career into the foremost ranks of contemporary scholarship, and achieved a phenomenal reputation. His life has been so often written that it is unnecessary here to do more than recapitulate its leading facts.

His father was a shepherd upon the "led" farm of Dunkitterick, half-way down the wild glen that leads from New Galloway to Newton Stewart. Here the future scholar first saw the light on 22nd October 1775. From the narrow means of his parents, and the remote situation of his home, his early life was attended with considerable asperities and privations, with which, as a naturally weak child, and short-sighted, he was ill fitted to cope. Especially was the road to knowledge, for which he soon evinced a thirst, blocked with unusual difficulties. His letters he learnt from the board of an old woolcard, on which his father used to draw them, with a piece of burnt wood or heather stem from the fire. In this primitive way he was taught to read and write; and to such purpose that, before he was nine years old, he became so proficient in the Bible and Shorter Catechism as to astonish the neighbours in the glen. For a few months in 1784, he attended school in New Galloway, staying with his grandfather; but, his health breaking down, he had reluctantly to return home. It was four years before he saw school again. Meanwhile he was occupied assisting the rest of the family in the work of the farm: at the same time reading voraciously whatever he could beg, borrow, or buy, as he watched the sheep on the hillside, or sat by the fire at night. For a short time during the winter of 1787-8, he taught some children in Kirkcowan parish. In May 1789, his father (who must have been nearly eighty-five years of age, for he was seventy when Alexander was born) removed from Dunkitterick to Drigmorn, only four miles from Minnigaff, where he had engaged as herd. This gave his son the opportunity of attending Minnigaff school, which at that time was under the care of Mr Cramond, one of the learned old pedagogues of former days. Here, and in a night school at Newton Stewart, he applied himself with such diligence, as not only to acquire a large amount of general knowledge, but also to lay, in the Classics, a solid foundation for that wonderful linguistic scholarship which he afterwards exhibited. His attendances at these schools stretched over four years, but were mostly confined to the brief period between Whitsunday and vacation; still, with these limited opportunities, he managed to gain a fairly accurate knowledge of French, Latin, Greek, German, and Hebrew, besides a passing acquaintance with Arabic, Abyssinian, Anglo-Saxon, and Welsh. Having tried his hand at verse, he travelled to Dumfries, and submitted some of his productions to the poet Burns, but was not encouraged to proceed with their publication. His talents, however, becoming widely known, a successful effort was made to get him entered as a student at Edinburgh University; where, from the first, by the extent and accuracy of his knowledge, he elicited considerable interest among his teachers, and gained the friendship of the Principal, Dr. Baird.

His course in Arts extended over five sessions, during four of which he attended a class in Greek, but only in one was a member of the Latin class. His previous proficiency in the

REV. ALEXANDER MURRAY, D.D.   257

Latin language probably obviated the necessity of further pursuing its study. Few students in those days took the M.A. degree, so that it is no disparagement of Murray's classical or philosophical attainments that, in 1797, he passed into the Divinity Hall, without possessing himself of that distinction.

Besides the names of the professors under whom he studied, little is known of his career in the Divinity Hall, owing to the fact that existing records only go back to the year 1830. Part of his time in winter, and, except for a holiday of a month or two, the whole of the summer vacations, seem to have been occupied in private teaching; young men, purposing

Eastern travel or employment, resorting to him for initiation into Persian, Arabic, Hindustani, and other languages. His close residence in Edinburgh brought him under the jurisdiction of the Metropolitan Presbytery, from whom he accordingly received his licence to preach on 14th April 1802. He was in no hurry, however, to undertake ministerial work: the bent of his mind was literary: and so, for four years he devoted himself to what work of that kind came to his hand. During the first six months, he held the editorship of the Scots Magazine, a position in which he was preceded by the well-known scholar, John Leyden, a man of tastes and acquirements kindred to his own. Thereafter he was invited by the publisher, Constable, to bring out a new edition of Bruce's "Travels in Abyssinia," the copyright of which had been secured from the traveller's son. For nearly a year he resided with the Bruce family at Kinnaird House in Stirlingshire, consulting and collating the manuscript notes and journals, that were supplied to him in profusion. His editing was characterised by such painstaking care and unusual erudition, that the publication of the work in 1805 brought him into considerable notice among scholars, and gained him admission into several learned societies. His life of Bruce, at first issued along with the travels, and afterwards published in a volume by itself, still further increased his fame.

Mr Murray was thus a man of established reputation when he returned to his native Galloway in June 1806, to take up the pastoral charge of Urr. The presentation was in the gift of the Crown, and was secured for him by the exertion of friends, the most active of whom was William Douglas, of Orchardton, afterwards a noted Eastern traveller. He had been a pupil of Murray's in Edinburgh, and had conceived so strong an attachment to him that, when Dr. Muirhead of Urr applied for an assistant and successor, he set himself to secure for him the appointment. The application to the Crown having been successful, and the consent of the retiring minister readily obtained, Murray travelled through to Urr in June, accompanied by another friend, Mr William Muirhead Herries of Spottes, the eldest son of Dr. Muirhead. In November, after several months' experience of his ministrations, a call was moderated among the people, and signed by all the heads of families in the parish. "If the day had been favourable," he says in one of his letters, "it would have been signed by everybody who can write, for there is not a single person in the place who has not declared for me, so that no call was ever more unanimous."

Considering the opportunities the people had had of hearing him preach before calling him, we may conclude that his manner in the pulpit was pleasing and effective. This would be somewhat of a surprise to his friends, who knew him only as a scholar, "timid, gentle, and reserved," whose style of speech in common conversation hardly did justice to his understanding. The exercise of preaching, however, must have developed in him a gift of fluent, as well as attractive discourse; for on occasion, as he himself records, he was able to hold the attention of the people for two hours, in a service lasting for three hours and a quarter. Part of this effect must doubtless be ascribed to the interesting and edifying matter which a preacher of his proved abilities and scholarly attainments would have at his command. There is every reason to believe that he was equally painstaking and profitable in the pastoral work of the parish, which at that time would be no light burden, as the old system of periodical catechising was still in force, and the population numbered between two and three thousand. For some time after his induction, Mr Murray, being only assistant and successor to Dr. Muirhead, resided with his uncle, William Cochrane, a farmer in the parish; but, after the death of the aged minister in May 1808, he entered into full possession of the benefice, and in December following was married to Henrietta Affleck, the daughter of the farmer in Grange. A new manse was soon afterwards provided for them, but it was not to be their fortune long to occupy it.

Whatever spare time he had was given up to his favourite literary pursuits; and it is truly surprising how much he was able to accomplish in this line, amidst the cares of family and social life, and the duties of a large and exacting parish. Besides reviews, articles, and translations, he laid plans, and gathered materials, for a large and exhaustive history of Galloway, which involved the personal inspection of many ancient ruins and places of interest. In March 1811, an incident occurred, which shews the estimation in which his knowledge of Eastern countries and their languages was held, as well as its uniqueness at the time. A letter was received by the British Government from the King of Abyssinia, written in his own language, which the Foreign Office, then under the charge of the Marquis Wellesley, the brother of the Duke of Wellington, had difficulty in finding any one to decipher. They were advised to send it to the manse of Urr; and, in a few days, Mr Murray translated and returned it. After his death, this service was remembered by the Government, and handsomely recompensed to his widow. His chief literary occupation, however, during his ministry in Urr, was the composition of his great work on "The History of European Languages." The first prospectus of it was issued in 1808, and it was intended to be published within two or three years thereafter; but, from various causes, chiefly from the ill-health of the author, the writing of it was protracted, and it was not finished till he left Urr for Edinburgh in 1812. His death supervened so quickly upon that event, that there was no time to bring out the book, and it lay in manuscript till 1823, when it was edited and published, with a memoir, by Rev. Sir Harry Wellwood Moncrieff, D.D. It is a work of great originality and profound erudition, anticipating many of the discoveries of the philologists of later years, and giving him a claim to a permanent place in the history of linguistic Science. It is enough here, by way of suggesting its nature and scope, to quote his own account of it. "I examine, in the First Part, the history of our own language, and the Teutonic in all its branches, from its origin, adverting to those general laws by which the parts of it were produced; in the Second Part, I apply the laws to the Greek, Latin, Sanskrit, Persic, Slavonic, and Celtic, concluding with a sketch of the rules by which philological research should be conducted, and extended to all the languages of the earth."

On 8th July 1812, after a keen contest, he was elected to the chair of Oriental Languages in Edinburgh University: at the same time the degree of Doctor of Divinity was conferred upon him. On 31st October, without as yet demitting the pastoral charge of Urr, he began his professorial duties. A hitherto unpublished letter, written at this time to one of the elders, Mr John Coltart, in Milton of Urr, and preserved in the family, is interesting for its bearing upon the circumstances. " Urr, Novr. 9th 1812. . . . . Dear Sir, ... As I am about to leave the Parish for a few months, I think it proper to inform you of this, and to request that you will be so kind as to give a short line to any member of the Congregation, entitled to privileges, that he may shew the same to any of my brethren nearest to him, and receive performance of the duty required. I have asked Messrs Cavet, Roddick, and Black to do the same, but I have given no order to our *Ruling* Elder, as he might again bring us into scandal. You know my health has for two years past been too infirm for doing the duties of this large and populous Parish. I have therefore determined to leave it, and I have accepted a place of less value in a worldly sense, but having less labour, and in which I hope with the divine assistance to do much good to the Church in general. Having got this place, I would have resigned the Parish before now, but this would have been unjust to my family that depends upon me. At no great distance of time I will give up my charge here, and I earnestly wish that it may fall into the hands of an able and religious minister. Of this there is a considerable prospect at present. As Mr Poole has undertaken to preach for me till I return, I believe that the parish will be satisfied with his doctrine. He is a fine scholar, and always preaches in an evangelical and practical way. It is no difficulty for him to give a discourse, and he is indeed well qualified for instructing a pious and unaffected audience. Affectation of fine discourses without force or feeling prevails far too much among many that go by the name of Christians. I have to acknowledge your kind and friendly countenance since I came into this parish. It has been agreeable to me, for I have always desired the friendship of good and sincere men, however far they may be from the noise of the times and the ways of the world. I have found many friends in a rank of life in which some would have been proud to find them, but to have well-wishers among those who neither will encourage vanity nor neglect duty is a blessing in any situation high or low. Let us then be thankful to God, who gives us the sure promise of eternal life through Jesus Christ, that He prepares us for that state by many mercies. Though affliction, decay, and death must be the portion of us all, our heavenly Father has not left any that believe in Him without comfort. Though our lot in this world may be very various, our condition is never forlorn, when we reflect on the good which He enables us to do for one another, and on the union by which all that love righteousness and truth are bound together. The day will at last come when no weakness of ours will remain to divide us from one another, or delay that perfection through which all shall be one in Christ. I am, with best wishes for your eternal welfare, My Dear Sir, Your very obedt. friend and servant, Alexr. Murray."

Unfortunately he was not destined to have a long tenure of office in Edinburgh. At the outset, he threw himself with enthusiasm into the work of his class, and prepared a small handbook for their use, entitled "Outlines of Oriental Philology." This was an abridgment of an earlier work, published

REV. ALEXANDER MURRAY, D.D.

twelve years before, "Principles of Oriental Grammar." Besides the ordinary work of teaching the rudiments of Hebrew, and reading the Old Testament with his students, he initiated a course of lectures upon more general subjects of Oriental and Biblical interest, which many outside of his class attended. His activity, however, was to be short-lived: the disease that had threatened him for years began rapidly to develop: pneumonia supervened upon consumption: and, before the end of the session, he was no more. His wife, who had remained at Urr, was sent for, but did not arrive till two days after his death, which took place on 15th April 1813. He was buried in Greyfriars' Churchyard; "close to the wall, on the north-west corner of the church." The Government conferred a pension of £80 a year upon his widow, "as a public acknowledgment of her husband's merits." She seems to have survived him about ten or twelve years. Dr. Murray left also two children, a boy and a girl. The latter died early, probably taking after her father in bodily constitution. The former, inheriting many of his mental gifts, was spared to manhood. Qualifying for the medical profession, he shipped as surgeon on board the Elizabeth, a merchant vessel trading to China, Quebec, and other places, but perished by shipwreck on his first voyage. He was deeply mourned by many affectionate friends, who, for his father's sake as well as for his own, were keenly interested in his career.

Two monuments have been erected to the memory of the great linguist by his admiring countrymen, especially in the south. The first, which is an obelisk of granite, rising to a height of seventy feet, stands upon a hill beside Dunkitterick, the place of his birth. The foundation stone was laid on 21st June 1834, with much ceremony, and amid a vast concourse of people of all classes gathered from the country round about. It was finished the following year, all but the inscription, which was added in 1877. In that year, also, a smaller, but handsome and well-proportioned monument, adapted to its surroundings, was raised over his burial place in Greyfriars' Churchyard. It, too, is of Galloway granite, and stands seventeen feet high. The feeling that prompted these tributes to his memory is worthy of all praise. Dr. Murray well deserves to be gratefully remembered: for his high gifts, his nobility of character, his strenuous and fruitful labours, and the encouragement to perseverance, even in the most adverse circumstances, that may be derived from the story of his life.

CHAPTER XVII

MINISTERS FROM 1813 TO 1909

REV. JOHN MCWHIR. 1813-1835

DR. MURRAY'S successor in Urr was a considerable contrast to himself: a man of action rather than letters: yet able and noteworthy in his own way. Possessed of clear and strong convictions, and endowed with an almost masterful firmness of disposition, he administered parochial affairs with a shrewdness, capability, and zeal, that have passed into a local tradition.

Mr John McWhir began his ministerial life as minister of the Chapel of Ease, Dunfermline, where he was ordained in 1810. Three years later he was transferred to Urr, his admission taking place on 7th October 1813. His career in Urr is simply a record of faithful and painstaking service. In his manse, it is said, he showed a love of orderliness and method, amounting almost to a passion. Anything out of place annoyed him: the routine of the day was definite and inviolable: at night he could not retire to rest, without personally satisfying himself that everything was shipshape and snug. It was this kind of spirit he carried into his parish work. Nothing escaped his notice: he was constantly employed putting things to rights: his hand was felt everywhere, exercising discipline, restraining laxity, maintaining and strengthening the parochial organisation and equipment. His first care was to get a new church built—the present church—which was opened for public worship in the autumn of 1815. At the same time a new set of communion tokens was obtained; and, later on, in 1823, the communion plate was overhauled and additions made to it. Throughout his ministry, he took particular pains with the administration of the Poor Funds, holding frequent meetings with his Kirk Session for their careful calculation and division. The church-door collections were still devoted to the support of the poor; but, as they were no longer sufficient for the growing demands upon them, Mr McWhir and his elders kept a sharp look-out upon other sources of revenue. Some arrears from Dr. Muirhead's time had remained in the hands of his executors: these were called in, and on 1st October 1815, the minutes record that "Mr W. M. Herries, for himself and brothers, gave the session an obligatory letter for £41, in respect of same; and the session record their approval of the honourable conduct and integrity of the Spottes family." A claim seems also to have been made on Dr. Murray's representatives; for, on 1st January, 1815, there was paid into the Treasurer's hands a sum of £6, "being a donation by the late Rev. Dr. Murray in aid of the poor, and as compensation for a collection lost, owing to the omission of the sacrament in the year the manse was building, with £1 as four years' interest." A sum of £100 had been left by Mr Michael Herries of Spottes in 1796, for behoof of the poor; this having been drawn upon in various emergencies, it was now decided to lift what remained of it from the Galloway Bank, make it up again to the original sum, and lodge it in the Bank of Scotland under Government security. Voluntary contributions to the Poor Funds were solicited from the leading heritors, and considerable sums were received from such men as Mr Thomas C. Stothart of Blaiket, Mr John Maxwell of Munches, and Mr W. M. Herries of Spottes. When all these sources failed to provide the requisite supplies, a full meeting of heritors was called.

The moral and spiritual welfare of the parish received the same minute attention and careful handling from Mr McWhir. Three months after his induction, in accordance with an old Act of Assembly (1648) the parish was divided into eight districts, over each of which an elder was appointed, who was expected to supervise the life and character of the people under his charge, and report to the Kirk Session any serious case that required their intervention. This duty seems to have been scrupulously performed, with the result, at least, that an interesting sidelight is occasionally thrown in the minutes upon the social condition of the parish. On 18th January 1818, there is such a bad report of the conduct of the people in Springholm, that a special inquiry is ordered. On 2nd March 1822, regret is expressed at the absence of many members from church, except at communion time, or when they want a child baptised, and it is agreed that the moderator should intimate from the pulpit, that these ordinances in future will be refused to such persons. On 21st September 1828, there are complaints of disorderly lodging-houses, and of the number of sturdy vagrants and strolling beggars infesting the parish, and it is resolved to make representations to the proprietors on the subject. On 9th August 1829, the lodging-houses in Dalbeattie are reported to be badly conducted, and three elders are deputed to investigate the matter. On 19th April 1830, the Session, having to certify applications for licence to sell ale and spirits, deplore the vice and drunkenness of the district, hope for the lessening of the number of licensed houses, and call upon the civil power and the constabulary to watch and punish offenders. On 3rd April 1831, certain persons are dealt with, who had come to the parish, and not produced their certificates of character, though requisitioned from the pulpit to do so. The discipline was strict in those days; and as individual offenders were numerous, the investigation and judgment of their cases entailed considerable labour on Mr McWhir and his Kirk Session. On occasions they sat for days together, exercising their judicial functions. There was no respect of persons with them, nor any narrow limit to the offences with which they dealt. The precentor in his box was no more secure than the man in the pew: even the elder had to submit to the judgment and rebuke of his brethren in the Session: and it was not flagrant moral faults alone of which notice was taken, but such milder delinquencies as swearing, Sabbath-breaking, quarrelling, and failure to attend church or take communion. The penitent had still to appear on several Sundays before the congregation, and suffer public rebuke from the minister; though signs begin to appear of a prospective change in this respect. In two instances recorded, one on 1st July 1830, and another on 3rd February 1833, the rule is departed from, and the rebuke administered by the moderator in presence of the Kirk Session only. It is distinctly stated, however, in the minutes, that these cases are not to be taken as precedents; but it happened with them, as with other relaxations of ancient customs; what at first were exceptions going to prove the rule, ultimately themselves became the rule.

In matters relating strictly to the church and its services, Mr McWhir was equally painstaking and conscientious. The Kirk Session was kept up to its full strength, by the prompt filling up of vacancies. A Treasurer was appointed to relieve the Session clerk of all responsibility for the funds, his remuneration to be a commission of four per cent. "on all poor money hereafter." The proclamation fees were twice revised: on the first occasion, they were fixed at 3s. 6d., when both parties belonged to the parish, and 4s. when one of them resided elsewhere: on the second occasion at 4s. for three Sabbaths, and £1 for one. The precentor was given a choice of salary, to begin with; either he might have a fixed sum of £5 per annum, or £1 10s. and the proclamation fees; but afterwards, perhaps because the income from proclamations showed signs of increasing, it was decided that he was not to get these fees, but a fixed salary of five guineas. The church officer's emoluments were also defined with scrupulous exactitude: on 19th November 1826, he complained of his small pay, and the Session, "considering he still uplifts corn from seatholders for cleaning their seats, decreed him 40s. a year, but he is to lose the sixpences he has hitherto had for each baptism." Everything about the church, as about the manse, received

Mr McWhir's personal attention, even the communion tent and benches being repaired under his supervision, and a wooden house erected in which to store them. The sacrament was still celebrated in the open air. One other matter may be mentioned, for its own peculiarity, and also as an instance of the excessive zeal with which Mr McWhir carried on his work. The minute of 5th June 1831 chronicles the appointment of several persons as deacons in the congregation. This is the only notice of such an appointment ever having been made in Urr; and, in point of law, a deacon's court forms no part of the constitution of the Church.

In these multifarious labours, he seems to have worn himself out, at a comparatively early age. Probably, too, he would have considerable worries and anxieties, as his strictness would no doubt raise animosity, and even hatred, against him, in some quarters. There is, indeed, a strong local tradition to the effect that he was shot at one evening, by a Roman Catholic, on his way home from Dalbeattie. In the spring of 1834, his health began to break down, and the Rev. Robert Kirkwood of Holywood was appointed temporary moderator of the Kirk Session. At the meeting on the 11th January 1835, Mr McWhir moderated himself, but it was for the last time. A pathetic note at the bottom of the minute records that " the moderator, from bodily weakness, is confined to his bed in a very frail state, and is unable to sign the minute." The strenuous rule was nearing its close: the rod was falling from the failing hand. He died on 8th February 1835, in the sixtieth year of his age. He was the author of A Doctrinal Catechism, and Some Forms of Family Prayer, which were published at Dumfries in 1815.

Mr McWhir's wife, whom he married on 10th December 1813, was Jean, daughter of Mr Alexander Fraser, S.S.C., Edinburgh. They had a family of four: a son, who qualified as a medical man, and died in Bengal, four years after his father, at the early age of twenty-three; and three daughters, of whom one died in infancy, another, Alison, married the Rev. Thomas D. Nicholson, Scotch Church, Nelson, New Zealand, and another, Amelia, married Mr James Mure, writer, Edinburgh.

REV. GEORGE M. BURNSIDE. 1837-1855

The death of Mr McWhir occurred at a critical time in the ecclesiastical life of the country. For years, patronage had been a bone of contention; and now, there was a large and growing party in the Church committed to its abolition. At any cost, they were determined to secure for the people a voice in the appointment of their own ministers; and, as Parliament showed no disposition to move in the matter, they took action themselves, and carried a measure through the General Assembly of 1834, called the Veto Act, which claimed the right for the Church to prevent the intrusion of any pastor upon a congregation against the will of the people, and declared null and void any presentation to which the majority of the parishioners objected. A plentiful crop of litigation immediately ensued: patrons continued to present: the people objected: the presbyteries upheld their objections: the presentee appealed to the secular courts, and they had no alternative but to support the patron in the exercise of his legal right. The result was to accentuate the strife, and precipitate the catastrophe of the Free Church Secession of 1843.

The coincidence of the vacancy in Urr with this state of matters was unfortunate for the parish. Such wrangling and division took place as prevented the settlement of a minister for over two years. A presentation by the Crown was duly made out and submitted to the people, but almost exactly the half of them cast their votes against it. Delays and interventions by the presbytery followed, in the midst of which some supporters of the presentee, Rev. W. Wallace Duncan, died, leaving his opponents in a slight, though clear majority. To save further trouble he beat an honourable retreat; and

THE REV. GEORGE M. BURNSIDE.
FROM A PORTRAIT BY JOHN ALEXANDER.

the presentation resigned by him was ultimately conferred upon Rev. George M. Burnside who was inducted into Urr in 1837. He was the son of the Rev. Cunningham Burnside of Dunscore, and had already been minister of Terregles for fourteen years.

Evidently the opposition to him, also, had been somewhat keen; for, at the first meeting of the Kirk Session after his induction, two elders, James Black and James Copland, and one deacon, Dougald McLaurin, tendered their resignations. The deacons inaugurated by Mr McWhir still continued to meet with the Kirk Session, but disappeared, with the abolition of their office, in 1844. Another elder, William Stothart of Cargen, resigned office shortly afterwards, but whether that had anything to do with the new appointment does not appear. With the help of a shrewd and kindly nature, however, and his considerable experience, Mr Burnside soon lived down any antipathy that may have met him in the parish, and made himself acceptable to all classes of the people. His goodness of heart is still vividly remembered: he could refuse nothing, even articles of clothing he required himself, to the poor: he encouraged innocent mirth, and was tempted into song himself upon occasion: he entered sympathetically alike into the joys and sorrows of his people. Over the canopy of his pulpit there was a gilt dove, bearing an olive leaf in its mouth: this once attracted the attention of a half-witted individual, who, when the congregation were all gathered, waiting for the minister, insisted on flapping his coat and crowing to it, until he was put outside. On the morning of the Disruption, it is said, the olive leaf was found dropped upon the ground. Certainly it is no longer in the mouth of the dove, which now, by a change of symbolism, adorns the front of the organ. Whatever may be thought of the story, there was no such spirit of partisanship in the minister; he remained in the Church of Scotland himself, and, by his tact and delicacy of feeling, was able to keep almost the whole of his people with him. About that time he revised the notice of Urr written by Mr McWhir for the Statistical Account of the Stewartry of Kirkcudbright, which was published in 1845. There attention was drawn to the abnormal length of the parish, and the necessity of having it subdivided for ecclesiastical purposes. Mr Burnside seems to have exerted himself to have this recommendation carried through; for, in 1842, a Chapel of Ease was established at Dalbeattie, and this afterwards led to the erection of the lower end of the parish into a parish quoad sacra. To a man of his amiability, the change in dealing with transgressors, which he was able to introduce in 1840, must have been particularly agreeable; thereafter they were no longer required to appear before the whole congregation for admonition and rebuke, but were dealt with in private by the Kirk Session.

That Mr Burnside was endowed with no mean intellectual gifts and powers of work, as well as a strong sense of duty, is amply attested: on the one hand, by the elaborate and costly monument raised to his memory, with its warmly appreciative inscription; and on the other hand, by the eloquent and sympathetic sermon preached in Urr church on the Sunday after his death, by the late Rev. Dr. Fraser of Colvend, copies of which are still cherished in the parish. Several of his own sermons were published; amongst them, one on the Nature of Unbelief, and another on the Irongray Martyrs. A man may be known by his friends as well as by his sermons; and one of Mr Burnside's most intimate friends was Rev. John Caird, afterwards the well-known Principal of Glasgow University. As a young man, rising into popularity, Mr Caird used sometimes to stay at the manse and occupy the pulpit of Urr. This friendship was confirmed by the marriage of Mr Caird to Mr Burnside's niece, a daughter of Rev. Dr. Glover, then of Crossmichael, afterwards of Greenside, Edinburgh. In 1894, it may be mentioned, on the occasion of extensive repairs upon the church of Urr, the reverend Principal, then nearing the close of his career, was asked to visit the parish, and preach the re-opening ser-

THE REV. JOHN MACRAE SANDILANDS, M.A.

mon. Unfortunately, his medical adviser at the time had interdicted him from public work; and with great regret, which was shared by Mrs Caird, he declined the invitation. Doubtless it would have been a sincere pleasure to them, in their old age, to have resumed acquaintance with a scene so closely associated with their early happiness. Mr Burnside himself had a sister to keep house for him, and did not marry till shortly before his death. That took place at the manse on 29th January 1855. His wife, Mary Morrin, survived him for over thirty years, dying at Redcastle on 18th October 1887.

Rev. John Macrae Sandilands, M.A. 1855-1891

With Mr Sandilands we come to such recent times that we can afford to be brief. A native of Ayrshire, he was educated at Edinburgh University, where he greatly distinguished himself, especially in the classes of Logic and Moral Philosophy. These, at the time, were respectively under the charge of the renowned teachers, Sir William Hamilton and Professor Wilson; and Mr Sandilands accomplished the feat of taking first place in both of them in the same year. Duly licensed as a preacher of the Gospel, he began ministerial work in Wellpark Church, Glasgow, as assistant to the minister of the Barony Parish. Thence he was transferred, in the same capacity, to the united parishes of Dunoon and Kilmun, where he soon established a reputation for himself, with natives and summer visitors alike, as an eloquent and inspiring preacher. In 1855, he received the call to Urr, and there, dismissing from his mind the thought of further promotion, he elected to spend the remainder of his days. Had he desired it, there is little doubt that, with his eloquence and abilities, he could have commanded a more prominent position; but, with little of personal ambition in his nature, and a great fondness for the pleasures and pursuits of the country, he preferred to seek his happiness and occupation in the life of a pastoral parish. That he found sufficient of both in his allotted parish is asserted by all who knew him. As a member both of the Parochial and the School Board, Mr Sandilands continued the interest of his predecessors in the care of the poor, and the education of the young: in other ways, also, as by the founding of a parish library with a large and carefully selected assortment of books, he exerted himself to advance the social and educational interests of his people. Eminently kind and benevolent of disposition, his sympathy and help were ever at the command of his parishioners; while his acuteness of intellect and loyalty to his friends made him the valued counsellor of his ministerial neighbours. The general transition, which began in his time, from older to more modern forms of thought and methods of worship, received his hearty countenance and support, and many improvements were made in the church services. He was especially happy in his preaching: possessed of a beautiful voice, a cultured mind, a sympathetic insight, and a great power of apt and telling expression, his sermons were elaborate, eloquent, and profoundly impressive; so much so, that they were in great demand for special services in other parishes, and many of them are faithfully remembered to this day. Bodily infirmity compelled him to relax his efforts for some time before his death, and even to seek the services of an assistant in the person of Rev. J. M. Campbell, now of Torthorwald; but, a few months afterwards, on 7th December 1891, he passed to his rest, leaving a widow and family behind him.

Rev. David Frew, M.A., B.D. 1892

Curiously enough, the present incumbent, who was ordained to Urr on 12th May 1892, also began his ministerial career as assistant in the Barony Parish, Glasgow, and afterwards served in the same capacity in the united parishes of Dunoon and Kilmun.

CHAPTER XVIII

ECCLESIASTICAL MATTERS GENERALLY—SINCE THE REFORMATION

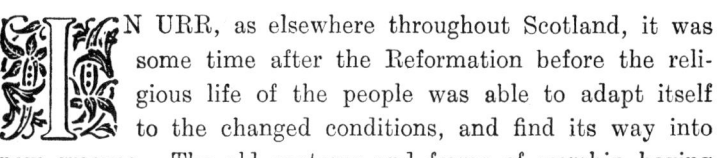

IN URR, as elsewhere throughout Scotland, it was some time after the Reformation before the religious life of the people was able to adapt itself to the changed conditions, and find its way into new grooves. The old customs and forms of worship having been abandoned, the new had to win their place in popular esteem, and acquire for themselves the necessary means of observance. In time, however, a full ecclesiastical equipment was secured, a regular system of services instituted, and an order of discipline established, upon Presbyterian lines. These have since been efficiently maintained, in keeping with the development of religious life and feeling in the country.

THE PARISH CHURCH AND MANSE

At first, of course, the necessity was not pressing for the erection of new ecclesiastical buildings. A stated pastor not as yet having been appointed, the services would be partial and occasional, as the readers, Mr Brown and Mr McCarmonth, had ability and opportunity to conduct them. The old Roman Catholic places of worship at Blaiket and Kirkland, with some internal alterations, would sufficiently meet the needs of the situation. Likely enough, too, there might be no great demand upon their accommodation, as many of the people would still have a hankering after the old faith, and, in the absence of its ministrations, abstain from worship altogether. This is rendered probable by the fact that the Roman religion never entirely disappeared from the parish, but continued for long years afterwards to be a source of trouble and concern to the ministers.

It was only upon the appointment of Mr Thomson in 1602, as first regular incumbent of the parish, that the erection of a new church and manse was decided upon. The old places of worship may have fallen into decay: in any case, the congregation had grown to such dimensions that it could not very well be accommodated in either of them. The site chosen for the new church was that which the present building occupies. This is amply borne out by the Statistical Account of the parish, written twenty years afterwards by Mr Robertson, in which he specifies the location of the different farms in the parish by their distance from the church. "Nether Kirkland," for instance, he speaks of, as "where the kirk is situat"; "Ower Kirkland" is "twa myll distant frae the kirk," and so on. All that remains of this original building (at least that can be identified, for part of it may be wrought into the present structure) is the pulpit panel already referred to, bearing the initials of Mr Thomson and the date 1606. According to old maps, the manse stood, not upon the present site, but on the south side of the church, in the little field lying between it and Kirkland, and still belonging to the glebe. The maps show the road of the time as passing between the manse and Kirkland, over the fields towards Torcatrine and Moss-side, where there is still a right of way.

For nearly a century and a half, these buildings seem to have sufficed for the wants of the people and their minister; at any rate, during that time there is no record of the reconstruction of either of them in the minutes of the Presbytery. If such took place, it could only have been during the troubled period of Mr Lyon's incumbency, and that is hardly probable. What stirring scenes they must have witnessed during their time of service! The outing of Mr Gledstains, the trouble and dissensions associated with Mr Lyon, the fiery denunciations of Mr Hepburn, and the disturbances of which he was the origin! Only on one occasion does anything seem to have been done to them. During the first suspension of Mr Hep-

URR PARISH CHURCH.

PHOTO. BY J. AND J. BROWN, CASTLE-DOUGLAS.

burn, advantage was taken of his absence to have some necessary repairs executed upon them. On 24th August 1697, the Presbytery made a visitation of Urr, and arranged that the vacant stipend should be applied to the repair of the church and manse, as well as of some useful bridges. The sum spent upon them was 1600 merks, or about £89 Sterling, which was a considerable amount for those days, and equal to nearly two years' stipend. Later on, when Mr Hepburn had finally disappeared from the scene, and Mr Wright had to make some necessary adjustments, the question was raised of the allocation of seats in the church. On 11th July 1727, a petition was presented to the Presbytery, representing that "some Heritors in the parish had more room in the church than their valuations did require, and some less, and some none at all; and desiring a visitation of the Presbytery for dividing of the said church more equally." The visitation was held on 1st August, and the record of it discloses some interesting facts regarding the form and dimensions of the church. According to measurements taken by two tradesmen deputed for the purpose, it was 62 feet long, and 18 feet wide; the space enclosed by it accordingly being 1116 square feet. From this there fell to be deducted a western area 16 by 3 feet; an eastern area 18 by 3 feet; a middle area for communion tables and movable seats or forms 28 by 6 feet; two entries 3½ by 6 feet; and the pulpit containing the minister's and reader's seats 8 feet square; or a total of 360 square feet; leaving 756 square feet to be divided amongst the heritors. This was done according to £100 valuations. There was also a small loft, in which some heritors were to be allowed to set up a seat. We can picture to ourselves the old-fashioned building—long and narrow; with the pulpit in the broadside of it, and a passage running lengthwise from east to west, doubled in width for about half its length in front of the pulpit for communion purposes, and a door at either end with spacious entries. The form is still preserved in some old churches, though, as a rule, the cruciform shape has been attained by the addition of a nave. Where the loft was situated, it would be difficult to say; probably it was in front of the pulpit.

By the time Mr McKinnell came to be minister of Urr, the old buildings could not be in a very satisfactory condition. Soon after his induction, he set about their renewal, beginning with the manse, which, in 1743, was rebuilt upon the same site. In this undertaking, he had the hearty co-operation of the heritors, who voluntarily assessed themselves for the expense. The workmanship was entrusted to John Frew, mason in Edingham, who, about this time, was much in consultation with the Presbytery about new churches and manses. He was also interested in the execution of other public works of some consequence, such as the bridge over the Urr Water, which has been already mentioned. The Presbytery met at Urr on 9th June 1743, inspected the new manse, and expressed their satisfaction with it. The workmen who assisted them reported " some small matters [evidently not in the original estimate] to be still necessary, which might cost 18s.; and advised that the lower rooms should be floored with dales, as they were exceeding damp, at a cost of £7 sterling; to all which the heritors present did cheerfully agree." Some interesting details are given with regard to the size and cost of the new building. In the estimates furnished to the Presbytery before the work was begun, it is said that the manse is to be 38 feet long and 15 feet wide within the walls; it is to have 11 windows, 1 door, 2 stairs, shutters, and 5 vents; the timbers, bands, locks, etc., of the old house are to be used as far as possible; the fresh timber required is to be brought from Whitehaven, and shells for lime from Colvend, to Dub of Hause, and thence to Urr by road. The total cost, including the repair of the office houses with thatch, is to be £97 13s. 2d. Evidently it was a narrow, two-story building of five rooms, two of which were on each floor, and one in the form of an attic.

GENERAL ECCLESIASTICAL MATTERS

A few years afterwards, Mr McKinnell began to draw attention to his church. At first, it was agreed to repair the old building; but, on 5th February 1751, he reported to the Presbytery that the heritors now thought it would be better to build a new one. Accordingly the Presbytery met again at Urr on 21st February, and had the usual consultations with heritors and tradesmen. It was agreed to have a new church built 61 feet long, 24 feet wide, and 13 feet high from foundation to easing; with 3 doors and 8 windows. This was judged ample for the accommodation of the inhabitants of the parish. Probably the internal arrangements were much the same as in the former church, though the new one was 6 feet wider. The old materials were to be used as far as possible; and the estimated cost, including £2 2s. 0d. to John Maxwell for preparing plans, and £6 8s. 0d. for collecting the assessment, was £134 10s. 0d. The church was duly finished and taken over by the Presbytery about a year afterwards. It is in this connection that we come, for the first time, upon what was called the Stent Roll of the parish. In the Presbytery minute of 4th September 1751, a record is given of the names of all the heritors, their valuations, and the respective amounts in which they were stented for the building of the new church.

No further change took place until Mr Alexander Murray came to the parish. Dr. Muirhead having vacated the manse for Spottes Hall, it was agreed by the heritors to have it taken down, and a new manse and offices built for the new incumbent. At the same time, it was wisely decided to remove to the present site, which is drier, more open, and detached from the graveyard. The new buildings were a great improvement upon the old ones. The manse consisted of two main stories, with four good, airy rooms upon each floor, extensive cellar accommodation, and two large attics; a stair, mostly stone, running from top to bottom. The outhouses were upon an equally liberal and substantial scale. The whole were finished and occupied by Mr Murray in 1809, the work being done by William Black, mason, and the cost over £900. With little alteration, these buildings have now completed their hundred years of existence. During the incumbency of Mr Sandilands, a new front was built to the manse at a cost of nearly £500, giving three additional rooms and some further hall space; but the offices remain as they were, and the old manse continues to be occupied as the main part of the present dwelling.

The shortness of Mr Murray's tenure of office precluded him from proceeding with the erection of a new church; but Mr McWhir, on succeeding to the benefice, at once took up that project. In 1815, he had the church rebuilt and enlarged to its present proportions, at a cost of £1000. The date is inscribed upon the small belfry over the western gable. Once again the old materials were used, giving the present building a certain hereditary connection—an association of substance, if not continuity of form—with its remotest predecessor, and making it, to the reflective mind, a symbol of the one religious life that has persisted through successive generations. In Mr Sandiland's time, a slight alteration was made upon the interior, by the substitution of fixed pews of the ordinary type for the old communion area, which was no longer required under the modern method of observing the sacrament. In 1894, on the present incumbent coming to the parish, an extensive scheme of improvement was carried through. The total cost was £650, which was made up by a contribution of £100 from the heritors, a similar contribution from the Baird Trust, and the remainder from the congregation. The whole interior of the church was renovated and reseated; a new heating apparatus and pipes were introduced; and a commodious vestry and two porches built in front of what had formerly been the main door. Three years later, a pipe organ was erected behind the pulpit; and in 1900, a handsome stained glass window was inserted in the western gable to the memory of Mr Thomas Biggar of Chapelton, the gift of his two re-

MANSE OF URR.

PHOTO. BY J. AND J. BROWN, CASTLE-DOUGLAS.

maining sons. Without pretensions to architectural elegance, the church is now a comfortable and convenient place of worship for the parishioners, in whose eyes it is hallowed by many sacred associations.

THE CHURCH SERVICES

While preserving a certain identity of form, the services of the church in modern times exhibit many points of departure from those to which our fathers were accustomed. In this respect, Urr has not been unaffected by the changes taking place generally in the Church of Scotland during the last fifty years. Briefly put, these have mostly been in a double direction: on the one hand, the tendency has been to make the services simpler and less protracted, and, on the other hand, to secure a better proportion between the devotional and the didactic elements in them. After the Reformation, the recoil from the elaborate ceremonial and stated festivals of the Roman Church expressed itself in religious habits of extreme austerity, and a church service almost destitute of forms. At the same time, the exigencies of controversy, and the clamant need for popular instruction in evangelical truth, had the effect of unduly emphasising the place and importance of preaching. Besides the lecture, which was simply a running commentary on the lesson for the day, there was also a sermon of at least an hour or two's duration. The singings were few and short, and confined at first to the Psalms, afterwards to the Psalms and Paraphrases; but the prayers, especially after they came to be extemporaneous, were more or less inordinate in length. The people stood at the prayers, and sat at the singings. The result was a service, which to the modern mind seems insufferably long and monotonous. Yet it continued in Urr, as in most other places, down almost to the middle of the last century. Nowhere, however, is the difference in the church services so marked, as in the observance of the sacrament of communion. One of the few elements of ritualism left to them at the Reformation, the people seemed, as time went on, to try how much, in their own way, they could make of it. For a while, it was regarded with increasing reverence and solemnity, until it came sometimes to be omitted for years, through fear of doing violence to it, and incurring mortal sin, by unworthy participating. This was the reason Mr Hepburn neither gave nor took the sacrament for sixteen years: he could not believe that, in the distracted condition of the country and the time-serving humour of the Church, the dispensation of the ordinance could be anything but displeasing to God. In the eighteenth century, however, feeling ran into the opposite extreme, and a change came over the habit of the people. The sacrament became in Urr, as elsewhere, a veritable " Holy Fair," as Burns has described it. The celebration took place, as a rule, once a year, and was of such a nature as easily admitted features of an unseemly and irreverent kind. Great crowds gathered, not only from the parish itself, but from surrounding districts; a preaching booth or tent was erected in the churchyard, from which a succession of ministers held forth from morning to night; at intervals, relays of the people sat down at the communion tables, and partook of the sacrament. It could not be expected that the worshippers could go all day without food; some form of refreshment was required to carry them through their prolonged devotions; and public opinion of the time did not prohibit those of an alcoholic kind. Some frugal people brought baskets of provisions with them; others resorted to the ale-houses which were usually placed in convenient proximity to the church; there was a good deal of indiscriminate drinking and mutual treating; so that, not infrequently, the sacrament degenerated into a merrymaking, if not a debauch. It is said that the servants of the neighbourhood, in hiring for the year, used to stipulate for a holiday, but were quite indifferent whether they got Urr sacrament or Kelton Fair. However that may be, the annual celebration of the ordinance must have

GENERAL ECCLESIASTICAL MATTERS 283

been a serious interruption to ordinary employment; for, besides the actual communion on Sunday, there were supplementary services on the Thursday (Fast-day) and Saturday preceding, as well as upon the Monday after. We can imagine the strain all this put upon the minister, though, of course, he was largely helped by his brethren.

It was well into the nineteenth century, before symptoms of coming change began to appear. Even in Mr McWhir's time, it was found necessary to have the communion tables and tent repaired. The old order, however, was doomed, and gradually gave place to the new. The celebration of the communion was confined to the interior of the church, and its duration considerably curtailed; the Saturday and Monday services in connection with it were given up. Until a generation ago, it was still dispensed four times in succession to relays of the people at what continued to be called "tables," with an address of some length before and after each table: it is now taken simultaneously, twice a year, and the whole service kept within two hours. The only distinctive relic of the past retained is the half-yearly sacramental Fast.

The communion plate belonging to the church consists of eight pieces—four silver cups, two pewter patens, and two pewter flagons. The cups were gifts to the parish, and bear inscriptions on them recording the dates and names of the donors. Two of them were presented in 1734 by James Moorhead, merchant in Dumfries; evidently, however, they have been recast and remoulded, to bring them into form with the other two, which were given in 1823 by William Stothert of Cargen. The flagons and patens were acquired by the church in 1821, and bear that date and the name of the church upon them. Besides these, which are kept in the manse, there is a bag of small leaden vouchers called "tokens," by which admission to the communion used to be regulated, but which have now given place to cards. They have the date 1850 upon them, and are numbered for four tables. Until recently, there were samples of older tokens in the manse, but these have now found their way into the hands of the irrepressible collector. Some of these went back so far as 1728, but most of them belonged to 1815, when a fresh stock of tokens was got by Mr McWhir, on the occasion of the opening of the new church, at a cost of £2 2s. 0d.

Kirk Session Minute Books and Trusts

The earliest remains of the minute books of Urr Kirk Session are preserved in the Register House, Edinburgh, and consist of odd leaves bound together in a single volume. They relate to the third quarter of the eighteenth century, and record somewhat irregularly the baptisms in the parish. From 1772 to the present time, the minutes are almost entire, and are contained in five volumes, the three oldest of which are in the hands of the minister, and the other two in those of the session-clerk. A good deal of information may be gleaned from them regarding the history of the parish; but, as usual in these old records, the greater part of the space is taken up with cases of discipline.

The only trust money now administered by the Kirk Session is a sum of £100, which, according to the minute of 9th June 1816, "was mortified for the poor of the parish of Urr by the late Michael Herries, Esquire of Spottes, under the management of the minister and kirk-session." This money is invested in a Clyde Trust Debenture, in the names of the minister and session-clerk, who uplift the interest and apply it under the supervision of the Kirk Session. Formerly there were three small endowments for education in the charge of the Kirk Session; but, on the passing of the Education Act in 1872, being relieved of this part of their function, they uplifted what remained of them, about £100, and paid it over to the School Board of the parish.

Glebe, Stipend, &c.

In pre-Reformation days, the old Roman Church possessed considerable tracts of land in the parish, now represented, as the names indicate, by the farms of Meikle and Little Kirkland. It was probably the fact of the latter being church land that determined the site of the first reformed church. Something like 100 acres in its immediate vicinity would have been devoted, from time immemorial, to the support of religion. It was only a small portion of the whole, however, to which the Church, after the Reformation, was able to serve itself heir. That is what now constitutes the glebe, and consists of 13 acres of good arable land, lying round the manse.

The stipend is what remains of the pre-Reformation tithes or teinds, proportions of the rent of lands granted to the Church for the support of religious ordinances. It was first fixed by the Commissioners of 1617 at eight hundred merks, or forty-five pounds Sterling; it was revised again in 1627, and gradually grew in value as the rent of land increased, until in Dr. Muirhead's time it amounted to £83 6s. 8d., with an allowance of £5 for communion elements. About the middle of the last century, it rose considerably with the increase in the prices of grain, but latterly fell away again to such an extent that, in 1883 and again in 1903, it was modified by the Court of Teinds, that is to say, revised and increased. It is now 26 chalders, or 208 bolls of meal and $151\frac{1}{2}$ quarters of barley, at the prices annually fixed by the Fiars' court, with an allowance of £10 for communion elements.

The Churchyard

The old God's acre of the parish lies close around the church, like an outer court of the dead, through which the living have to pass to the performance of their devotions. Previous to the acquisition of a cemetery by Dalbeattie, it was the common burying-place for town and country; consequently it has a directly personal interest for a considerable number of people.

Besides, it has a certain interest of its own; for many of its inscriptions not only awaken reflections of a general kind, but corroborate or throw fresh light on points of local history.

In the absence of other evidence, the date of its origin can only be inferred from the stones which it contains. These indicate that it did not come into use till after the Revolution of 1688; for the earliest of them, which lie to the south and east of the church, and are of the sowback and through-stone type, do not carry us further back than the end of the seventeenth century. It is not surprising that nearly a hundred years should pass, after the first church was erected upon the present site, before interments began to be made in its vicinity. The old burial-ground of the church at Kirkland would be still available, and even preferred by the people on account of its associations. It would be hallowed to them, if not by the formal act of Roman consecration, at least by the cherished memories of the generations that slept in it. Tradition says, indeed, that it continued to be a place of burial, not only after the removal of the church, but long after the present churchyard came into existence. It is even averred that an interment took place in it, at a comparatively recent date—somewhere in the early part of the last century.

The present churchyard is evidently a growth from the original nucleus on the south and east of the church. Gradually it would extend itself round the other sides of the church, and outward upon the adjacent land, as occasion required. According to the heritors' minutes, some readjustment and repair of boundary dykes took place in 1816, the year after the present church was built. In 1893, a considerable addition was made and suitably enclosed, and a new entrance-gate erected, at the expense of the heritors, to the north of the church. At the same time, for sanitary and other reasons, an old sexton's house was removed, which had long stood at the church gate, with its back deeply embedded in the graveyard soil.

The oldest gravestone so far discovered is a fine sowback specimen, lying well out on the south side of the church. It is worked in relief with the usual emblems of sand-glass, skull, and cross-bones, and bears the inscription: "Heir lyes Robert Herries who leived in Houphead. Depairted Anno 1695. Aig 67." Nearer the church, and close to the conspicuous monument of Dr. Samuel McKeur, there is a flat stone to the memory of George Macartney of Blaiket, who died in August 1704. It has a long inscription, fast being obliterated, which tells of the good testimony he bore in the time of King Charles II, and the sufferings inflicted on him for his fidelity to the truth. George Macartney is otherwise known to have figured very largely in the troublous times of the persecutions, and the subsequent dissensions associated with the incumbency of Mr John Hepburn. From this sturdy stock, it may be mentioned, there came some notable descendants, such as General Macartney, and the Earl of Macartney—raised to the peerage for distinction in the diplomatic service.

Within the railing that surrounds Dr. McKeur's place of interment, there is another noteworthy stone, the inscription on which may be given in full—

"In memory of John Thomson in Blaiket: he died 1751, aged 81.
He feared not the face of man in defence of Scotland's Covenanted Religion and with zealous courage contended much for it.

This zelous wrestler in the dust lay down
In full assurance of a glorious crown."

Evidently he, too, was a partisan of Mr Hepburn, and a keen supporter of the dissenting congregation that arose after his death.

With the exception of Dr. Alexander Murray, the ministers

of the parish, from Mr Wright downwards, are all interred in the churchyard. Most of them have costly and elaborate monuments to their memory, with quaint and fulsome epitaphs, occasionally in poetry, according to the fashion of their times. "Mixing their kindred dust" with them, lie several of the ministers of the Secession Church—Mr Milligan, Mr Biggar, and Mr Storrar. On the north side of the church, enclosed within an iron railing, is the burial-place of the Kerr family, who were tenants of Redcastle for many years. Here rest the remains of Robert Kerr, "The Ploughman Poet of Urr," a man not unakin to Robert Burns in his gifts, and not unlike him in his personal history. Born at Midtown of Spottes on 2nd September 1811, and educated at the Parish School at Hardgate under Mr William Allan, he spent most of his life at Redcastle, in the pursuit of the ordinary farm avocations. For a few years, like many young Scotsmen from the southern counties, he tried his fortune at the "Pack" in England; but, being unsuccessful, gladly gave it up, and returned to his native vale. He died at Redcastle on the 30th September 1848, at the early age of 37, "to the inexpressible grief of all who knew him." Many of his poems were not intended for publication; and, though possessed of considerable merit, did not get beyond manuscript form and oral repetition. Others appeared in various periodicals, and earned him distinction beyond the immediate circle of his friends. In 1891, a collection was made of those suitable for publication, and edited with a memoir, by Mr Malcolm McL. Harper, Castle-Douglas, under the title of "Maggie o' the Moss, and Other Poems." It was published in Dalbeattie by Mr Thomas Fraser.

Beside the resting-place of Robert Kerr, there is a large open vault or tomb, in which are deposited the remains of Mr Michael Herries of Spottes, a benefactor of the parish, his wife, and son. There are many other memorials of persons, rich and poor, who served their day and generation well, and in most cases left descendants who maintain the good tradi-

ROBERT KERR, REDCASTLE.
FROM A PORTRAIT BY JOHN ALEXANDER.

tions of their families. In the remote south-eastern corner of the churchyard stands a monument to which a peculiarly pathetic interest attaches. It was raised by public subscription to commemorate six Springholm children, who met their death together by falling through the treacherous ice of Auchenreoch Loch on Sunday, 16th February 1873. Not far from it is the burial-place of the Stewarts of Dalbeattie, the last survivor of whom is the Rev. Dr. William Stewart, the distinguished Professor of Biblical Criticism, and Clerk of Senate, in Glasgow University.

Apart from the eulogies on the monuments of the ministers, which are sometimes whimsical enough, and the caustic epitaph of the Laird of Kipp already given, the only other inscription which is calculated to provoke a smile is that upon a stone at the north-eastern corner of the church, which records the death of a man, " aged 101 years, by his own account."

CHAPTER XIX

Urr United Free Church

THIS is one of the oldest dissenting churches in the country. For the origin of it we must go back nearly two centuries, to the stirring times of that great protagonist of dissent, the Rev. John Hepburn. Though certainly not contemplated by him, it was an aftergrowth of the movement he set on foot.

During the lifetime of Mr Hepburn, as we have seen, his friends and adherents were more or less estranged from the ordinary life of the Church, and frequently found themselves in opposition to the judgments of its courts. After his death in 1723, many of the members of the congregation of Urr, including the whole of the Kirk Session, abstained from joining in the call to Mr Christopher Wright, and withdrew themselves from his ministrations. For a time, the position of these nascent dissenters was unsettled and undecided. Some of them joined the MacMillanites, but the great majority refrained from any ecclesiastical connection. These, however, formed a kind of Society amongst themselves, and met together, as time and place were convenient, for prayer and meditation on the Scriptures, their favourite rendezvous being Blaiket, which was still in the possession of the Macartneys, a staunch old covenanting family.

This state of affairs continued until the rise of the Secession Church in 1733, through the withdrawal of the Rev. Ebenezer Erskine and three other ministers from the Church of Scotland. The immediate causes of their withdrawal were the restoration of patronage in 1712, and the consequent troubles and distractions thereafter associated with the settlements of ministers; but other forces, especially those put in action by

Mr Hepburn, helped to accelerate the movement. In 1736, the Associate Presbytery, as it was called, was joined by other four ministers, and the Secession rapidly gained ground in the country. From the first, it had the sympathy, and soon it received the adherence, of many of the old Societies to which Mr Hepburn had ministered. Their views were very similar, and their sentiments congenial, to those of the new dissenters. Though not among the first to do so, the Society in Urr was not long in acceding to the Presbytery, and becoming one of its congregations. Thereafter, until they acquired a church and minister of their own, they had the occasional services of a Secession preacher at their meetings, once in two months being the average.

At an early stage of its existence, the Secession Church itself suffered a disruption, as a result of the controversy over the Burgess Oath. This oath required a profession of belief in the religion of the country, and allegiance to the reigning sovereign. Some of the Seceders took up a moderate attitude to it, and advised that it should be left to the determination of the individual conscience. Others had an insurmountable objection to it, and contended that it could not be taken by the members of their church, consistently with their principles. Feeling grew so strong on the subject that, in 1747, a separation took place: the more tolerant party taking the name of the Associate or Burgher Synod, while the party which condemned the oath formed themselves into the General Associate Synod. Popularly they were known as Burghers and Antiburghers. It was quite in keeping with the antecedents of the Urr congregation that they should throw in their lot with the more extreme section. They became Anti-burghers, and continued such for a hundred years, when another change of name took place. In 1847, the old Secession and Relief Churches united to form the United Presbyterian Church, and Urr became a congregation in the conjunct body. Still another transmutation was in store for them. When the United Presbyterian Church joined forces in 1900 with the Free Church of Scotland, the new name of United Free Church was introduced, and Urr received the appellation by which it is now known.

The first church was built for the congregation in 1743, a little above the present farm-house of West Glenarm, in what is now a small meadow by the roadside. The manse was situated somewhat further down the road, almost in front of the farm-house. The site chosen for these buildings, it may be observed, would be about midway between those of the old pre-Reformation churches of Blaiket and Meikle Kirkland. The manse continued to be occupied almost to the close of the century, and its ivy-covered ruins may still be seen, at the side of the Glenarm road; but the church does not seem to have been long in use, and no trace of it now remains. Probably it was of a temporary and insubstantial character, and the site not so convenient as could be wished. At any rate, so early as 1760, a second church was built at Hardgate. This also had a comparatively short existence, giving place in 1798 to a larger building, which is said to have cost £400, and to have had accommodation for 480 sitters. About the same time, the old manse at Glenarm was given up, and another built on the present site adjacent to the church. For over half a century thereafter, these buildings served the needs of the congregation, which during that period was of growing dimensions, being largely supplemented from the rising town of Dalbeattie, where as yet there was no place of worship of the same denomination. In 1860, however, it was found necessary to remodel the church, when the walls were raised considerably, and about eight feet added to the width; and eight years afterwards, a new and commodious manse was provided for the minister. Within the last three years, the congregation had the church and manse done up, and some additional conveniences provided, by means of a successful sale of work; but, unfortunately, on 11th April 1909, which was Easter

Sunday, a disastrous fire broke out in the church, about nine o'clock in the evening, and practically destroyed it. Nothing remained beyond the four bare walls, but the work of reconstruction was at once begun, and is now nearing completion.

The first minister's name found in connection with the congregation is that of the Rev. John Cleland. While a probationer, he was sent down by the Associate Presbytery to preach to the dissenters of Urr, on the second and third Sundays of April 1741, while yet they met as a Society at Blaiket. Afterwards he became minister of the Secession church at the Holm of Balfron. The first attempt to obtain the services of a regular pastor was made in 1745, when a call was presented to Mr J. Swanston, afterwards of Kinross, which he did not see his way to accept. The reasons for his declinature were regarded by the Synod as so unsatisfactory that they administered to him a public rebuke. It was not until after the Burgess Oath controversy that a regular settlement was effected; and since then eleven ministers have presided over the charge.

1. REV. JOHN MILLIGAN. He came from the South Church, Sanquhar, and was inducted to Urr on 16th September 1748. After a ministry of 47 years, the longest on record in the congregation, he died on 26th January 1795, at the age of 80, and was interred in Urr churchyard. According to the Old Statistical Account, Mr Milligan was "a gentleman equally venerable as a minister, and respectable as a citizen," and the Antiburgher Seceders in the parish in his time consisted of 30 families.

2. REV. JAMES BIGGAR. He belonged to the district, but was no relation of the present family of Biggars in the parish. His father, according to the family stone in the churchyard, was James Biggar of Killymingan, who died on 20th March 1806, at the age of 97. He was called both to Auchtermuchty in Scotland and Newtonards in Ireland. Accepting the call to Newtonards, he was ordained to that charge on 13th April 1785, but resigned it in a few years, and returned to Scotland.

After itinerating as a probationer for some time, he was admitted to Urr in 1797. Loosed from his charge in 1813, he built the residence of Summerhill for himself, and lived there till his death on 4th November 1820, in the 73rd year of his age and 36th of his ministry.

3. REV. JAMES BLYTH. He came from Abernethy, and had calls to Kinkell, Rothesay, and Moniaive, as well as to Urr. He was ordained to Urr on 2nd September 1817. Resigning on account of his health on 4th February 1833, he removed to Perth, and died there in 1844, in the 60th year of his age.

4. REV. WILLIAM PULLER, from Barrhead. He was ordained on 10th July 1834, but for some reason or other resigned little more than a year afterwards, on 18th November 1835. He continued as a probationer of the Church till 1844, when he left the connection.

After his departure the congregation called the Rev. James R. Dalrymple from Wallacetown, Ayr; but he preferred to go to Thornliebank, whence he emigrated to America, and afterwards to Australia.

5. REV. WILLIAM BURGESS, A.M. He came from Annan, and had calls both to Dumfries and Urr. Ordained to the latter church on 24th November 1836, he remained till 28th April 1842, when he was translated to Eglinton Street, Glasgow.

6. REV. DAVID WILSON BAYNE, from Balbeggie. He was ordained to Urr on 4th April 1843, but resigned on 5th May 1853, and was deposed by the Synod on 3rd June 1856.

The congregation then called the Rev. James Hill from Edinburgh, but he preferred the charge of Scone, to which he had also received a call. In 1863, he proceeded to New Zealand.

7. REV. JAMES BLACK. He came from the West Church of Dunse, and was ordained to Urr on 10th October 1854, but on 26th May 1857 was translated to St. Andrews. Afterwards he became minister of Wellington U.F. Church, Glasgow, and a Doctor of Divinity.

8. REV. JOHN CLARK. He was admitted a probationer from the Free Church by the Synod of the United Presbyterian Church in May 1858. He was ordained to Urr on 23rd December 1858, and laboured there till his death in 1886. He was a prominent member of the first School Boards in the parish. His son is a minister of the United Free Church.

9. REV. WILLIAM STORRAR. He was a native of Fifeshire, and was ordained to Urr in February 1887. Cut off early in life, after barely eight years' ministry, he is remembered affectionately in the parish, for his earnest labours and genial disposition. To mark the esteem in which he was held, shortly after his death a handsome granite monument was erected to his memory in the parish churchyard, where his wife and one of his children now repose beside him.

10. REV. DAVID R. ALEXANDER, B.D. For some time before Mr Storrar's death, Mr Alexander had taken charge of the congregation, and after that event, which occurred on 20th April 1896, he was ordained to its ministry. He was translated to Dunblane in 1907.

11. REV. THOMAS McEWEN, M.A., the present incumbent. He came from Arbroath, where he had been assistant for a time, and was ordained to Urr on 14th February 1908.

CHAPTER XX

THE CHURCHES OF DALBEATTIE

DALBEATTIE PARISH CHURCH

IN accordance with the system of the Church of Scotland, the rise of an industrial community in the lower end of Urr has been followed by the erection and endowment of a separate ecclesiastical parish. At the beginning of Mr Burnside's ministry, the population of Dalbeattie and the immediate neighbourhood had reached the considerable figure of 1600; yet there were only two places of worship in the town—the Roman Catholic chapel and the Cameronian meeting house. The adherents of the Church of Scotland continued to attend Urr church, and depend upon its incumbent for religious ministrations. The development of the town, however, had already caused the inconvenience of this arrangement to be felt, and a desire had arisen for a better supply of religious ordinances than the parish church alone could provide. A movement in that direction was accordingly initiated, the result of which has been the complete independence and equipment of the district as a quoad sacra parish, and the building up of one of the largest and most active congregations in Galloway. The new parish embraces the whole of Urr to the south of a line running between the two Firthheads across to the Kirkgunzeon road at Newfield. So far, of course, as civil matters are concerned, it still forms part of the original parish.

The first step was taken in 1839, as soon as Mr Burnside had settled down in the district. If it did not entirely originate with him, it seems at least to have had his hearty approval, though it promised a considerable reduction in the number

RICHORN LOCH, NEAR DALBEATTIE.
PHOTO. BY ARCH. GILLESPIE.

THE CHURCHES OF DALBEATTIE

of his congregation, as nearly seventy of his male communicants, out of a total of 173, resided in Dalbeattie. The heritors of the parish, and especially the laird of Munches, Mr John Herries Maxwell, entered sympathetically into the movement, and ensured its success by their countenance and support. With them was associated a committee of the people of Dalbeattie, consisting of Messrs Hugh Lindsay, James Heron, James Corrie, and Thomas Rawline, the two former being elders of the parish church. The response of the general community was such that in a short time the promoters of the undertaking were able to realise their immediate aim in the formation of a Chapel of Ease. Sufficient funds having been provided, and a sufficient congregation gathered together, the old meeting house in Burn Street was acquired from the Cameronians, and converted into a comfortable place of worship, capable of accommodating 500 people. The purchase was made in 1842, and in the following spring an ecclesiastical district was assigned, and arrangements were made for calling a minister to the new charge. On 2nd March 1843, Rev. James Mackenzie was ordained first minister of the church of Dalbeattie. For some time he had been in charge of the mission station at Southwick, and consequently was already well known in the district. His ministry, however, was of the briefest, as the Disruption in the Church of Scotland took place a few months after his induction; and, his sympathies being with the seceding party, he relinquished his charge, and proceeded to form a new congregation in the town in connection with the Free Church. The majority of his former members having adhered to him, it required all the enthusiasm and devotion of those who remained in the parish church to preserve its infant existence. The charge was declared vacant on 13th June 1843, and over eighteen months elapsed before a successor to Mr Mackenzie was able to be inducted, in the person of the Rev. Alexander Arthur. His ordination took place on 23rd January 1845, but he only held the charge for three years, demitting it on 14th March 1848.

The ministry that followed Mr Arthur's may be said to have witnessed the real making of the church and parish of Dalbeattie. The Rev. Duncan Stewart was ordained to the charge on 20th July 1848; and for nearly thirty years he laboured with such acceptance and success, that not only was the ground lost at the Disruption recovered, but the foundations were laid of that strong and healthy congregational life, which has ever since been maintained. About the time of his appointment, an addition was made to the ecclesiastical equipment by the erection of a manse and offices in Burn Street, on the feu immediately adjoining the church. The site had been given in 1842, by Mr William Copland of Colliston, to the original promoters of the scheme for an independent church in Dalbeattie; but the congregation had been unable to utilise it, till about the time Mr Stewart became their minister. The buildings erected then continue to be the minister's abode, though substantial alterations and additions have been made to them in recent years. A further advance was made in 1864, when the church was duly endowed with a minimum stipend of £120 a year, and the district it had hitherto served was created into a quoad sacra parish. A proportion of the funds for this purpose was received from the Endowment Committee of the Church of Scotland: the remainder was raised among the people and their friends. A constitution was granted in the usual form, under which the proprietors of Munches, Aucheninnes, and Edingham were nominated trustees of the church and parish, with others of an ex-officio character. Mr Stewart died on 11th September, 1877, and was succeeded by the Rev. John Mackie, who was ordained on 13th December of the same year.

During the short but energetic incumbency of Mr Mackie, several important works were carried through, and the congregation continued to increase in number and activity. Within a month of his settlement, a movement was set on foot for the erection of a new church, the old Cameronian meeting

THE CHURCHES OF DALBEATTIE

house, which had served the purpose of the congregation for 37 years, having become totally inadequate to its growing demands. The population of the parish had risen to over 4000, and the membership of the congregation had proportionately increased; so that a more commodious and convenient place of worship was urgently required. The movement was generously supported, and soon resulted in the handsome ecclesiastical edifice that stands at the end of Craignair Street. The plans were prepared by Messrs Kinnear & Peddie, Architects, Edinburgh, and provided accommodation for 850 worshippers, besides the usual conveniences. The site was a gift from the leading trustee of the church, Mr Wellwood H. Maxwell of Munches, who also defrayed the cost of the graceful, pointed spire which adorns the new building. Exclusive of the site and spire, the total expense incurred was £3876 8s. 3d., towards which sum grants were received of £1000 from the Baird Trust, £250 from the Ferguson Bequest Fund, and £245 from the Home Mission Committee of the Church of Scotland. The remainder was made up by individual subscriptions, and the sale of the old church, which has since been converted into an Armoury. The memorial stone was laid by Mrs Maxwell of Munches on the 24th December 1878, and the church was completed and opened for worship on Tuesday, the 27th January 1880, when the Rev. James Barclay of Montreal, Canada, who had been assistant minister in the time of the Rev. Duncan Stewart, preached the sermon. About two years afterwards, the name and labours of Mr Stewart were appropriately commemorated by the placing of five stained glass windows in the apse, depicting the eleven apostles viewing the ascension of Christ. In October 1888, a suitable communion table was obtained; and, quite recently, a handsome mural tablet of local granite was inserted in the wall beside the pulpit, to the memory of Mr Maxwell of Munches, a lifelong friend and benefactor of the church and parish.

In the same year in which the church was opened, the efficiency of the congregation was further augmented by the acquisition of a set of rooms in Burn Street, comprising a large hall, four smaller apartments, and a kitchen. The front portion of the present building had been erected by Mr Maxwell as club-rooms, for the use of the working men of Dalbeattie. In 1880, these club-rooms were made over by Mr Maxwell to the church; and, after being enlarged and refitted, were opened for use as a church hall and offices on 10th December of the same year. The cost of the alterations and additions was about £500, which was met by a grant of £300 from the Baird Trustees, and a loan of £200 from the donor of the building, a considerable portion of which was afterwards remitted by him, when it came to be repaid. These rooms have been of great service to the congregation, not only in connection with its Sabbath School work, but in the prosecution of many other branches of Christian activity.

After other five years of active and successful work, Mr Mackie resigned the charge on 30th September 1885, and departed to Canada, where he is now minister of St. Andrew's Church, Kingston.

The Rev. Roger S. Kirkpatrick, B.D., was appointed to the vacancy, and ordained on 18th February, 1886. During his devoted ministry, the traditions of the church were worthily upheld, its organisations maintained at the full measure of their working power, and various improvements made in the conditions of congregational life and worship. In 1894, when the number of members on the church roll had risen to nearly 600, a scheme was projected for repairs upon the church, extensive alterations upon the manse, and an addition to the suite of congregational rooms. To assist in carrying through this scheme, a bazaar was held in September of that year, the total receipts of which, after deducting expenses, were £494 8s. 7d. To this sum were added a grant of £50 from the Baird Trustees, a donation of £150 from Mr Maxwell of

THE CHURCHES OF DALBEATTIE

Munches, one of £50 from Mr Kirkpatrick, and other contributions to the extent of £60 5s. 10d., which brought up the total funds available to £804 14s. 5d. The various works were carried out, to the great improvement of the properties concerned; but, as the cost amounted to £1031 3s. 4d., the congregation was left with a deficit of £226 8s. 11d. Two years afterwards a fresh enterprise was undertaken by the congregation, and an organ erected in the church at a cost, with water motor and other expenses, of £540. The contract was given to Messrs Forster and Andrews of Hull, and the instrument was completed and fitted in its place by 30th April 1897, when there was a formal opening. To defray the expenditure incurred, subscriptions were received from members and friends of the church to the extent of £370, in which sum was included a donation of £100 from Mr Scott, Johannesburg. A deficit was thus left upon the organ of £170 which, with the previous deficit upon the improvements, brought up the whole indebtedness of the congregation to nearly £400.

It was not to be Mr Kirkpatrick's fortune to enjoy the increased comforts and conveniences which he had been largely instrumental in procuring for the minister and people of Dalbeattie. In October 1896, when the movement for the organ was only getting under weigh, he was called to the parish of Jedburgh; whence, a few years later, he was transferred to Govan, one of the largest and most important charges in the Church.

In succession to Mr Kirkpatrick, the Rev. James P. Wilson, B.D., who was a son of the minister of St. Quivox, and who had been assistant in Dalserf for a time, was ordained to the charge on 25th February 1897. Two months after his settlement, the organ was completed and installed; and thereafter the equipment of the church was as complete as could be desired. The only material drawback to the contentment and zeal of the congregation was the debt of £400 which still rested upon it, and this it soon characteristically resolved to make a strong effort to liquidate. Another bazaar was accordingly held in September 1900, which met with such success that sufficient funds were provided, not only to clear off the debt, but to repaint and decorate the church. The energies of the congregation being now unhampered, a period of quiet but unremitting activity set in, during which prosperity continued to attend it. Under the careful supervision and painstaking ministrations of Mr Wilson, the various departments of its life and work were efficiently carried on, its organisations maintained and developed, and relations cultivated with other congregations in the town, which tended to promote the general interests of religion. Profound regret was felt in the district, though not unmingled with pleasure at the compliment paid to his worth and abilities, when in the summer of 1906 he was called to the parish of St. Quivox, to succeed his father, and minister to the people among whom he had been brought up.

The present incumbent of Dalbeattie is the Rev. Lewis McGlashan, M.A., formerly assistant in St. John's, Edinburgh, who was ordained on 11th January 1907. At that date the communion roll contained 639 names.

Colliston United Free Church

This is the present name of the former Free church of Dalbeattie which, as already indicated, was founded in 1843, the year of the Disruption. In May of that year the Rev. James Mackenzie, minister of the Chapel of Ease in Dalbeattie, seceded from the Establishment; and, as almost the whole of his people adhered to him, it was at once resolved to form a new congregation in connection with the Free Church of Scotland. For a short time the possession of the church in Burn Street was disputed by the followers of Mr Mackenzie, who were loath to leave the building which they had been largely instrumental in providing, and to which they considered they had an indefeasible claim. They retained the use of it

THE CHURCHES OF DALBEATTIE

for several Sundays, notwithstanding the protests of the remnant who elected to remain in the Establishment; but, on 17th June, legal interdict was obtained against them, at the instance of Mr Copland of Colliston and Mr Maxwell of Munches, and they were forced to give it up. The ground of their claim, which they believed to be warranted alike in law and equity, was that " the church in which they worshipped previous to the Disruption, having been built by general subscription, and attached to the Establishment on the understanding that its minister should be a recognised member of all Church Courts—a condition which the Civil Courts declared to be illegal—the congregation were entitled in justice to continue in the use of their place of worship, though resigning all connection with the Establishment." Whatever cogency the argument possessed, it did not prevail with the administrators of the law, and nothing was left to the seceders but to find themselves another place of worship.

So little time was lost in providing for this urgent want that the foundation stone of a new church was laid by Mr Mackenzie on 7th August of the same year. On that occasion there was a full gathering of the congregation, including Messrs Robert Shennan and James Heron, elders. Amongst others present was the Rev. William Andson, a young minister who had been in charge of Southwick Mission Station, and who became the first Free Church minister of Kirkmahoe, dying quite recently at the advanced age of 92. The exterior of the church was completed in less than four months, during which time the congregation had no other meeting place than an open timber yard, the use of which for their Sunday worship was granted them by Mr William Martin of Castle-Douglas. So soon as the walls were finished and properly roofed over, Mr Mackenzie and his flock moved into their new quarters which, in spite of the absence of internal fittings, would still be preferable to the open air. The fact of their holding together and maintaining religious ordinances under such discouragements and discomfort is an eloquent testimony to the strength of their convictions and the warmth of their zeal. It was not till the winter of 1844-45, after a full year's experience of worshipping within bare walls, that the church was completed internally, and furnished with the usual conveniences. Then they were able to occupy it, not only with some degree of comfort, but with the added satisfaction that it was practically free of debt.

Mr Mackenzie continued to minister to the new congregation till 11th June 1845, when he was translated to the Free church of Annan, whence he was afterwards called to a more important charge in Dunfermline. He seems to have been a man of enthusiastic temperament and abounding energy, with sufficient strength of character to shape a clear and decided course amid the controversies of his time. Firmly convinced of the principles that actuated the Free Church in the Disruption, he was earnest and insistent in his advocacy of them, and did much to promote their acceptance in the southern districts of the country. At the same time, he was possessed of considerable literary gifts, and found time in the stress of current controversies and daily pastoral work for some able and successful publications. Besides "Our Banner and its Battles," he wrote a "History of Scotland," which was long used as a text-book in the Scottish schools. He was also the author of the first part of the Life of Principal William Cunningham, D.D., of the New College, Edinburgh; the second part of which was the work of the late Principal Rainy.

After the removal of Mr Mackenzie from Dalbeattie, the church remained without a settled minister for nearly three years. On 11th May 1848, the Rev. George Dudgeon was ordained as his successor in the charge. Two important events took place at the outset of his ministry: the building of a manse for the minister, and the opening of a school for the children of the denomination. These undertakings are an indication of the resources already possessed by the congregation; and there was no diminution of their prosperity during the incumbency of Mr Dudgeon. He is said to have been a genial, kind-hearted man, popular with all classes of the congregation, and particularly interested in the poorer members. He died on 22nd August 1865, at the early age of 46. The next minister of the church was the Rev. Robert Wright, who was ordained on 22nd February 1866. A capable and energetic pastor, he laboured devotedly in the interests of the congregation for thirteen years. Elected a member of the first School Board of Urr in 1873, he had the distinction of presiding at its first meeting. During two terms of office, he threw himself heartily into the work of organising the education of the parish upon the lines of the new system, and providing the proper equipment of school accommodation and teaching staffs. In the midst of his work, and of his plans for a new church to replace the old Disruption building, the general unsatisfactoriness of which had begun to be felt, he was laid aside by severe illness, which ultimately terminated his promising career on 26th April 1879, at the age of 44. For some time before his death, the work of the church was carried on by an assistant, the Rev. Mr Henderson, whose performance of the duties gained the good opinion of the congregation, and who acted for a short time as a member of the School Board.

The Rev. James A. Paton, M.A., succeeded Mr Wright, and continues to occupy the charge. He was called from Portmoak in Kinross-shire, the parish in which the Rev. Ebenezer Erskine, the founder of the Secession Church in Scotland, began his ministerial career, and was inducted on 27th November 1879. Shortly after the settlement of Mr Paton, a fresh start was made with the movement for rebuilding the church upon modern lines. Erected in haste, as we have seen, at the Disruption, to meet the immediate wants of Mr Mackenzie and his followers, its architectural features, like those of many of the early Free churches, left much to be desired; its conveniences were inadequate to the growing life of the congregation; and a considerable outlay was annually required to keep it in proper repair. A new building was planned upon a more handsome and generous scale, the foundation stone of which was laid by Colonel Neilson of Queenshill, in the presence of a large gathering of the congregation and their friends, on 19th July 1881. Previous to the actual ceremony, a brief history of the congregation was read by Mr William Thomson, the last teacher of the Free Church school, whose services had been transferred to the School Board. The work was completed and the church reopened for worship in July 1882, when an inaugural service was conducted by the Rev. Walter C. Smith, D.D., the Moderator of the Free Church of Scotland for that year. The total cost of the new church was £2300. It is a beautiful edifice, in the Romanesque style, with a commodious gallery, and a spire 100 feet high, which is not only a credit to the congregation, but an ornament to the town. In the vestibule a mural tablet has been placed to the memory of Mr Wright, the inscription on which bears that " he was a faithful and zealous pastor, enjoyed the esteem of an attached congregation, and departed this life in the full enjoyment of the rich consolations and promises of the Gospel."

Four years ago, the semi-jubilee of Mr Paton, as minister of the church, was suitably celebrated by the congregation, when ample testimony was borne to the faithfulness and success of his ministry. The conscientious attention, however, which he has always given to his immediate pastoral duties, has not prevented him entertaining interests of a wider kind, and engaging himself in questions of social and national concern. For three years, at the outset of his ministry, he occupied a seat upon the School Board. The temperance cause has always appealed most strongly to him, and commanded his unwearied advocacy and support. A keen upholder of the purity of Reformation principles, he has not hesitated to enter the arena of controversy, on the least appearance of danger, and has written many miscellaneous letters and articles upon the questions at issue with Ritualism and Rome. In particular, he contributed to the "Protestant Standard" some time ago a series of weekly articles, which ran for over a year, contrasting the doctrines of the Reformed and Roman Catholic Churches, and covering a large field of controversy. He has also appeared in the "Christian Leader" as the author of a long series of articles upon the Names of Christ. His most important literary production, however, is a book entitled "Honouring God," which was favourably received by the press, and obtained a considerable circulation in the southern counties. It deals with the relations between religion and science, and expounds the more outstanding implications of the Christian faith.

At the union of the Free and United Presbyterian Churches in 1900, it was necessary to change the name of Dalbeattie Free church; and since then it has been known as Colliston United Free church, the ground on which it is built having been feued from Colliston estate, and Colliston public park, a gift from Miss Copland of Colliston, being in the immediate vicinity. Mr Paton was favourably disposed to the union, and desires to see it carried to its legitimate conclusion in the amalgamation of some of the smaller congregations. During the vacancy which occurred in Burnside church, through the translation of the Rev. A. M. Johnston to Ayr, he put every facility in the way of the two congregations, to enable them to unite, if they had been so disposed; but the time was not ripe, for besides other difficulties to be overcome, neither congregation was prepared to give up its separate existence. An amalgamation of the two churches, if harmoniously effected, would probably be to their mutual benefit, and conducive to the religious life of the town; but meantime it is postponed for future consideration.

BURNSIDE UNITED FREE CHURCH

This was originally the United Presbyterian church of Dalbeattie, but has been known by its present name since the union of the Free and United Presbyterian Churches in 1900. Its origin takes us back to the year in which Dalbeattie acquired the dignity and privileges of a Police Burgh. Before that time, the only place of worship belonging to the United Presbyterian denomination in the parish was the church at Hardgate, to which, with an adherence to principle that rendered them indifferent to physical inconvenience, a number of the inhabitants of the town were accustomed to resort. The regularity of their appearance at their chosen sanctuary, in spite of its distance from their homes, is still a matter of remembrance in the district. The growing size and importance of the town, however, at length suggested the feasibility, as well as the desirability, of a more adequate arrangement; and only the occasion was awaited for beginning a movement in favour of an independent church. In May 1857, the Rev. James Black was called away from Hardgate, and thereafter a difference of opinion in the congregation, which had been simmering for a time, developed into active disagreement. During his ministry, a "band" or choir had been introduced, as a help in the service of praise. Though constrained to tolerate it while he was with them, some of the members had taken strong exception to it from the beginning; and, on his removal, they approached the Presbytery at Dumfries, and obtained an order for its discontinuance. There was naturally some disappointment among the members who had supported and sympathised with the innovation; and, as many of these belonged to the lower end of the parish, it was not long till steps were initiated for the erection of another church in Dalbeattie.

On 27th March 1858, a meeting for the consideration of the matter was held in the house of Mr John Kerr, Maxwell Street; as the result of which a petition was drawn up to the United

THE REV. DAVID KINNEAR, B.A.

THE CHURCHES OF DALBEATTIE 309

Presbytery of Dumfries, requesting them to arrange for the opening of a preaching station. The signatories to this document were Messrs R. Thomson, Edingham; James McRobert, Reedweel; James Wright, Munches; and Thomas Maxwell, W. Reid, W. Heughan, Thomas Rawline, John Kerr, and James Grieve, Dalbeattie. The petition was favourably received, and its crave granted, by the Presbytery on 3rd May following. No time was lost in getting the new station formally under weigh. On 23rd May, service was conducted in the hall of the Commercial Hotel by the Rev. M. N. Goold of Dumfries; and on 28th May, a second meeting was held in the house of Mr W. Heughan, to make further arrangements for the carrying on of the station. At that meeting the following committee was appointed to manage the affairs of the incipient congregation: Messrs Kerr, Heughan, Renton, Thomson, Grieve, Maxwell, Rawline, Paterson, and McRobert. The enthusiasm of the leaders, however, was not to be satisfied with a preaching station; and, as the prospect soon appeared to them to warrant a forward measure, another meeting was held on 3rd August, at which a petition to the Presbytery was promoted for the establishment of a regular charge. The Presbytery acceded to the petition, and sent a deputation of their number to Dalbeattie on 21st September, to arrange with the petitioners for their formation into a congregation of the United Presbyterian Church. Some members of the Free church, and other churches in the town, associated themselves with the new congregation, which shortly afterwards proceeded to hear candidates with a view to the calling of a minister. The candidates were required to occupy the pulpit for two successive Sundays; and to one of them, the Rev. Mr Murray, fell the duty and honour of presiding over the first celebration of the Communion in connection with the new charge. It took place on 3rd November, and was attended by 34 communicants. A fortnight later, a staff of office-bearers was elected, a missionary committee appointed, and a regular constitution drawn up and adopted. It only remained for the congregation to complete their organisation by the selection of a permanent pastor.

A number of preachers having been heard, the choice fell upon the Rev. David Kinnear, B.A., from Buckhaven, to whom a unanimous call was offered on 19th April 1859, the congregation promising to raise £120 a year towards his stipend, and to provide pulpit supply for an annual holiday of four weeks. Mr Kinnear accepted the call, and was ordained to the charge on 30th August 1859, the service being held in the old Established church in Burn Street, the use of which was granted for the occasion. It was his first and last appointment. He remained in Dalbeattie for the rest of his life, a period of 44 years, and during that time had the gratification of seeing the youthful charge grow under his hands into a vigorous and stable congregation. From the beginning, as might have been expected, the praise was led by a "band," the conductor of which was Mr James Tait, at one time of Lochrutton, and latterly of Culvennan, who had occupied a similar position in the old Hardgate "band." At the date of Mr Kinnear's ordination, the number of members upon the roll was only 55: in less than fifteen years it had increased to 155: it is now 140.

With the settlement of Mr Kinnear, it was felt that the time had come to proceed with the building of a place of worship. Various sites were considered, especially one in Station Road, where the Temperance Hotel now stands; but ultimately the present site in John Street was selected, and a feu charter obtained from the proprietor, Mr Maxwell of Munches. One of the conditions of the charter was that the building proposed to be erected, as well as the dwelling-house which, it was anticipated, might be subsequently added, should be used for no other purposes than those of a church and manse. In the recent discussion of the question of union with Colliston United Free church, it was pointed out that, under

THE CHURCHES OF DALBEATTIE

this condition, the congregation could not dispose of their church and manse, except to some other religious body, without the sanction of the proprietor. In the meantime, however, there is no likelihood of the congregation abandoning their ecclesiastical buildings, which are in good condition, and convenient to the town. The church was designed to seat 350 people, with a provision for a gallery, should it be required, which would increase the accommodation by 250. The estimates amounted to £885, but the actual cost exceeded £1000. Towards this sum a grant of £250 was received from the Ferguson Trustees, and another of £120 from the Debt Liquidating Board; the remainder was made up by the congregation and their friends; and the church was opened practically free of debt in October 1861. The leading parts in the opening services were taken by two distinguished divines— Dr. Macfarlane of London, and Dr. Eadie of Glasgow; and a feature of the occasion was the introduction for the first time in the neighbourhood of the modern postures of devotion, namely, a standing attitude at praise, and a sitting one during prayer.

An interval of ten years passed before the congregation was in a position to face the erection of a manse, but this convenience was at length obtained, at a cost of over £700. It is built of granite, like the church, which it immediately adjoins, and accords with it in design. In 1894 a further addition was made to the ecclesiastical equipment in the shape of a hall and session-house, which have been found of great service in the work of the church. For the use of the meetings in the Hall, an instrument was presented by Mrs Kinnear; and this soon led to a desire for instrumental music in the church, which was met by the gift of an organ from one of the members, Mrs Grieve. In Mr Kinnear's time, too, the church was renovated and refloored, and the seats and heating apparatus were improved. These undertakings, considered in conjunction with the ordinary work and liberality of the congregation, testify to the zeal and energy of the minister, as well as the enterprise and generosity of his members. Mr Kinnear was a man well adapted for the life-work that fell to him: he had all the qualities of the pioneer and the builder-up: a marked individuality, a resourceful disposition, strong convictions, and a forceful character. The schemes he took in hand at different times were all carried through by voluntary contributions, without resort to a bazaar or sale of work; and none of them were allowed to interfere with the scrupulous attention which he regarded as due to the purely spiritual duties of his office. These were always his chief concern; and the manner in which he fulfilled them won the deep attachment of his people, and still gives him a cherished place in their remembrance. At the same time, he had interests beyond his own congregation, and was able to take a considerable part, not only in the educational affairs of the parish in which his lot was cast, but in the general concerns of the denomination to which he belonged. For a long time he was a leading member of Urr School Board, and took a special interest in the development and welfare of Dalbeattie Public School; his speech at the closing of the school for the holidays, after the annual religious examination, being one of the events of the day. In the courts of his Church, he was a prominent figure; and his influence in their counsels, his power as a speaker, and knowledge of ecclesiastical law were recognised in 1895 by his elevation to the Moderator's chair of the Synod, a distinction which gave peculiar gratification to many friends in Dalbeattie, besides the members of his own congregation. The proposals for union between the United Presbyterian and the Free Churches had a strong advocate in him; and, when the union became an accomplished fact, he was pleased to enter into the new confederacy as minister of the Burnside United Free church.

Mr Kinnear survived the union about three years, and died on 26th November 1903. His devoted people not only placed a mural tablet in the church to his memory, but, as he had left no family, decided to charge themselves with the care of the memorial in Dalbeattie Cemetery, which marks the spot where he and his wife, who predeceased him, are laid; thus paying him a peculiarly touching, and somewhat unique tribute of esteem.

On 9th June 1904, the Rev. A. M. Johnston, B.D., who had been for a time an assistant minister in Edinburgh, was ordained and inducted to Burnside church, in succession to Mr Kinnear. He laboured for four years in Dalbeattie with great acceptance, interesting himself particularly in the young men of the town, a large number of whom he gathered together weekly in a Sunday afternoon class. In his time, a sale of work was held in connection with the congregation, the precedent set by Mr Kinnear thus being broken. On his removal to Ayr, in the spring of 1908, an attempt was made to bring about a union of the two United Free churches in Dalbeattie; but that attempt failing, the congregation of Burnside proceeded to take the usual steps for filling their vacant charge, and in due course gave a call to the Rev. D. A. Dick, B.D., assistant at Dreghorn, who was ordained on 29th July 1908.

The only remaining member of the church, it may be mentioned, who is known to have taken an active part in the institution of the congregation, is the present preses, Mr John Paterson, baker, Dalbeattie. Another of the original company survives at the time of writing, Mr James McRobert, but is now resident in London. Besides these, there are other two survivors of those who sat down at the first Communion: Mr James Tait, Culvennan, and Mrs Armstrong, Dumfries.

Evangelical Union Congregational Church

In the same month (May 1843) in which the Free Church seceded from the Establishment, another denomination was formed in Scotland by the separation of the Rev. James Morison of Kilmarnock and three other ministers, with their congregations, from the United Secession Church. The new body took its name from the character of the movement of which it was the outcome, and became known as the Evangelical Union. The leading principles for which it stood were the freedom of the human will, and the universal significance and applicability of Christ's atonement, as distinguished from the Westminster Confession doctrines of predestination, election, and reprobation. Some time previously, views of a similar kind had found lodgment in Dalbeattie, and a small congregation had been formed, called The United Christian church, under the charge of Mr John Osborne, who had been expelled from the Reformed Presbyterian ministry. In 1830, Mr Osborne was succeeded by Mr Roseman, who kept the congregation together till 1836. After his removal, however, it gradually melted away, and soon became defunct, though some of its members continued to cherish the beliefs which had been the means of bringing them together. There was, therefore, a certain preparation of the ground for the congregation which was afterwards formed in connection with the Evangelical Union.

It was in 1863 that the first definite steps were taken towards this object. In that year a number of those who sympathised with the principles of the Evangelical Union began to hold meetings in a hall of the town, and were accorded preaching supply by the Home Mission Committee of the Union. In 1866 a church was built, and a minister called and inducted, in the person of the Rev. John Inglis of Coatbridge. At the same time, one of the remaining members of the old United Christian church presented the communion plate which had been used in it to the new congregation, "because it stood up for the principles for which Mr Roseman had contended." During the ministry of Mr Inglis, a manse and small school house were built. After the passing of the Education Act of 1872, the latter was no longer required by the denomination, and was let to the School Board for use as an Infant school

THE CHURCHES OF DALBEATTIE

until the present public school was built. It has since been converted into a dwelling-house for the caretaker.

Mr Inglis remained in charge for six years, and saw the congregation fairly launched upon its way. Since his time the following ministers have held office in the church: Rev. Thomas D. Hogg, 1873-1874; Rev. Robert Robertson, in whose time the church was improved and enlarged, 1875-1877; Rev. John M. Sloan, 1878-1880; Rev. John Cameron, 1881-1892; Rev. John Penman, 1892-1900; Rev. J. Livingstone Gower, 1900-1909; and Mr James Dobie, the present incumbent. Mr Cameron, it may be mentioned, is the author of an interesting local work upon the Buchanites, and of several theological books; while Mr Sloan has the following works to his credit: " New Aids to Reflection," 1889; " Quintin Doonrise, a Study in Human Nature," 1892; " The Carlyle Country," 1904; and " Galloway Described," 1908.

Since 1896, when the Evangelical and Congregational Unions joined forces, the church has been known as the Evangelical Union Congregational church of Dalbeattie.

CHRIST CHURCH (EPISCOPAL)

The Episcopal Church in Scotland, having adopted the Thirty-nine Articles of the Church of England in 1804 and the Prayer-book in 1863, is closely related to the great Church of the southern kingdom, not only in its method of government but in its forms of belief and ritual. Its services are accordingly in request by members of the Anglican communion who happen to be resident in Scotland; and it was to meet the requirements of such in Dalbeattie that the congregation of Christ Church was formed. In 1873 a considerable number of English granite workers were employed in the quarries of Messrs Shearer, Smith and Company; and services were started for them in a hall in the town, by the Rev. W. M. Ramsay, M.A., St. Ninian's church, Castle - Douglas. The mission met with such success that, in 1875, it was decided to proceed with the erection of a church; and the result is seen in the present building, a chaste little edifice, in the early English style, with accommodation for 164 worshippers. The first clergyman appointed to the church was the Rev. J. Tandy, LL.D., who had charge of it from 1878 to 1882. Since his time, the following have been incumbents: Rev. W. Marlow Ramsay, 1882 to 1885; Rev. Arthur Stephen, M.A., (First Term) 1885 to 1888; Rev. J. M. Jackson, 1888 to 1892; Rev. John Strachan, M.A., 1892 to 1894; Rev. W. Graham, D.D., 1894 to 1898; Rev. Lennox R. Gloag, 1898 to 1899; Rev. Arthur Stephen, M.A., (Second Term) 1899 to 1908. In the summer of the last-mentioned year, Mr Stephen was compelled by the state of his health to relinquish the charge, after a total incumbency of twelve years, during which he established himself in the general esteem of the community, and materially advanced the interests of the church. Externally, he had the church buildings put into good repair and surrounded by a handsome stone wall and iron railing; internally, he succeeded, through the liberality of friends of the congregation, in effecting many improvements, both in the way of adornment and convenience. A few years ago, a suitable parsonage was built, and occupied free of debt; the site—an acre and a half of land in the vicinity of the church — having been granted by Miss Copland of Colliston. During Mr Stephen's time the communion roll increased; and, on his retiral, he had the satisfaction of leaving the congregation in a promising condition. His successor is the Rev. H. F. Plant, who was inducted to the charge on 15th April 1909.

St. Peter's R. C. Church

It is doubtful whether the Roman Catholic religion entirely disappeared from Urr at the Reformation, or continued to have its secret followers among the people. That the latter was the case is suggested by the fact that the earliest existing records of Dumfries Presbytery reveal the presence of what

THE CHURCHES OF DALBEATTIE

were called "malignants" in the parish, whom it was the business of the minister to discover and bring to book. On 23rd November 1647, it was reported to the Presbytery that Edward Morisone in Edingham had given satisfaction for his "malignancie": on 26th January 1649, process was begun against James Jardine for "malignancie and other offences": on 8th January 1650, Catherine Broune, spouse to John McBairnie of Culmain, was cited for popery: and on 10th August 1658, Robert Herries in Dalbeattie was ordered to be dealt with for popery, and refusing to subscribe the Covenant. At this time, George Maxwell was proprietor of Munches. He held the property from 1637 to 1683; and, being a Catholic, gave his countenance and support to the adherents of the ancient faith. As he was a judge-ordinary of the county, and a man greatly esteemed among all classes, he was not only left comparatively undisturbed himself, in the exercise of his religion, but was able to shelter many of his co-religionists from the rancour of the times. Munches became the rallying-place of the Catholics from a wide area; and services were provided for them by successive generations of Maxwells, who preferred the old ways. Throughout the eighteenth century, the Chapel at Munches was a great place of religious resort, people gathering to it, not only from Buittle and Dalbeattie, but from Castle-Douglas, Kirkcudbright, and Newton-Stewart. That severe ecclesiastical measures continued to be taken by the minister of Urr against members of his flock who went over to the old religion is attested by the Presbytery minutes. On 7th January 1729, Mr Christopher Wright reported that he had dealt with Helen Wylie, a "pervert" to popery in Meikle Dalbeattie; and on 7th April 1747, Mr Thomas McKinnell informed the Presbytery of steps he had taken against three "apostates" in Dalbeattie, Samuel Coupland, Helen Concher, and Mary Neish. No overt demonstration, however, was made against the house of Munches, except on one or two occasions when, by authority, search was made in it for Catholic books and vestments. The only books of a compromising nature discovered were an illuminated New Testament and a treatise entitled "The Faithful Farrier"; the former coming under the ban of the authorities by reason of its illustrations, and the latter through the misreading of its title as "The Faithful Friar." They were carried to Dumfries, and publicly burned on Corberry Hill; a proceeding on which Dr. Muirhead makes the quaint comment, "there have been greater mistakes both in religion and politics."

About the year 1794, when the Old Statistical Account was published, there were 28 families of Roman Catholics in Urr, who resorted to Munches Chapel for worship. In the early years of the nineteenth century, this number was so largely augmented by incomers from Ireland and other places that it was deemed advisable to have a place of worship in Dalbeattie. Land was obtained from the proprietor of Munches, and in 1814 a church was erected which, with the school and priest's residence adjoining, continues to serve the needs of the congregation. Among the earlier priests was a Father Geddes, who afterwards rose to high position in the Catholic Church. In 1832, the Rev. Andrew Carruthers, a future Archbishop of Glasgow, was in charge; and his immediate successors, each of whom held office for a short time, were the Rev. Peter Forbes, the Rev. Stephen Keenan, and the Rev. John Cowie, who became Rector of Valladolid College. From 1835 to 1857, the Rev. John Strain was incumbent, an able and energetic man, who ultimately filled the position of Archbishop of Edinburgh. During his residence in Dalbeattie, he took an active part in the business of the Poor's Board and its successor, the Parochial Board; attending most of the meetings, and occasionally acting as chairman. He was succeeded in St. Peter's by the Rev. Alexander Gordon, who remained in charge for twenty-three years, and earned the respect and esteem of the whole community, by his kindly, genial disposition, fine character, and active interest in public work.

THE CHURCHES OF DALBEATTIE

Like Father Strain, he did good work on the Parochial Board; he was also a member of the first School Board, and, after an interval of three years, was re-elected in 1879, the year before he left the town. His favourite recreation was bowling, a game of which he was a keen exponent, and his presence was no less welcome than familiar on the green. In his later years, contrary to the custom of the clergy in his Church, he wore a long, flowing, white beard, which gave him a very patriarchal appearance. He is still held in grateful remembrance by many of the older people in the town in no way connected with St. Peter's congregation. Since his time the succession of priests has been: Rev. P. Agnew, 1880-1882; Rev. P. Murphy, 1882-1883; Rev. John Lee, 1883-1885; Rev. D. McCartney, 1885-1898; Rev. C. O'Malley, 1898-1907; and the present incumbent, Rev. H. J. Langley.

APPENDICES AND INDEX

APPENDIX A

NAMES AND OWNERS OF LANDS

AUCHENGIBBERT (G. *Achadh an tiobair*, field of the well.)
1672, James Gordon; Robert Gordon; 1676, Roger Gordon; 1799, William Bushby; 1819, Hon. Fletcher Norton; R. K. Howat of Mabie; 1866, James Affleck, 1902, J. H. Hacking.

AUCHENREOCH (G. *Achadh an riabhach*, little grey field) UPPER AND NETHER
15th cent., Dougall McClelland Johnstone or Dungalson; 1490, Alexander Gordon; John Gordon; John Gordon; Alexander Gordon; 1607, George Gordon; 1616, George Gordon; 1622, George Gordon; John Gordon; 1624, John Hamilton; 1671, John Hamilton; 1715, John McGeorge; 1729, Thomas and William McGeorge: (UPPER) 1799, David Maxwell of Cardoness; 1813, Alexander Blair of Dunrod; Hugh Blair; 1878, Alexander, Patrick, and Hugh Blair. (NETHER) 1799, Rev. David Lamont, D.D.; William Lennie; Trustees of William Lennie (Town Council of Edinburgh).

BARBEY (G. *Barr beith*, hill of birches.)
Part of Crochmore; John Morraine; 1628, Albert Biggar; 1799, William Ireland; John G. Clark of Speddoch; John H. Gilchrist Clark; Mary E. Gilchrist Clark.

BARFILL (G. *Barr phuill*, hill of the pool.)
1799, Lady Winifred Constable; 1819, William Maxwell of Nithsdale; Hon. Marmaduke Constable-Maxwell of Terregles; Frederick H. Constable-Maxwell; 1873, Alfred Peter Constable-Maxwell; Herbert Constable Maxwell Stewart.

BLAIKET (A. S. *Blaec wudu*, black wood.)
1472, Walter Porter; John Gordon; 1576, Edward Makmorane; 1587, Eupheam Gordon; 1607, John Gordon of Beoch; 1610, John Gordon of Airds; 1616, John Brown, Mollance; 1628, Grizell Gordon; 1662, John Macartney; 1680, George Macartney; 1717, John Macartney; 1740, Ann Macartney, spouse to James Hill, surgeon, Dumfries; Robert Kirkpatrick; 1780, James Stothert of Cargen; 1819, William Stothert; 1867, Alexander Forrester of Arngibbon; William Forrester; 1908, Harvie A. Forrester.

BRANDEDLEYS (A. S. *Branded* or *Brannit leáh*, brown or burnt meadow.)
1819, William McMurdo; George Dunn.

BURNBRAE AND MILTON MILL.
Formerly part of Milton of Urr; 1869, James Henderson; 1886, William Reid.

CHAPELTON
1623, Robert Mure; 1632, John and Janet McNaught; 1646, Sarah Lockhart or McNaught; 1799, Alexander Copland of Colliston; 1819, William Copland; 1857, Thomas Biggar; 1900, James Biggar; 1906, Trustees of James Biggar.

COCKLICK (G. *Coic llech*, a hiding place?) MEIKLE AND LITTLE 1532, Edward Maxwell of Lochrutton; 1585, Edward Maxwell of Drumcoltran; 1601, George Maxwell; 1634, John Maxwell; 1644, Jean Guthrie; 1704, John McGore or McGeorge; 1726, John McGeorge (married the daughter of the Rev. John Hepburn): (MEIKLE) 1751, John McGeorge; 1799, John Lowden-Muir; John Muir-Lowden; John Lowden of Clonyard; Mrs Alison Harkness; 1906, William Reid: (LITTLE) 1747, Joseph Frissell or Fraser; 1750, Hugh Fraser; 1799, James Fraser; 1803, Trustees of James Stothert; 1825, Thomas Gibson; William Forrester; 1908, Harvie A. Forrester.

COURTHILL
Formerly part of Milton of Urr; John Cumming Sloan; 1869, James Rogerson; John Rogerson.

CRAIGLEY (G. *Creag liath*, the hill pasture.) AND WHITEHILL 1611, George Maxwell of Drumcoltran; 1679, John Maxwell; 1799, Robert Nasmyth; Mrs Judith Irving; Robert Nasmyth Irving; William Reid.

CROCHMORE (G. *Cruach mor*, great stack or hill.) 1696, Robert McBrair; 1799, Charles Sharpe of Hoddam; 1819, General Matthew Sharpe; James Beattie; James Smith; Mrs Catherine Smith.

CULLOCH (G. *Cullach*, a boar?) LITTLE 1666, James Morrison; 1671, John Herries; 1674, William and James Herries; 1704, James Herries; 1799, William McGeorge; William Gillespie; John W. Hutchison; Trustees of J. W. Hutchison.

CULMAIN (G. *Cul min*, the smooth back?) LITTLE 1625, John Brown of Carsluith; 1712, John Aiken; 1750, Hugh Fraser; 1751, Joseph Fraser; 1799, William Fraser; 1819, William Stothert of Cargen; Maxwell Clark; John Gibson.

CULMAIN MEIKLE
John Lowden; 1791, William and James Lowden; 1819, conjoined with Fell.

DALBEATTIE, MEIKLE AND LITTLE
1488, John Redik; 1557, Paul Redik; William Redik; John Redik; 1678, John Redik; conjoined with Meikle and Little Richorn.

DALMUN OR DALMONEYSIDE (G. *Dal muine* or *monadh*, field of the thicket or moor.)
Part of Meikle Firthhead.

EDINGHAM AND MEIKLE CULLOCH (*Eidheann*, ivy?)
1529, Elizabeth Gordon; 1553, Alexander Livingstone; Alexander McGhie; 1611, Robert McGhie; 1612, John Morrison; 1626, Edward Morrison; 1630, John McGhie; 1659, John Morrison; 1666, Henry Morrison; 1677, James Affleck: (EDINGHAM) 1799, James McVicar Affleck; 1819, William Maitland of Auchlane: (MEIKLE CULLOCH) John Morrison; 1752, James Morrison; 1799, Hugh Corrie; 1828, Thomas Corrie: (EDINGHAM AND MEIKLE CULLOCH) William Maitland; Mrs Matilda E. Maitland Kirwan of Gelston; John W. Hutchison; Trustees of J. W. Hutchison.

FELL (N. *Fell*, a hill.)
1685, John Maxwell; 1692, George Maxwell; 1799, George Sofflay; 1819, Robert Carrick; John Carrick-Moore; James Carrick-Moore; Sir David C. Buchanan; David W. R. C. Buchanan.

FIRTHHEAD, MEIKLE AND NETHERYETT
John Brown of Carsluith; 1625, John Brown; 1658, Thomas Brown; 1687, John Brown; 1751, John McGeorge of M. Cocklick; 1760, David Bean; 1799, James McMichan; James Welsh; Trustees of James Welsh.

FIRTHHEAD, LITTLE
Formerly part of M. Firthhead; 1799, James Graham; 1859, Thomas Rawline; 1897, James Biggar; 1906, Trustees of James Biggar.

GARMARTIN (G. *Gar*, near, and *Martainn*, a man's name, or the word for a kite.)
1799, David Maxwell of Cardoness; 1819, Sir David Maxwell; (GARMARTIN AND WHITECAIRN) Sir William Maxwell.

GLENARM (G. *Glenairne*, the glen of sloes or wild plums.) EAST
1607, George Gordon; 1633, John Gordon; 1665, Elizabeth Adair or Gordon; 1754, Thomas McGeorge; 1799, Rev. George Maxwell; 1813, James Niven; 1833, John McMorine; George McMorine; 1871, Thomas Duncan; James Duncan.

GLENARM, WEST
1607, George Gordon; 1630, John Gordon; 1665, Elizabeth Adair or Gordon; 1719, George Maxwell; 1799, Rev. George Maxwell; 1819, Gordon Maxwell; Dr. Alexander McNeillie; Mrs Jessie G. Kissock; Alexander McN. Kissock; Trustees of A. McN. Kissock.

GLENSHALLOCH (G. *Gleann sealg* or *seileach*, glen of the hunting or willows.) AUCHENINNES (G. *Achadh an inis*, field in the island.)
NOW NETHER DALBEATTIE
1623, Robert Mure; 1696, John Maxwell of Barncleugh; 1730, Alexander McBriar; 1734, Thomas Copland; 1736, Alexander Copland; 1819, William Copland; 1851, Charles Copland; Eliza M. Copland.

HERRIESDALE (G. *Dal*, a portion of land.) FORMERLY TOWN OF URR
1799, John McGown; 1819, John Lowden; 1830, Mrs Helen Welsh; John Mackay; 1885, James Gillespie; 1907, John Dempster.

KINGSGRANGE (King's farm) FORMERLY LITTLE SPOTTES
1590, Robert Maxwell, second son of Lord Herries; 1596, John Redik of Dalbeattie; 1621, Matthew Hairstanes; 1629, John Hairstanes; 1632, John McNaught; 1646, Sarah Lockhart or McNaught; 1664, Robert Gordon of Troquhain; James Gordon; 1688, Roger Gordon; 1708, Mrs Ann M. McLellan or Telfer; 1760, Patrick Gordon; 1799, Alexander Copland of Colliston; 1819, William Copland; Thomas Rainson Gray; 1874, Thomas Gladstone; 1904, Mrs Gladstone.

KIRKLAND MEIKLE
1619, John Maxwell; 1753, Thomas McGeorge and John Kirk; 1799, William McGeorge; 1819, William Stothert of Cargen; Alexander McNeillie; William McNeillie of Castlehill; Trustees of W. McNeillie.

KIRKLAND LITTLE
1799, John Burgess; 1819, James McMichan; Trustees of J. McMichan; 1881, Alexander McKean; 1900, George Wilson; Trustees of G. Wilson.

LARGLANGLEE (G. *Leargan liath*, grey hillside.)
1510, Andrew, second Lord Herries; 1622, Robert Grierson of Lag; 1632, John Herries; 1659, Robert Grierson; 1669, Robert Grierson; 1671, James Gibson; 1679, Robert Grierson; 1686, John Douglas; 1746, Mary McGeorge or Sofflaw; William McGeorge; 1819, Robert Gordon; David Hutchison Gordon; 1878, Jonathan Townsley; 1909, Trustees of J. Townsley.

LARG (G. *Learg*, a hillside.) MEIKLE
1705, Charles Herries; 1736, James McGeorge; 1750, John McGeorge; 1799, James Biggar of Maryholm; Edward Eccles; James Eccles.

LARG LITTLE
1799, —— Bryces; 1803, James Cavet; Alexander Cavet; James Cavet; John Stobo; John Wallace.

MILLHALL
William Wood; 1908, Robert Macartney.

MILTON OF URR, ETC.
John Maxwell; 1753, William McWilliam; 1769, Sarah Welsh or McWilliam; 1799, John Boyd; Mrs Maria le Maitre Davies: (MILTON MAINS) 1869, John Thomson; 1899, Mrs J. Thomson.

MILTON LITTLE
1799, John Fleck; 1819, conjoined with FELL.

MOTE OF URR
1550, Robert Maxwell; 1604, John Maxwell; 1619, Robert Maxwell;

1767, Sarah Crosbie McWilliam; 1799, James Walker; 1856, John Walker; John Walker; 1907, William E. Paterson.

NEWARK (N. *Virki* or *wark*, a fortification.)
Formerly part of MILTON; 1869, James Henderson; 1886, Thomas Henderson.

REDCASTLE
1543, William, third Lord Herries; end of 16th cent., Stephen Laurie; 1638, John Laurie; 1669, William Laurie; Robert Laurie, second son of John Laurie of Maxwellton, and father of "Annie Laurie"; 1698, Robert Laurie; 1722, Walter Laurie, minister at Stoneykirk; 1745, James Laurie; 1772, Andrew and Mrs Margaret Laurie; 1799, Walter Sloan Laurie; 1813, Walter Bigham Laurie; Mrs Jane Bigham Craig or Sinclair; 1857, Rowland Craig-Laurie; 1896, Col. John Craig-Laurie; 1901, Col. John Birney; 1901, John Gordon Birney.

RICHORN (A. S. *Read aern*, red house.) MEIKLE AND LITTLE (MEIKLE) 1604, Robert Gordon; 1623, Robert Mure; 1628, John Gordon; 1635, John, Viscount Kenmure; 1645, Robert Gordon; 1664, Robert McBrair; 1698, John Gordon; 1752, John Somervail; (LITTLE) 1550, Robert Maxwell; 1604, John Maxwell; 1619, Robert Maxwell; 1666, James Gordon; 1696, John Maxwell of Barncleugh; 1732, James Neilson; (M. AND L. RICHORN WITH M. AND L. DALBEATTIE) latter part of 18th cent., George Maxwell and Mrs Agnes Maxwell; 1819, Mrs Clementina Herries Maxwell; John Herries Maxwell; 1843, Wellwood Herries Maxwell; 1900, William Jardine Herries Maxwell.

SHENRICK
Formerly part of Auchengibbert; 1819, Samuel Ewart; 1842, John Ewart; James Kerr; Trustees of James Kerr.

SPOTTES
1529, Robert, fifth Lord Maxwell; 1546, Sir John Maxwell, Lord Herries, and Agnes, Lady Herries; 1582, Sir Robert Maxwell; 1615, Sir Robert Maxwell, first baronet, of Orchardton; 1681, Sir Robert Maxwell, second baronet; 1693, Sir George Maxwell, third baronet; 1719, Sir Robert Maxwell, fourth baronet; 1729, Sir George Maxwell, fifth baronet; 1746, Sir Thomas Maxwell, sixth baronet; 1754, Sir Robert Maxwell, seventh baronet; 1767, Robert Riddick of Corbieton; 1783, William Riddick of Corbieton; 1784, Michael Herries; 1800, William Muirhead-Herries; 1823, William Young-Herries; 1872, Alexander Young-Herries.

STEPEND
John Paterson; William E. Paterson.

TORCATRINE (G. *Torr creachan*, summit of the hill?)
1604, Robert Gordon; 1628, John Gordon; 1635, John Gordon; 1645, Robert Gordon; 1677, John Hannay; 1698, John Gordon; 1743, Hugh

Aitken; 1779, Mrs Kirkpatrick; 1819, Dr. John Macartney; R. T. J. and A. Maxwell; John W. Hutchison; Trustees of J. W. Hutchison.

The derivations of names are mostly taken from Sir Herbert E. Maxwell's *Studies in the Topography of Galloway*. The lists of proprietors follow P. H. McKerlie's *Lands and their Owners in Galloway*, but are amended in places, and brought down to date.

APPENDIX B
ELDERS IN THE CHURCHES
PARISH CHURCH

1647 John Macartney, Blaiket.
John Herries.
1648 John Macjore.
1650 John Muirhead.
1692 George Macartney, Blaiket.
1694 John Hanna, Culmain.
1699 William McGeorge, Larg.
Thomas McGeorge, Glenarm.
John McGeorge, Kirkland.
John Colvin.
Andrew Colvin.
1726 Hugh Aitken, Torcatrine.
John McKill, Richorn.
James Calland, Glenarchie.
John Black, Halmyre.
John McMinn, Chapelton.
John Mcjore, Garmartin.
1735 John McGeorge, M. Cocklick.
James Coltart.
1770 John Parker.
William McGowan.
1772 John Gelston, Chapelton.
William Copland, Dalbeattie.
1774 John Bushby.
1777 James Robertson.
William Sloan, Dalbeattie.
1784 John Boyd, Milton.
1797 James Cavet, L. Larg.
John Coltart, Milton.
1806 John Anderson.
James Black, Edingham.
John Riddick, Kirkland.
1814 William M. Herries, Spottes.
Robert McMillan, Newbank.
James Copland, teacher, Dalbeattie.
Alexander Blair, Auchenreoch.

1821 William Stothert, Cargen.
William Allan, teacher, Hardgate.
1827 Hugh Lindsay, Dalbeattie.
William Thomson, Bush o' Bield.
James Heron, Edingham.
1831 Robert Burnie, Midtown.
Archibald Marchbank, L. Richorn.
Alexander Cavet, L. Larg, *deacon*.
John Smith, Milton, *deacon*.
Dougald McLaurin, Dalbeattie, *deacon*.
1856 John Thomson, Blaiket.
John Murdoch.
John Valentine, Crocketford.
Joseph Tait, Burnbrae.
1857 Thomas Biggar, Kingsgrange.
Alex. Thomson, Chapelton.
1870 Alex. McNeilie, Redcastle.
Maxwell Clark, Culmain.
John Menzies, teacher, Hardgate.
1882 John Reid, E. Glenarm.
William McAlister, teacher, Springholm.
John Smart, teacher, Milton.
Andrew McKie, Blaiket.
1894 James Biggar, Kingsgrange.
*Joseph Brown, Hermitage.
*James Dinwoodie, Corbieton.
*Andrew Farish, Stonehouse.
*James Gillespie, Herriesdale.
Andrew Kirkpatrick, Auchengibbert.

URR UNITED FREE CHURCH

1801 William Bain.
1808 John Ker.
1837 Robert Howard, Netheryett.
  William Charteris, Crocketford.
1849 Joseph Welsh, Urr.
  Robert Renton.
  James Hyslop.
1856 William Heughan.
  Willian Dunn.
  John Scott, Drumhumphry.
  Alexander Kirk.
1864 Robert Rutherford, Arnmannoch.
  James Sanders, Crocketford.

1866 John Ewart, Shenrick.
  Henry Rankine, Castle-Douglas.
1870 James Menzies, Hardgate.
  James Rogerson, Courthill.
  —— James Hiddleston, Conniven.
  William Halliday, Nethertown.
1887 *William Ewart, Culmain.
  *Robert Scott, Drumhumphry.
  John Nivison, Blackhall.
1905 *Samuel Ewart, Firthhead.
  *Robert Slater, Hardgate.
  *William Thomson, Branetrigg.

DALBEATTIE PARISH CHURCH

1864 Hugh Lindsay.
  William Bryce.
  James McAndrew.
  John Ritchie.
1870 John Coltart.
  Andrew Beveridge.
1873 Alexander Davidson.
  *William Kerr.
  George Ritchie.
  William McBride.
1878 William Jack.
  *George Shaw.

1878 David Paterson.
  John Maxwell.
  *Alexander Wilson.
  William Milligan
  George Grant.
1892 William Baird.
  William Smith.
  *James Little.
1899 *Dugald McLaurin.
  *James Irving.
  *Robert Maxwell.
  *Alexander McPherson.

COLLISTON U.F. CHURCH, DALBEATTIE

  Robert Shennan.
  James Heron.
1844 James Black.
  William Heughan.
  William Milligan
  Gilbert McCready.
1848 James Brown.
  Thomas Maxwell.
1855 William Moffat.
1861 Robert Rain.

1861 John Stewart.
  Robert Robson.
1876 Walter Kirkpatrick.
  Francis Armstrong.
  James Murdoch.
  *William Maxwell.
1881 *Henry Gillespie.
  Henry Rankine.
  *John Clark Bell.
  William McClymont.
  John Haugh.

APPENDIX B

COLLISTON U.F. CHURCH, DALBEATTIE *(Continued)*

1891 *Robert Lindsay.
Thomas Baird.
William Welsh.
*John McVinnie.

1896 *David Kissock.
*John McClymont.
*James Buchanan.
1908 *Anthony Thomson.

BURNSIDE U.F. CHURCH, DALBEATTIE

John Kerr.
William Heughan.
Robert Renton.
Thomas Maxwell.
James Grieve.
James Kimm.
Robert Armstrong.
James Wright.
*John Paterson.
*Andrew Stevenson.

George Fotheringham.
John Thomson.
Joseph Heughan.
*John Lindsay.
*Robert Milligan.
Andrew Craik.
*Walter Rae.
*William Lindsay.
James Hyslop.
*John Taylor.

*Those marked with an asterisk are still members of the respective Sessions.

APPENDIX C

MEMBERS OF PUBLIC BOARDS
POOR'S BOARD

1842 John Sinclair of Redcastle.
J. C. McMichan of Corbieton
Alex. McNeilie of W. Glenarm.
John McNeilie of Kirkland.
John McMorine of E. Glenarm.
Thomas Maxwell, Dalbeattie.
Thomas Crosbie, Kirkland.
James McKenzie, Springholm.
William Dickson, Crofthead.
Anthony Rigg, Torcatrine.
John Ewart, Shenrick.
Rev. G. M. Burnside.
William Allan, Hardgate.
Hugh Lindsay, Dalbeattie.
Robert Burnie, Midtown.
James Heron, Edingham.
John Bell, Auchenreoch.

1842 Alexander Cavet, L. Larg.
Dr. James Currie, Dalbeattie.
1843 Wellwood H. Maxwell of Munches.
Thomas Gibson of L. Cocklick.
Samuel Thomson, Markfast.
1844 James Lowden, Haugh-of-Urr.
John Shaw, Dalbeattie.
Thomas Rawline, Dalbeattie.
Samuel Brown, Dalbeattie.
James McLaurin, Dalbeattie.
Rev. John Strain, Dalbeattie.
Robert McNaught, factor for Torcatrine.
1845 Thomas Biggar, Kingsgrange.

PAROCHIAL BOARD
Present at first meetings in 1845 and 1846

John Sinclair of Redcastle.
John McMorine of E. Glenarm.
Rev. G. M. Burnside.
John M. Lowden of Cocklick.
James Lowden, Haugh-of-Urr.
John Ewart, Shenrick.
Samuel Thomson, Markfast.
James McLaurin, Dalbeattie.

Robert Burnie, Midtown.
Rev. John Strain, Dalbeattie.
Dr. James Currie, Dalbeattie.
John McNeilie of Kirkland.
James Hyslop, Auchenreoch.
Hugh Lindsay, Dalbeattie.
James Kissock, M. Culmain.
John Carswell, Dalbeattie.

APPENDIX C

PAROCHIAL BOARD *(Continued)*

Present at last meeting in Dalbeattie Town Hall on 29th March 1895

Wellwood H. Maxwell of Munches.
Rev. David Kinnear, Dalbeattie.
Rev. R. S. Kirkpatrick, Dalbeattie.
Rev. David Frew, Urr.
Dugald McLaurin, Dalbeattie.
J. D. McClymont, Dalbeattie.
Thomas Fraser, Dalbeattie.
James Paterson, Dalbeattie.
John Craik, Dalbeattie.

In the interval, besides the ministers and elders, a large number of the leading heritors and ratepayers took part in the business of the Board.

PARISH COUNCIL

BURGH MEMBERS.

- 1895 John Craik.
  - *Josiah Ferguson.
  - Thomas Fraser.
  - James Garmory.
  - *J. D. McClymont.
  - John Wright.
- 1898 Andrew Craik.
  - John Jack
- 1904 J. H. Gallagher.
  - *W. J. H. Maxwell of Munches.
  - J. E. Milligan.
- 1906 *Robert Wilson.
- 1907 *Thomas Fraser (second time).
  - *Dugald McLaurin.

LANDWARD MEMBERS.

- 1895 *Joseph H. Brown, Hermitage.
  - *Rev. David Frew, Urr.
  - *W. D. Herries, yr. Spottes.
  - Andrew Hyslop, Auchenreoch.
  - Andrew Kirkpatrick, Auchengibbert.
- 1898 James Gillespie of Herriesdale.
- 1901 *James Dinwoodie, Corbieton.
- 1907 *James Gilchrist, Blaiket.

*Present members of Parish Council.

SCHOOL BOARD

- 1873 Rev. Alexander Gordon.
  - James Grieve.
  - Wellwood H. Maxwell.
  - Dr. McKerchar.
  - Rev. Duncan Stewart.
  - Rev. David Kinnear.
  - Rev. Robert Wright.
  - Rev. J. M. Sandilands.
  - Rev. John Clark.
- 1876 Maxwell Clark of L. Culmain.
- 1878 Rev. John Mackie.
- 1879 Rev. Mr Henderson.
  - Rev. James A. Paton.
- 1882 James Biggar, Kingsgrange.
  - James Paterson.
- 1885 *Thomas Fraser.
  - James Little.

SCHOOL BOARD *(Continued)*

1885 *Dugald McLaurin.
Walter Kirkpatrick.
Alex. Livingstone, Edingham.
1888 *William Biggar, Chapelton.
Andrew McKie, Blaiket.
1893 Andrew Kirkpatrick, Auchengibbert.

1900 Ivie A. Callan.
*W. J. H. Maxwell of Munches.
1903 *James Dunn, Brandedleys.
*Robert Maxwell.
Rev. J. P. Wilson.
1906 *J. E. Milligan.

* Present members of School Board.

APPENDIX D

COMMISSIONERS AND TOWN COUNCILLORS OF DALBEATTIE SINCE 1858

Robert Clark.
John Carswell.
John Elliot.
Alexander Lindsay.
Thomas Maxwell.
James McLaurin.
David Paterson.
Thomas Rawline.
Thomas Helme.
Dr. McKnight.
George Nisbet.
James Grieve.
Joseph Newall.
James Newall.
Dr. J. P. Lewis.
William McDowall.
William Herries.
John Hair.
James Ritchie.
Thomas Halliday.
David McNish.
John Muir.
Rev. A. Gordon.
John Murdoch.
George Kimm.
John Martin.
James Glendinning.
James Carswell.
Robert Grieve.
James Paterson.
Josiah Ferguson.
John Ritchie.
John Stewart.
William McBride.
W. J. Hamilton.
Mr Kennedy.
Francis Armstrong.
George Ritchie.
Hugh Robson.
James Heughan.
Alexander McGowan.
James Ferguson.
W. R. Sibbald.
John Lindsay.
Walter Kirkpatrick.
James Matthewson.
John Paterson.
Alexander Ross.
John Raleigh.
Joseph Heughan.
George Shaw.
James McMorrin.
Thomas Fraser.
James Tait.
Thomas Allison Cunningham.
Dugald MacLaurin.
Samuel Sibbald.
Robert Wilson.
George Nisbet (son of previous G. Nisbet).
John Craik.
William Jack.
Samuel Cowan.
William Herries.
William Clark.
*William Davie.
*David Newall.
J. D. McClymont.
James Tait (son of previous James Tait).
*Josiah Ferguson.

COMMISSIONERS AND TOWN COUNCILLORS OF DALBEATTIE
SINCE 1858 *(Continued)*

Dr. S. A. D. Gillespie.	Alexander Smith.
*William Dornan.	*John James Clark.
James Murdoch.	*Robert James Shennan.
John Rae.	*Walter Rae.
*John Jack.	*David Mundell.

* Present members of Town Council.

INDEX

ABERCROMBY, Sir Ralph, 122
Abbey, Dundrennan, 14, 17
Abbey, Holm Cultran, 11, 20
Abbey, Holyrood, 20, 21, 210, 211
Abbey, New, 14
Abyssinian king's letter, 260
Affleck, James, 76
Agnew, Rev. P., 319
Agricola, 5
Agricultural Society, Dalbeattie, 70-71
Agricultural Society, Stewartry, 60, 61
Agriculture, 13, 18, 24, 25, 41, 44-47, 50, 60-76, 114
Aird, Quintin, 94, 150, 165, 168
Aitken, Roland, 157, 158
Alexander, Rev. D. R., 295
Alexander, John, artist, 90, 92
Alexander III., 20
Alexander, William, 97
Allan, Rev. Mr, 100
Allan, William, 149, 150, 163, 165
Anderson, Dr. A., 144
Andson, Rev. William, 303
Angles, 7
Animism, 203
Arthur, Rev. Alexander, 297
Auchengibbert, 6, 56-58, 76
Austin, James M., 139, 145, 167

BACON Curing, 96, 103, 118
Baliol, Eustace, 20, 211
Baliol, John 8
Bank, Commercial, 141
Bank, Failure of Ayr, 46
Bank, Union, 114, 128
Barclay, Rev. James, 299
Barr, Rev. James, 34
Basques, 10
Baxter, Alexander, 159
Bayeux Tapestry, 176
Bayne, Rev. D. W., 294
Bean, David, 46
Beck, James, 152, 155
Bell, James, 143
Bell, John, 96
Beltane, 204, 205
Bernicia, 7

Beveridge, Andrew, teacher, 156
Biggar, Rev. James, 89, 293
Biggar, James, 65, 68-71, 76
Biggar, Thomas, 62, 68, 70, 73, 74, 76, 120, 280
Biggar, William, 68
Birney, J. Gordon, 94
Black, Rev. James, 294, 308
Blair, Alexander, 64
Blair, George, 86
Blair, Margaret, 86
Blyth, Rev. James, 294
Board, Parochial, 164-167
Board, Poor's, 163, 164
Board, School, 150, 152, 153, 158-161
Bone dust, 63, 64
Bordland, Assault at, 19
Bothwell Bridge, Battle of, 31
Boyne, Battle of the, 34
Bowl, King Robert's, 180
Braid, David H., 129
Bridge, Buittle, 43
Bridge, Craignair, 44, 113, 123
Bridge, Foot, 171
Bridge, High Street, Dalbeattie, 132
Bridge of Urr, Old, 32, 36
Bridge over Spottes Burn, Old, 34
Bridge, Military, 83
Bridgehall, 85
Bridget, Saint, 20, 209, 212
Broadfoot, Anthony, 118, 124
Broun of Boghead, Andrew, 248
Broune, John, 19
Brown, John, reader, 205, 213-215, 275
Brown, Joseph H., 76, 106
Brown, Robert, 155
Brown, Samuel, 130
Bruce, Captain, 31, 32, 33
Bruce, Edward, 8
Bruce, King Robert, 8, 12, 15, 20, 179, 180
Bruce's Travels in Abyssinia, 258
Buchanan, Peter, 51
Buchanites, 54-59, 76, 102, 103, 104, 105
Burgess, Allan, 97

HISTORY OF THE PARISH OF URR

Burgess, John, 169
Burgess, Rev. William, 294
Burgh of Dalbeattie formed, 129
Burghers and Antiburghers, 291
Burnie, James, 70, 128
Burns, Robert, 121, 253, 257
Burnside, Rev. G. M., 33, 270-273, 296
Buthergask, Andro, 12

CAER-BANTORIGUM, 5, 6, 179
Caird, Dr. John, 272
Cairnses of Dalbeattie, 110
Cairns, George, of Kipp, 251
Callan, Ivie A., 143, 145
Calpes or Caupes, 16
Cameron, Rev. John, 315
Candlemas Bleeze, 151
Canmore, Malcolm, 8, 207
Carlingwark, Murder at, 23
Carlyle, Thomas, 121
Carruthers, Rev. A., 318
Carswell, John, 70, 120, 130, 132
Castles, Norman, 14, 177, 178
Castle, Buittle, 12, 15, 16, 43, 44
Castle Clare, 106
Castle, Crugeltoun, 12
Castle, Edingham, 35, 181, 185, 186
Castle Hardships, 106
Castle, Thrieve, 8, 15, 16
Castle, Wygton, 12
Catechising, Ministerial, 191-193
Catlick Burn, 84
Causey, 86
Celts, 3-5, 10
Cemetery, Dalbeattie, 167
Censures, Privy, 247
Chalmers, Andrew, 28
Chalmers, Dr. Archibald, 104
Chalmers, James, 31
Changes, Modern, 195-197
Chapels, 186, 211, 212
Chapelton, 76
Charles I., 26, 29, 218
Charles II., 29, 34, 219
Cholera, 91, 104, 105
Christison, Dr., 175
Church, Blaiket, 186, 207-211
Church, Burnside U.F., 308-313
Church, Cameronian, 99-101
Church, Christ, 315, 316
Church, Colliston U.F., 302-307
Church, Dalbeattie Parish, 272, 296-302
Church, E.U. Congregational, 313-315

Church, M. Kirkland, 186, 207, 208,
Church, Parish, 216, 246, 265, 275-281
Church, St. Peter's R.C., 316-319
Church, Urr U.F., 290-295
Churchyard, Urr, 285-289
Clachrie, Charles, 119
Clark, David, 119
Clark, Rev. John, 295
Clark, J. J., 145
Clark, Maxwell, 65, 73
Clark, Robert, 130
Claverhouse, 30, 33
Cleland, Rev. John, 293
Clubs, Dalbeattie, 146
Coals, 47, 112
Coals, Tax on, 47, 49
Coins, Roman, 6
Coles, F. R., 172, 174, 182
Collections, Church, 161
Coltart, John, 82, 261
Communion, 236, 247, 250, 281, 282
Comyn, Alexander, 8
Constantine, Saint, 20, 208, 209, 212
Copeland, Merchant, 114
Copeland, Thomas, 124
Copland, Alexander, 47, 49, 112
Copland, James, 111
Copland, James, schoolmaster, 116, 155
Copland, Miss, 139, 145, 146, 147, 316
Copland, Nathan, 119
Copland, William, 64, 116, 298, 303
Corrie, James, 297
Council, County, 69, 73, 78
Council, Parish, 78, 167, 171
Courthill, 81
Covenant, The Solemn League and, 26
Covenanters, 26, 29-34, 219
Cowie, Rev. John, 318
Craik, Andrew, 167
Craik, David, 157
Craik, John, 145, 167
Craik, Mrs, 157
Crocketford, 3, 58, 61, 72, 80, 84, 101-108, 109, 113, 153, 159
Crofts at Haugh-of-Urr, 89
Crofts at Springholm, 96
Cromwell, Oliver, 29.
Crosbie, Thomas, 163
Cunningham Village, 112
Curates, The, 30, 36, 220, 221
Curling Club, Parish, 168, 169

INDEX

Currie, Dr. James, 129, 163, 165, 169
Currie, Miss, 129

DAIRIES, 74
Dalbeattie, 2, 49, 53, 61, 72, 73, 75, 80, 84, 100, 109-147, 164, 168, 296-319
Dalbeattie, Meikle, 43, 110, 111
Dalbeattie, Little, 110, 111
David I., 8, 12, 207
David II., 12, 20, 21
Davidson, Alexander, 156, 158, 159
Davie, William, 140, 144, 145, 146
Deacons in Parish Church, 269, 271
Dempster, John, Springholm, 98
Dempster, John, Haugh-of-Urr, 88
Denniston, John, 121
Dick, Rev. D. A., 313
Dickie, Rev. John, 246
Dickson, William, 163
Dickson, W. Stephen, 153
Dinon, Mote of, 176
Dinwoodie, Thomas, 65
Discipline, 218, 251, 267, 268
Disruption, The, 157, 271, 297
Disturbances at Parish Church, 233, 235
Donaldson, James, 98, 155
Donaldson, Thomas, 95
Dornan, Councillor, 145
Douglas, Archibald, The Grim, 8
Douglas, William, of Orchardton, 258
Douglases, The, 15, 16, 20
Drainage, Dalbeattie, 134, 136
Droving, 45, 46, 104
Druidism, 204, 205
Dudgeon, Rev. George, 304
Duncan, Rev. W. Wallace, 270
Dunn, Andrew, 159
Dunse Law, 29

EADIE, Dr., Glasgow, 311
Edingham, 6, 21
Education, 24, 36, 52, 53, 148-161
Edward I., 12, 13
Elliot, John, 122, 130
Elliot, William, 122.
Enclosing the land, 42
Episcopacy, 26, 220
European Languages, History of, 260
Ewart, John, 99.
Exchequer Rolls, 175, 178
Exercise and Addition, 243
Exogamy, 191

FAIRS, 41
Fair, Haugh-of-Urr, 92
Fair, Dalbeattie, 116, 117
Famines, 19, 20
Farish, J. B., Schoolmaster, 156
Fast Day, 283
Faulds, Springholm, 98
Fergus, Lord of Galloway, 8, 210
Ferguson, Josiah, 139
Fergusson, George, 98
Fergusson, Samuel, 98
Firthhead, Little, 75, 76
Fisher, John, 98
Fisher, Mrs, 152
Flag, Hepburn's, 40, 239
Flodden, Battle of, 17
Forbes, Rev. P., 318
Forsyth, John, 118
Fort, Milton Loch, 182
Fort, Waterside, 183
Fowlis, James, 130
Fraser, Rev. Dr., 272
Fraser & Young, 125
Fraser, Thomas, 142, 143, 145 167
Frew, Rev. David, 94, 145, 167, 168, 274
Frew, John, 43, 278.
Friendly Societies, 146
Fuel, Scarcity of, 47, 112

GAELIC, 3, 5
Gallgaidhal or Gallwyddel, 7
Galloway, Early History of, 3-9
Galwegians, 7
Gas Company, Dalbeattie, 131
Geddes, Father, 318
Gibson, Thomas, 65, 169
Gibson, William, 87
Gillespie, Miss, 129
Gillespie, Dr. S. A. D., 136, 144, 167
Gillhole, 86
Gladstone, Thomas, 79
Glebe, The, 245, 285
Gledstaines, Rev. George, 30, 218, 219
Glendinning, Thomas, 143
Gloag, Rev. Lennox R., 316
Golf Course, 44
Goold, Rev. M. N., 309
Gordon, Rev. Alexander, 318
Gordon, Alexander, 17
Gordon, Edward, Martyr, 32, 33
Gordon, Grisell, 27, 217, 218
Gordon, Jock, 92
Gordon, John, 17
Gordon, John, Martyr, 32, 33

Gordon, Patrick, 46
Gordon, Robert, 17
Gower, Rev. J. L., 315
Graham, Rev. Dr., 316
Granite Industry, 123-127
Graveyards, Old, 186, 208, 286
Gray, Thomas Rainson, 79
Grierson of Lag, 30, 31, 32, 33
Grieve, James, 70, 71, 128, 130, 140, 309
Grieve, Robert, 142
Griffith, Miss, 157
Gunn, Alexander, 93

HACKING, J. Harold, 76
Hall and Library, Urr, 93, 94
Hall, Dalbeattie Town, 127, 137, 138
Halliday, William, 98
Hamilton, John, 28
Hamilton, Rev. Mr, Holywood, 246
Hardgate, 3, 54, 72, 83-95, 149, 150, 154, 159
Harkness, Robert, 152
Harrison, William, 92
Haughhill, Tradition of Lady of, 32
Haugh-of-Urr, 3, 34, 44, 54, 62, 72, 77, 80, 82, 83-95, 109, 113, 119, 157, 164, 168
Health of Parish, 51, 104, 107
Health of Dalbeattie, 136
Hebronians, 39, 230
Helme, Messrs, 121
Helme, Thomas, 130, 135
Hendersons of Newark, 83
Henderson, Rev. Mr., 305
Hepburn, Rev. John, 39, 40, 81, 99, 213, 221, 222, 276
Hepburn, Rev. John, Calls to Urr, 227.
Hepburn, Rev. John, Disputed Induction, 227, 229
Hepburn, Rev. John, Aims and Methods, 229, 230
Hepburn, Rev. John, Preaching, 230-232
Hepburn, Rev. John, First Suspension, 232-234
Hepburn, Rev. John, Imprisonment, 234
Hepburn, Rev. John, Second Suspension, 234-235
Hepburn, Rev. John, Deposition, 235
Hepburn, Rev. John, Restoration, 236

Hepburn, Rev. John, Anti-Jacobitism, 237-239
Hepburn, Rev. John, Death and Family, 239, 240
Hermitage, 76, 212
Heron, James, 116, 297, 303
Heron, Robert, 113
Heron, William, Martyr, 32, 33
Herries, Alexander Dobrée, 79, 95
Herries, Alexander Young, 78, 91, 94, 169
Herries, Andrew, 19
Herries, Lord, 12, 17, 19
Herries, Michael, 77, 161, 254, 284, 288
Herries, Miss, 121
Herries, Robert, 111
Herries, William Dobrée, 78, 94, 167
Herries, William Muirhead, 254, 259, 266
Herries, William Young, 62, 64, 77, 85
Heughan, Joseph, 137
Heughan, William, 309
Highland Society, 67, 73, 74, 75
Hillhead, 44
Hogg, Rev. Thomas D., 315
Hogmanay, Old, 187-189
Holehouse, 61
Horticultural Society, 168
Hotel, Grapes, 95, 98
Hotel, King's Arms or Commercial, 114, 115, 122, 130, 132
Hotel, Laurie Arms, 88
Hotel, Maxwell Arms, 70, 114, 115, 122, 129
Hotel, New Inn, 103
Hotel, Temperance, 310
Houston, William, 157
Howcroft, 86
Hugo of Hurr, 11
Hurricane of 1839, 91
Hutton, John, 23
Hyland, William, 44
Hyndman, John, 64
Hyslop, James, 65

IMPROVEMENTS Committee, 139, 144
Inglis, Rev. John, 314.
Inn, Bacon Ham, 98
Inn, Brown Cow, 114, 122
Inn, Coach and Horses, 98
Inn, Commercial, 103
Inn, Dog and Duck, 87
Inn, Fish, 88

INDEX

Inn, George, 103
Inn, Plough, Crocketford, 103
Inn, Plough, Dalbeattie, 114
Innes, Andrew, 58, 59
Invasion, Alarm of French, 247
Ireland, 7, 87, 105
Ireland, James, 84

JACK, John, 145
Jackson, Messrs, 121
Jackson, Rev. J. M., 316
Jacobite Rebellion of 1715, 16, 39, 40, 41, 237-239
Jacobite Rebellion of 1745, 41
James VI., 22, 26, 215
James VII., 34.
Javelin, Roman, 6
Johan, Vicaire de Urres, 210
Johnston, Rev. A. M., 313
Johnston, D. C. G., 107
Johnston, Dr. James, 89
Johnston, Miss, 157, 158
Johnstone, John, Dalbeattie, 157
Johnstone, John, Millbank, 85
Johnstones, Barbey, 83
Johnstones, Millbank, 85
Jubilee Celebration, Dalbeattie, 144-147

KEENAN, Rev. S., 318
Kelly, Miss, 157
Kenmure, Lord, 23, 39, 237, 239
Kerr, James, 121
Kerr, John, 308
Kerr, Robert, 94, 288
Kingsgrange, 76, 79
Kinnear, Rev. David, 310
Kirk, John, 124
Kirk, John, Grocer, 130
Kirkconnel Family, 11
Kirkpatrick, Mrs, 121
Kirkpatrick, Rev. R. S., 300
Kirkstyle, 86
Knox, John, 18
Kurour, Wiliam, 19

LAKE Dwellings, 4
Lamond, Rev. Dr., 95, 99, 253
Langley, Rev. H. J., 319
Langside, Battle of, 17
Lardner mart cow, 16
Larghill, 2, 33, 57, 58, 102
Larglanglee, 2, 31
Laurie, Rev. George, 100
Laurie, Walter Bigham, 87
Laurie, Walter Sloan, 84
Lawson & Henderson, Messrs, 121

Lee, Rev. John, 319
Legacies for education, 160
Levellers, The, 42, 43
Lewis, Dr. J. P., 130, 133-137, 165
Lewis, William, 118, 130
Leyden, John, 258
Library, Dumfries Presbytery, 243
Liddle, Miss, 152
Lime, 47, 64
Lindsay, Alexander, 130
Lindsay, Mrs Alexander, 157
Lindsay, Hugh, 116, 118, 297
Lithgow, Traveller, 25
Little, James, 141, 145, 161, 168
Loans, School Board, 160
Lochenkit Moor, 31, 32
Lochs, 2, 135, 169
Lodging houses, Dalbeattie, 115, 116
Longevity, Instances of, 51
Lowden, James, 88, 169
Lowden, John, 88, 161, 165, 169
Lowden, John McGowan, 130
Lyon, Rev. John, 31, 36, 220-225, 227, 276
Lyon, Rev. John, Trial of, 221-225

MACFARLANE, Dr., London, 311
Machinery, Farm, 66
Mackenzie, Rev. James, 297, 302
Mackie, Rev. John, 298
Maitland, William, 64
Major, Nathan, 117
Malignants, R.C., 218, 237, 316, 317
Man, Isle of, 7, 45
Manse, Parish, 246, 259, 275, 281
Manures, Artificial, 66, 73
Margaret, Queen, 12, 13, 207
Marl, 3, 44, 45, 47
Marshall, William, 43
Martin, James, 112
Martyrs of Lochenkit, 31, 32
Martyrs' Tomb and Monument, 33, 34.
Mary, Queen of Scots, 17
Matthewson, James, 143
Maxwell, David, 23
Maxwell, Sir David, 64
Maxwell, George (1637-1683), 317
Maxwell, George (1715), 40
Maxwell, George (1780), 112
Maxwell, John, 43
Maxwell, John Herries, 64, 297
Maxwell, Robert, 165
Maxwell, Sir Robert, 23

Maxwell, Samuel, 158
Maxwell, Thomas, 130-132, 157, 167, 309.
Maxwell, Wellwood, 142, 144, 145
Maxwell, Wellwood Herries, 67, 70, 71, 127, 131, 132, 137, 161, 165, 167, 299, 300, 303, 310
Maxwell, William, 40
Maxwell, William Jardine Herries, 68, 71, 128, 140, 145, 146, 147, 161
Maxwells of Logan, 23
Mechanics' Institute, 127, 128
Menzies, John, 150, 151, 165
Mersey Dock and Harbour Board, 123
Mill, Corn, 64, 112, 118
Mill, Flax, 64
Mill, Lint, 49, 112
Mill, Paper, 49, 113, 118
Mill, Saw, 64, 118, 143
Mill, Woollen, 118
Millhall, 96
Milligan, Hugh, 118
Milligan, Rev. John, 293
Milligan, John, 114
Milligan, J. E., 71.
Milligan, Mrs. Haughhead, 160
Milligan, William, 71
Milton, 3, 26, 27, 44, 80, 81-83, 84, 149, 151, 154, 159
Milton Mill, 81, 83
Minister's Man, The, 194, 195, 252
Minutes, Kirk Session, 284
Moir, Henry, 128
Mollance, 19, 41
Moncrieff, Sir H. Wellwood, 260
Montgomeries, Haugh-of-Urr, 84, 85
Morrison, Rev. James, 313
Morrisons, Haugh-of-Urr, 84
Moss, Minister's Peat, 246
Mosses, 2, 3, 6
Mote, Edingham, 181
Mote, Little Richorn, 181
Mote of Urr, 5, 6, 11, 21, 171-180, 183, 184
Mote of Urr, Situation of, 171
Mote of Urr, Description of, 172-174
Mote of Urr, Roman connection with, 174
Mote of Urr, Houses on, 174, 175
Mote of Urr, Origin and History of, 175-179
Mote of Urr, Tradition of, 179, 180
Mount, The King's, 179

Muir, Adam, 153
Muir, John, 130, 132
Muirhead, Rev. Dr. James, 41, 44, 46-54, 86, 112, 148, 161, 185, 248-254, 258, 279, 318
Muirhead, James, Dumfries, 248
Muirhead, William, Carlisle, 160
Mundell, David, 145
Mundell, Dr., Wallace Hall, 40
Murphy, Rev. P., 319
Murray, Rev. Dr. Alexander, 61, 161, 249, 255-264, 266, 279
Murray, Rev. Dr. Alexander, Early Days, 255-257
Murray, Rev. Dr. Alexander, Edinburgh, 257-258
Murray, Rev. Dr. Alexander, Urr, 258-261
Murray, Rev. Dr. Alexander, Professor, 261-263
Murray, Rev. Dr. Alexander, Death and Monuments, 263-264
Murray, David, 115
Murray, Elizabeth, 97
Murray, Regent, 17

McADAM, John, 36, 224
McAlister, William, 153, 169
McAndrew, James, teacher, 156
McCartney, Rev. D., 319
Macartney, George, 31, 222, 228, 287
Macartney, John, 31, 217
McBriar, David, Richorn, 28
McCaig, James, 87
McCarmonth, Alexander, 215, 275
McClune, John, 96
McClymont, J. D., 143, 145.
McCormick, John, 114
McCroskie, Alexander, 130
McDermid, Rev. J., 33
McDougall, Dougall, 21
McDougall, Miss, 153
McEnallie, Thomas, 151, 155, 157
McEwan, Andrew, 137
McEwen, Rev. T., 295
McGeorge, Jeanie, 97
McGeorge, Thomas, 222
McGeorge, William, 222
McGill, David, 86, 91
McGlashan, Rev. L., 302
McGregor, Donald, 153
McKean, Matthew, 82
McKenzie, Dr. James, 163
McKerchar, Dr. 144
McKerlie, P. H., 21, 210, 219

INDEX

McKie, Catherine, or Livingstone, 19
McKinnell, Rev. T., 111, 244-248, 278, 317
McKinstray, John, 19
McKnight, Dr. Thomas, 130, 132, 165
McLauchlan, Rev. Mr, 100
McLaurin, Dugald, 118, 131, 167
McLaurin, James, 70, 118, 130
McLeod, James, 88
McMillan, John, 96
McMillan, Robert, 98
MacMillanites, The, 230
McMorrine, James, 130
McMorrine, John, 163, 164
McMorrine, John, Culshan, 99
McMorrine, Peter, 96
McMorrine, William, 96
McNab, R. W., 71, 128
McNaight, Rev. John, 193
McNaught, John, 19, 23
McNaught, Marion, 23
McNaught, William, 154
McNeillie, Dr. Alexander, 169
McNish, David, 137
McRobert, James, 309, 313
McRobin, or McCubbin, Alexander, 32
McWhae, Joseph, 84, 85
McWhir, Rev. John, 89, 156, 161, 265-269

NATURALS, 92
Neilson, Col., of Queenshill, 306
Nether Place, 17, 19
Nether Place, Murder at, 19
Newall, Andrew, 123, 130
Newall, Charles, 123, 125
Newall, David, 123, 124
Newall, David (another), 126
Newall, D. H. and J., Messrs, 119, 124, 125
Newall, Homer, 123, 124
Newhouse, 58
Newspapers, 142, 143
Nine-mile Bar, 102, 105
Ninian, Saint, 205, 206
Nisbet, George, 70, 130
Noggie, The, 155
Norsemen, The, 7, 8, 206, 207

O'BRIEN, Frank, 101
O'Malley, Rev. Charles, 319
Osborne, Rev. John, 100, 115, 314
Outlines of Oriental Philology, 262

PARISH, Description of, 1-3
Parish, Erection of, 12, 207
Parish, Condition of (1200-1300), 13, 14
Parish, Condition of (1300-1603), 18-21
Parish, Condition of (1627), 24-26
Parish, Condition of (1707), 35-36
Parish, Condition of (1750), 41
Parish, Condition of (1790), 46-54
Parish, Condition of (1800-1820), 60-61
Parish, Condition of (1820-1850), 62-65
Parish, Condition of (1850-1900), 65-76
Panel in Pulpit, 216
Parishes, 12, 207
Parks, Public, 139, 140, 146
Parsonages, 210, 211
Paterson, David, 70, 114, 130.
Paterson, John, 313
Paton, Rev. J. A., 305
Patronage, 38, 39, 211, 237
Payne, William, 92
Percy, Henry de, 12
Persecutions, 29-34
Philiphaugh, Battle of, 29
Picts, 4, 7
Pig Killing, 90, 96, 104
Pinkiecleuch, Battle of, 17
Plagues, 20
Plant, Rev. H. F., 316
Plate, Communion, 283
Pont, Timothy, 111, 112, 185
Pool, The Boat, 44
Poole, Rev. Mr, 262
Poor, Relief of, 51, 161-167, 250, 265, 266
Population of Parish, 24, 48, 62, 64, 75
Population of Crocketford, 105, 107
Population of Dalbeattie, 120, 121, 127
Population of Haugh-of-Urr and Hardgate, 87, 93
Population of Milton, 82
Population of Springholm, 96
Post Office, Crocketford, 107
Post Office, Dalbeattie, 115, 128, 129
Post Office, Haugh-of-Urr, 93
Post Office, Springholm, 97.
Potatoes, Introduction of, 44
Principles of Oriental Grammar, 263
Proclamations, Marriage, 268

Proprietorship, 20, 21, 64
Provosts of Dalbeattie, 130-140
Ptolemaeus Claudius, 5, 179
Public-Houses, 97, 98, 103, 115
Puller, Rev. William, 294

RACING for the Napkin, 189, 190
Rae, Councillor, 145
Railway, 71, 107, 131, 171
Ramsay, Rev. W. M., 315, 316
Randolph, Thomas, 12
Rates, Parish, 160, 161, 162, 163, 164, 166
Rawline, Thomas, 70, 75, 114, 119, 130, 297, 309
Readers, The, 214, 215
Redcastle, 83, 84, 85, 94
Redik, John, 28
Redik, Paul, 17
Rediks of Dalbeattie, 110
Reformation, The, 5, 18, 19, 22, 23, 211, 212, 213.
Registrars, 165
Registrum Magni Sigilli, 175
Reid, James, 96
Reid, John, 6
Reid, William, of Broadlea, 76
Reid, William, Springholm, 96
Reid, William, Dalbeattie, 309
Religion, Early, 203-207
Religion, Early Christian, 205
Religion, Norse, 206, 207.
Religion of Catholic Times, 207-212
Religion in 1790, 52
Religion of Present Day, 196
Rents of Farms, 25, 46, 65, 75
Rental of Parish, 48, 62, 64, 75
Revolution, The, 34, 39, 221, 229
Riddick, Charles, 119
Riddick, Mrs, 157, 158
Riding of the Bruise, 190, 191
Rigg, Anthony, 163, 169
Roads, 3, 16, 36, 43, 44, 61, 62, 80, 83, 87, 95, 101, 102
Robertson, Rev. Alexander, 24, 36, 110, 216-218
Robertson, Rev. Robert, 315
Robinson's Field, Jennie, 114
Robson, Miss, 152
Roddick, John, 98
Roman Remains, 5, 6
Roseman, Rev. Mr, 314
Rutherford, Rev. Samuel, 23

SALUTATIONS, 197-199
Samhain, 204, 205
Sandilands, Rev. J. M., 94, 160, 165, 273-274, 280

Sanitation, 133
Sanquhar, Meeting at, 235
Schools and Schoolmasters, 24, 36, 53, 112, 149-161, 224
Schools, Adventure, 154
Scott, Sir Walter, 6
Sea-going Trade, 118, 141, 142
Seats, Allocation of Church, 242
Secession Church, 290, 291
Selby, Sir Walter, 180
Selgovae, 4, 5
Services, Church, 281-284
Shaw, George, 137-140, 145
Shaw, John, 119.
Shearer, Curteis & Co., 125
Shearer, Field & Co., 125
Shennan, Councillor, 145
Shennan, Robert, 303
Sibbald Manuscripts, 185
Simpson, John, 128, 145
Sinclair, John, 64, 163
Sinclair, William, 19
Skirvings of Croys, 254
Slaters, Hardgate, 89
Sloan, Rev. J. M., 315
Sloan, William, 155
Smart, John, 152, 165
Smith, Janet C., 82
Smith, John, Grange, 19
Smith, John, Dalbeattie, 128
Smith, Robert, 82
Smith, Thomas, 153
Smith, Rev. Dr. W. C., 306
Smith, William, 159
Smuggling, 45
Societies, Christian, 229
Soffley, George, 160
Spearheads, Roman, 6
Spottes, 77, 85
Spottes, Burn, 1, 34, 62, 77, 84
Spottes, Glen, 77
Spottes, Lake, 2, 169
Springholm, 3, 61, 72, 80, 84, 95-101, 109, 113, 119, 120, 152, 154, 155, 159, 164
Sprott, Hugh, 211
Sprotte, Mark, 180
Sprottes of the Mote, 21, 180
Stage Coaches, 72, 87, 97, 103, 104, 107, 117
Statistical Account of 1627, 24, 110, 208, 212, 216
Statistical Account of 1794, 46, 84, 112, 174, 185, 318
Statistical Account of 1845, 63, 120, 153, 271
Steamships, 63
Stephen, Rev. A., 316

INDEX

Stewart, Rev. Duncan, 298
Stewart, William, registrar, 165
Stewart, Professor W. D.D., 289
Stewart, William, Martyr, 32, 33
Stone, Standing, 184
Storrar, Rev. William, 295
Stothart, Thomas C., 266
Stothert, William, 64, 162
Stipend, 215, 216, 245, 253, 285
Strachan, Rev. John, 316
Strain, Rev. John, 318
Streets, Dalbeattie, 117, 121, 134, 138
Summerhill, 88, 89
Superstitions, 18, 19, 37, 81, 204
Swanston, Rev. J., 293

TAIT, James, 310, 313
Tait, Johnny, 92
Talbot Papers, 17
Tandy, Rev. J., 316
Teinds, Tithes, 207, 211, 214
Thomas, son of Hugo of Hurr, 11
Thomson, Alexander, 70, 73, 169
Thomson, James, 73
Thomson, James, Kirkstyle, 86
Thomson, Rev. James, 215, 216, 276
Thomson, Rev. James, Cameronian, 99, 100
Thomson, Jean, 86, 155
Thomson, John, Blaiket, 70, 73, 74, 75, 169
Thomson, John, Haugh-of-Urr, 85
Thomson, R., 309
Thomson, Samuel, 163, 169
Thomson, Thomas, 28
Thomson, William, 141, 158, 159, 306
Thomsons of Milton Mains, 83
Tile Drains introduced, 63
Tokens, Church, 283, 284
Town Clerks of Dalbeattie, 140, 141
Train, Joseph, 6
Tripod, Roman, 6
Trusts, Kirk Session, 284

UCHTRED, 8
Ulster, Men of, 6

Union of the Crowns, 22
Union of the Parliaments, 38, 39, 237
Union of the U.P. and Free Churches, 307, 308
Urn, 6
Urr, Barony of, 11, 12, 20, 207
Urr, Derivation of, 10, 11
Urr Navigation Trustees, 142, 145
Urus, 3

VEITCH, Rev. Mr, 228, 231
Vessels, 119
Vicarages, 210, 211
Villages, 3, 53, 54, 80-108
Volunteers, 144

WAGES, 50, 65, 66
Walker, Jean, 34, 35
Walkers of Mote, 175
Wallace, John, Martyr, 32, 33
War Committee, 24, 26-29, 81
War, French, 60, 62, 87, 114
Water Supply, Dalbeattie, 134, 135, 136
Watson, Isabella, Life of, 128
Webster, Andrew, 157
Welsh, Robert, 155
Welshes, Haugh-of-Urr, 91
White, Rev. Hugh, 55-59
Wilkinson, William, 122
William and Mary, 34
Wilson, David, 98
Wilson, Captain George, 70, 119
Wilson, Rev. J. P., 301
Wilson, Miss, 152
Wilson, Robert, 139, 145
Wilson, William, 130, 146
Wilson, Paper Manufacturer, 113
Wilsons, Burnfell, 83
Wood, Fergusson, 169
Wood, John and Alexander, 98
Wright, Andrew, 118
Wright, Rev. Christopher, 43, 241-244, 277, 317
Wright, James, 309
Wright, Rev. Robert, 305
Wright, William, 87
Wycliffe, 18

ERRATA.

Page 51, line 32: For "*limts*" **read** "*limits.*"
Page 80, line 24: For "*1858*" **read** "*1859.*"
Page 87, line 8: For "*William*" **read** "*Walter.*"
Page 165, line 2: For "*Poor*" **read** "*Poor's.*"
Page 194, line 8: For "*Historigrapher*" **read** "*Historiographer.*"